DOG

Words and Music
JERRY LEIBER
MIKE STOLLE

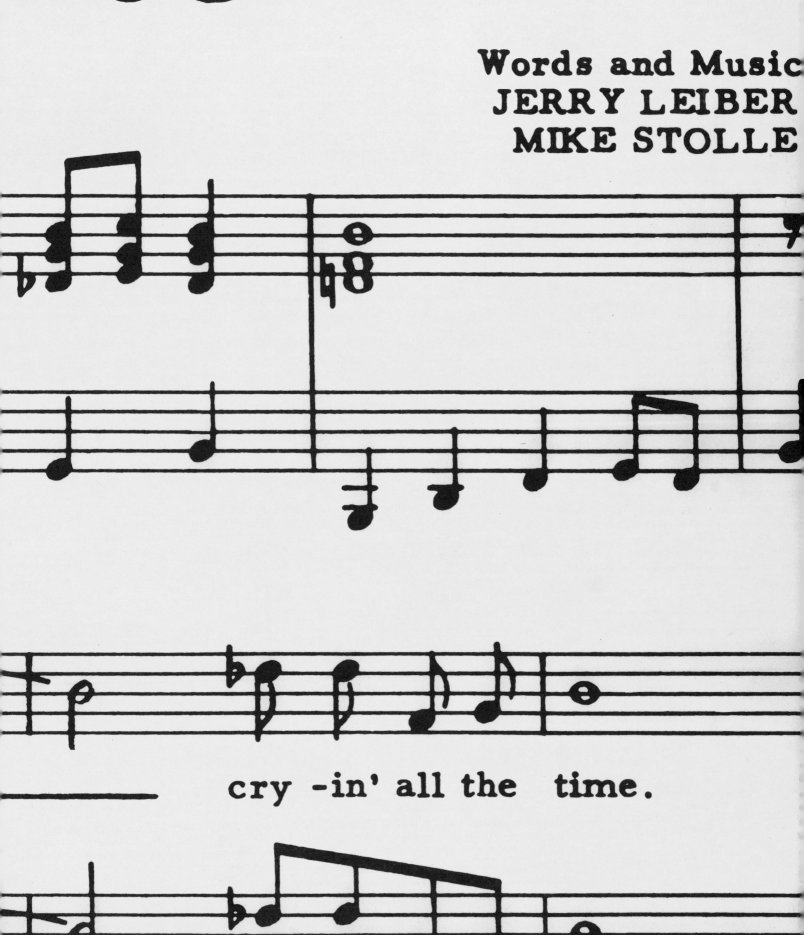

cry -in' all the time.

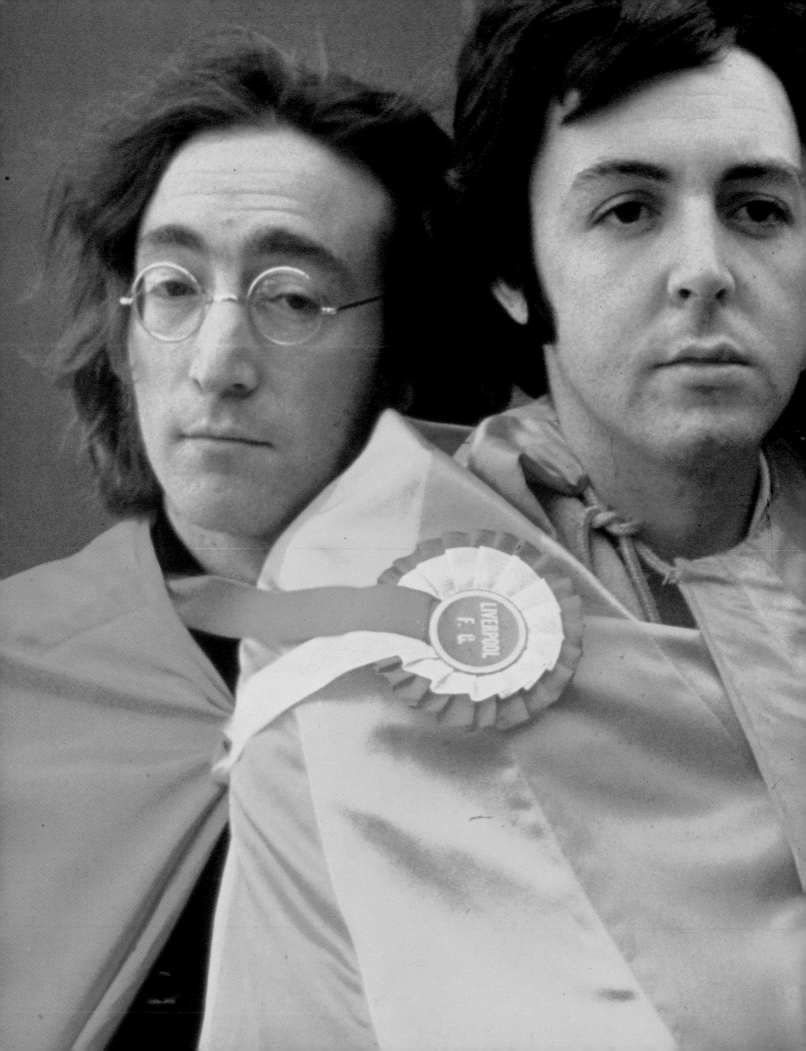

ROCK STARS

BY TIMOTHY WHITE

DESIGNED BY J. C. SUARES

STEWART, TABORI & CHANG

PUBLISHERS, NEW YORK

Editor: Roy Finamore
Photo research: Leora Kahn

Library of Congress Cataloging in Publication Data

White, Timothy.
    Rock stars.

    Includes index.
    1. Rock musicians—Biography.   2. Rock music—History and
criticism.   I. Title.
ML3534.W55   1984   784.5′4′00922   [B]   84-2531
ISBN 0-941434-50-8

The essay on Sting originally appeared in a different form in *Penthouse*.
The essays on James Taylor, Carly Simon, Stevie Nicks, and Rickie
Lee Jones originally appeared in a different form in *Rolling Stone*.

Published by Stewart, Tabori & Chang, Inc.
300 Park Avenue South, New York, New York 10010

Distributed by Workman Publishing
1 West 39 Street, New York, New York 10018

Printed and bound in Japan

PRECEDING PAGES
Pages 2–3: the Beach Boys in the 1980s (Michael Putland/Retna Ltd.).
Pages 4–5: the Beatles in the late 1960s (David McCullin/Magnum
Photos).
Pages 6–7: the Rolling Stones in the 1980s (Michael Putland/Retna
Ltd.).
Page 8: Elvis Presley, electric balladeer (Frank Driggs Collection).
RIGHT
Mick Jagger, lean and mean (John Bellissimo/Retna Ltd.).

Mick Jagger, lean and mean
(John Bellissimo/Retna Ltd.).

INTRODUCTION

After silence, that which comes nearest to expressing the inexpressible is music.
—ALDOUS HUXLEY

THERE'S AN OLD DOMESTIC TRAVEL PROMOTION SPIEL: "See America First." That's precisely what rock and roll aims to do—with the top down, the radio blaring, and the gas pedal stomped to the floor. Make no mistake about it: only America, the greatest social laboratory in the history of the planet, could have produced a cultural phenomenon as singularly violent, plaintive, reckless, tender, risky, lurid, threatening, heart-wrenching, grotesque, corruptible, and vital as rock and roll. It took a land where every soul had a fairly decent shot at the awesome state of freedom *with* license to hatch an art form so triumphantly incendiary.

When the Puritans landed on these shores, part of their master plan was to create a strict province of orthodox piety in the wilderness. These and other scrupulous colonists failed to comprehend that America, by its very nature, was and is a permanent wilderness, a wilderness of the spirit. For their part, the guilt-crippled Puritans saw their fiercely independent fellow settlers as necromancers and demons all. Rather, they were mortals possessed with self-realization, each consumed by the concept that, in this boundless territory, they could completely reinvent themselves.

In *Roll, Jordan, Roll: The World that the Slaves Made*, Eugene D. Genovese writes, "The idea of original sin lies at the heart of the Western formulation of the problem of freedom and order. In time it tipped the ideological scales decisively toward the side of individual freedom in its perpetual struggle with the demands for social order." In other words, Americans decided that if you've got the Devil to pay simply for being *born*, you might as well have fun counting your change. While the Puritans may have agonized over why God created both good and evil, and executed "witches" in a vain attempt at purging the world of the painful paradox, the rest of America slowly learned to see the bonfire for the flames . . . and then became drawn to those flames.

FACING PAGE
Jerry Lee Lewis, the Killer (John Shea/Sygma).
ABOVE
Elvis, all shook up (Gabi Rona/CBS).

Is rock and roll predicated on personal excess? Not necessarily. It depends on the practitioner. While there are those rock stars who deem rock and roll to be a declaration of war, others hunger for a quiet place, a still pool for reflection. Some need to know if they can rise above the howling tumult, feeling sure that the only way to find out is to plunge into the thick of it. One longs to unravel mysteries. Another wants to unravel psyches. But these are longings, and it is the American in all of us, whether we're from Tallahassee or Hong Kong, that fires them.

When the young heart is impossibly heavy, when the crowded mind grows ineffably lonely, when urges seem too dizzying to dare act on—and yet you do act on them because they're a part of *you*—you're *rocking*. Rock and roll is the darkness that enshrouds secret desires unfulfilled, and the appetite that shoves you forward to disrobe them. As Jerry Lee Lewis can tell you, if you want to rock, you do not go gently into that good night.

JERRY LEE LEWIS HAS SAID, IN NO UNCERTAIN TERMS, THAT HE'S GOING TO hell for playing rock and roll. And Jerry Lee—a whiskey-lapping, woman-squeezing, wild-eyed Louisiana roadhouse roustabout with no more sense of restraint, decorum, or social conscience than a shark on a July afternoon at Virginia Beach— is exactly right. Don't think for one minute that he merely stumbled onto this momentous path. Jerry Lee's parents sent their child to a fundamentalist Bible college in Waxahachie, Texas, to learn the difference between the Darkness and the Light. And he did—with a vengeance. Slipping down into each magnetic midnight on a Jacob's Ladder of knotted bedsheets, he'd dash off to downtown Dallas to seek out every forbidden pleasure the Good Book had alerted him to. And any time there was an upright piano handy to help him improvise a soundtrack to his gloriously tawdry personal saga, he'd shift his hips, bring his right boot heel down hard on High C, and start pumping out some bastardized black spiritual with all the lowdown hillbilly abandon he could muster, his quasi-Apache war whoops providing ultra-coarse counterpoint.

In a country composed of more different sets of competing and conflicting rules, dogmas, prejudices, pietistic predilections, and doctrinaire obsessions than a Chinese puzzle factory, Jerry Lee Lewis declined the role of joiner. Rather, he moved to embrace the big picture. Some folks in his hometown got spitting mad at a white boy banging out black music, so he egged them on with a ringing barrage of backalley chordplay. Others raged that setting church music to the rhythms of a

barroom or a bordello was sacrilege! Jerry Lee served up a dose of coal-cellar boogie-woogie just to see the furnace in their eyes. And shook his skinny ass at them for good measure.

On the lam from everything his devout forebears held dear, driven by an unbridled lust to own the moment, Jerry Lee looked at what he had wrought and saw that it was good—good rock and roll. Jerry Lee had elected, for better or worse, to explore every nook and cranny of who he hoped and feared himself to be, swallowing the gigantic promise of America in one shivering gulp and washing it down with a scalding double swig of Night Train wine.

He made his choice, crossed the line, and began devouring great balls of fire for breakfast, pushing himself to every unholy limit he could perceive in his own private universe. In so doing, Jerry Lee remade himself in the image and likeness of a rock star. And so he continues to be, through bouts with loaded pistols, overturned Rolls Royces, bags of Biphetamines and Placidyls, bottles of grain alcohol, five wrecked marriages, and seven shades of almighty mayhem swirling around eighty-eight ivories that rattle with a music bent on exorcism through possession. He dances on tombstones, bays at the moon, and pisses icewater in the faces of all who go to bed too early or remain there too long. Until, on the appointed day, at an hour known only to the Lord (or perhaps the Devil), Jerry Lee will lay down his massive, self-imposed burden and confess, probably in a wobbly whisper, "Take me now, Big Man, for I am finally *spent.*"

ABOVE
Professor Longhair, the "Bach of Rock" (David Gahr).

EWIS AND OTHERS LIKE HIM LOOKED TO THE STORIED divertissements of Louisiana for their earliest inspiration. In New Orleans' Congo Square, in the early 1800s, slaves were permitted by their masters to congregate on certain days and play their native instruments. To chase their despair and alienation, to enrich their fragile sense of community, and to beguile and bewilder their captors, these displaced Ashanti, Yoruban, and Senegalese people combined their own riveting rhythms with new ones that had bombarded them during their difficult passage and in their new surroundings: hymns, sea chanteys, flamenco tempos, and brassy quadrilles.

This was a scandalous but necessary evil—in the opinion of polite society. But, in time, the torrid outdoor displays evolved into an accepted exhibition and rallying point. And when the Africans' admiration of the martial cadences of European processional rites induced them to include these rhythms in their own elaborate burial rites, the groundwork was laid for an enduring Crescent City institution: funeral marching bands. Among the youths who grew up following, and then playing in, those street parades were Joe "King" Oliver, Louis "Dippermouth" Armstrong, and one Henry Roeland Byrd—better known as Professor Longhair, the legendary "Bach of Rock," whose barrelhouse mambo-rhumba piano figures would profoundly influence Fats Domino, Huey Smith, Allen Toussaint, Mac "Dr. John" Rebennack, and by extension, every keyboard carouser from Ray Charles to Sly Stone.

A thousand miles away in Salem, Ohio, the patrons of the Golden Fleece Tavern would gather around the owner and his sons as they performed "The Arkansas Traveler," a traditional skit that tells the tale of an impressionable hayseed just returned from his first trip down to Louisiana. It is the story of a traveler who can't get this nagging New Orleans jig out of his fool head, and he takes up a fiddle in a fitful attempt to reproduce it. His efforts are accompanied by a vaudeville of give-and-take chatter with a passing stranger who repeatedly demands that the silly traveler stop jawboning and "finish the tune!"

The tipplers at the Golden Fleece would sit through every hoary straight man-buffoon exchange with gleeful anticipation, knowing full well that the stranger would ultimately take up a fiddle himself and duel the traveler to a furiously dexterous finale. It was through these workaday jam sessions and frolics—and

ABOVE
Little Richard, "Whoooo!" (Frank Driggs Collection).
FACING PAGE
Elvis, pulling in the big bucks (Frank Driggs Collection).

through others of endlessly quirky variety (field hollers, chain-gang chants, bunkhouse and saddle singalongs, immigrant street songs, marching tunes)—that one vast, hodgepodge nation, drunk on its own adolescence, eventually gave birth to the ominously adrenalized spectacle of rock and roll.

This development occurred as the land's myriad social conventions grew more rigid, and its class, racial, religious, and sexual lines had become more dangerous, even lethal, to cross. And yet, as embodied by its major exponents—the true rock stars—rock and roll has less to do with rebellion than with an exquisite self-absorption in which there is no tug of war, only a swift, steady pull. Barriers don't exist in the minds of the most gifted rockers; their thoughts are elsewhere, locked into a feeding frenzy. At its high end, rock and roll not only eats its young, it eats everything in sight. Beyond gluttony, beyond selfishness, beyond caring, it is a banquet nonpareil, oblivious to *all* consequences. For the rapacious rocker believes that all history, whether personal history, rock history, or human history, is redeemed by eternity.

THERE IS AN ENDURING SUPERSTITION IN THE RURAL SOUTH THAT EVERY great bluesman and blueswoman had an otherworldly tutor who taught them to arrest listeners with the inky side of their souls; that they had a secret handshake with the Angel of Death, who enabled them to live so recklessly, ever-flirting with dissolution while drawing others into their damning web.

It is ironic that, to an extent, rock and roll began in church, when Johnny Shines raised his voice as a child in a Memphis chapel and marveled at the sound of it, realizing there was only one John Ned Shines and he was never gonna come again. So he and Robert Johnson split from the tabernacles that had inspired them with the Lord's greatest gift—singularity—and they hit the treacherous black hobo trail to chart the parameters of their amazing onlyness. They wrote songs about sinister women, nights of nameless terror, the nearness of Satan's grip. They sang of "conjurers" who worked spells or "mojos" in boneyards after dusk, combining snakeskins, horsehair, and grave dirt into potions that might forestall the grim final reckoning. Further, one of the first times Jerry Lee Lewis played piano was at the Holiness Church Meeting of God Assembly in Waxahatchie, and all he wanted the man in the pulpit to explain was: if God created pretty young virgins, fast cars, summer nights, and the fixings for bourbon, why couldn't he celebrate His handiwork?

PRECEDING PAGES
John Lennon and Mick Jagger, after the ball (Ron Galella).

F YOU WANT TO GET A HEALTHY YOUNG MAN OR WOMAN PLENTY thirsty for something, all you've got to do is forbid it. Then stick to your guns. No liquor. No sex. No drugs. No release from fear. No accurate picture of who you really are, good or bad.

To help codify these raw rituals of denial, Carl Jung coined a term for the personality traits and smoldering drives all men refuse to acknowledge—the "shadow." Jung didn't live to hear the Beach Boys harmonize on Brian Wilson's "I Just Wasn't Made for These Times" or witness Mick Jagger and Keith Richards whipping into "Sympathy for the Devil" or see Boy George cavorting through "Karma Chameleon" and then telling reporters, "I'm not interested in gay rights because to me gay is normal, being free to do what you want to do." But Jung would have understood the dynamic within their messages, as well as the nature of the All-American Universal Rock and Roll Ethic: what you don't see, ask for.

By 1983, the Police, a British-American band which openly craved superstar status before such temporal achievements evaporate in what they believe is the millennial onrush of a nuclear Armageddon, released *Synchronicity*, an album based on Jung's theories. The record, which became one of the biggest-selling LPs in rock history and made the Police the most popular group on the planet, was an icy assessment of the shadow side of human nature. It put forth the plea that the most significant task of any individual is to achieve harmony between the conscious and the unconscious; that is, the only antidote to evil is self-knowledge, because our dreams are the very harbingers of our potentially monstrous malevolence.

Raw self-revelations and dark admonishments are only part of the rock star's intent, however, for rock and roll craves an audience. The rock concert is a tribal rite in which an option-addicted culture is allowed to blow off its enormous stores of nervous energy. But after the show, the true rock star keeps on rocking; he or she is the potential nemesis of social order—an energy vampire eager to sate himself while there's still time—and any particular audience is merely another course in a desperate feast.

Considerable energy is expended to keep the party going; each day, the capability to invoke glorious and grotesque rock and roll visions escalates. When American popular music first became linked with electricity, a unique brand of sensory sorcery bloomed. Nobody is entirely certain how the phenomenon of electricity works, no physicist comprehends the precise chemistry of the particles of

ABOVE
Pete Townshend, at the hop (Ebet Roberts).

charge as they repel each other and create a propulsive new force; it's a modern sort of alchemy. Likewise, the power to fill entire arenas with the reverberating voltage of rock and roll, drums rumbling with the tumult of mountains falling, roaring guitars and synthesized keyboards keeping several thousand craniums humming, represents a quantum leap into new realms of preternatural exultation, mesmerization, and assault—the blunt death of musical limits.

When you confront your own shadow in all its incarnations, you're inside rock and roll. And when you do it musically, onstage, in a terrible, wonderful, chilling contract with your audience, succeeding at encouraging them to stir some measure of their shadows into the spiraling maelstrom, then you're a rock star.

This is the story of rock and roll—past, present, and future—and some of its greatest stars. It is told through the fabric, texture, and dimensions of the stars' inner voracity, their art becoming their life, their life becoming their art, all of it of a piece. It explores a world apart from the normal codes of behavior, from commonplace concepts of responsibility, of loyalty, of duty, of professionalism. Unlike most other schools of musical thought, rock and roll virtually discards conservatorylike rubrics concerning study, dedication, and virtuosity. Theater traditions and showbiz ethics become blurred or trampled underfoot in the onrush of its peculiar imperatives. The show mustn't necessarily go on; rock and roll is self-absorbed almost to the point of ignoring itself.

The book is divided into three sections: the Ancestors, who laid the groundwork for the rock and roll disposition; the Descendants, who expanded the parameters of its impropriety; and the Inheritors, who are striving to find new applications for the uncommon conduct pioneered by their role models. The choices made herein were intended not only to isolate personal styles and seminal musical contributions, but to advance the bizarre saga itself. The book is meant to be read in sequence, as a kind of story with a cumulative lesson, rather than as an exclusive encyclopedic collection. In this way, a plot emerges, one figure learning from, influencing, exciting, threatening, and spurring another. The risks become greater, and the sense of dark heritage deepens in the mind of each participant as they collide with their commingled destinies.

Any truths in the book emerge organically, whatever momentum that's achieved builds on itself, the process becomes the reward, and it is rich with the energy of living. As the torch is passed, an ethos is forged. The conscience is confronted. The truth is felt. And, in time, the soul is sold.

FACING PAGE
Boy George, ballsy gender bender (Richard Corman for L'uomo Vogue).

CHAPTER

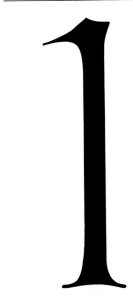

THE ANCESTORS

FACING PAGE
Neatness counts—Buddy Holly and the Crickets (Frank Driggs Collection).
OVERLEAF
Little Richard, Lula Hardaway, her son Stevie Wonder, and Chuck Berry, at the Grammys (Derek/Photo Trends).

ROBERT JOHNSON

FOR THE POOR BLACK, LIFE ON THE MISSISSIPPI DELTA IN THE 1930s had an acrid flavor, and those who learned to stomach it came to exist in a curious pocket of time, set apart from the uncomprehending white world that coursed around them. The lowly sharecropper was in terminal debt to one of a vast network of corrupt white landlords whose larcenous, comically inflated fees he could barely hope to meet. The landless day laborers who worked the cotton plantations were treated like ghosts: expected to appear at sunrise, toil without complaint in the unspeakable heat, and vanish at the smoky first hint of dusk. What other sustaining labor that existed was to be found on the levees that strained to hold back the tides of the fickle Mississippi. Since the levees required constant inspection and maintenance, work camps grew up around them, often peopled by convicts from prison farms in the district. The camps were vile, squalid places that produced criminality of the most notorious sort. Violent incidents usually erupted on the weekends, when parties were held on the riverbanks; prostitutes and sporting women would be brought in by wagon or truck, and entertainment was provided by the more daring local blues musicians. Such musicians were a highly mobilized underclass of the delta caste system. These men—and a very few women—elected to drift from town to town playing a circuit of "jook joints," country picnics, and streetcorners where the deputy wouldn't collar them.

Country picnics were rambunctious Saturday-night affairs (and direct rivals of Sunday-morning church services) that took place in remote fields. Invitation was by word of mouth; bottles of coal oil, with a burning rag for a wick, would be hung in trees to guide people to the sites. The highly popular jooks (probably from the West African word *joog*, meaning to "shake up") served as the mainstay of many an itinerant bluesman. Jooks were shacks, usually bootlegger-run, hidden deep in the woods, where one could find beer, bad gin, "hooch," casual sex, and dancing fed either by live music or the "vendor," as the first crude jukeboxes were called. The musicians at picnics and jooks might be given a small fee, but usually they had to depend on the generosity of the tanked-up patrons when it came time to pass the hat.

Competition among the players to hold the floor was as keen as the spirited wooing of the available women, and fists and razors would fly over both issues. The best way to remain top dog in the "headcutting" contests that could ensue between two or more contentious bluesmen was to develop instantaneous, encyclopedic mental access to the chord patterns and lyrics of every blues record currently popular, as well as the latest output of your immediate adversaries. The trick was to concoct a well-rhymed response to an opponent's wiliest stanza, either building on or reinterpreting the man's own words, and then shifting the balance by slipping in a piping-hot verse of your own creation. Headcutting was both a way of blowing off steam and tempering your command of the craft. However, the better you were at it, the greater the odds of getting your ear torn off by a sorely enraged loser.

Vocalion

Not Licensed for Radio Broadcast

(SA 2586)

Vocal Blues with Guitar Acc.

TERRAPLANE BLUES
-Robert Johnson-
ROBERT JOHNSON

03416

U.S. PAT 1,637,544 &4 JR. SWICK RECORD CORPORATION

Vocalion

Not Licensed for
Radio Broadcast
(SA 2580)

Vocal Blues
with
Guitar Acc.

KIND HEARTED WOMAN
BLUES

-Robert Johnson-

ROBERT JOHNSON

03416

I T WAS INTO THIS REALM OF INDENTURE, SORROW, SIN, AND DESPERATION that Robert Johnson was born. The date was May 8, 1911; the place was Hazelhurst, a little hamlet south of Jackson, Mississippi. His mother was Julia Ann Majors, and his absentee father was one Noah Johnson. Julia had married Charles Dodds, Jr., a prosperous cabinetmaker and landowner, several years before Robert was born, but Dodds was chased out of town in 1907 by a lynch mob after he'd had an altercation with two prominent white businessmen. Julia stayed behind in Hazelhurst, and Robert was the result of a liaison, during Dodds's forced exile, with sharecropper Johnson, who moved on shortly afterward. Robert wound up living in Robinsonville, Mississippi, with his mother and a man named William "Dusty" Willis. Johnson would never know his real father, and in adulthood he would vacillate between contemptuous disinterest in him and a distempered desire to locate him.

As a boy, Robert took up the jew's-harp and the harmonica as distractions and would regularly sneak off to jooks in the Robinsonville area to listen to and learn from such delta blues greats as Charley Patton, Willie Brown and, later, Eddie "Son" House. Robert became known as something of a pest, dogging the bluesmen's heels as they made their stops, scrutinizing their solo and group playing, and asking to be shown chords and fingering techniques. Still, it seemed that music might be no more than a hobby for Robert. In 1929, he married sixteen-year-old Virginia Travis. But when Virginia died in childbirth a year later, taking their infant son with her, Robert's few fragile roots in the world were ripped out, and he adopted the ways of a determined rounder.

Moving back to the vicinity of Hazelhurst, he took up with an Alabama-born guitarist named Ike Zinnerman, an obscure figure who boasted that his mastery of his instrument stemmed from some graveyard conjury. Johnson then faded from sight. He resurfaced in Robinsonville a year later, attacking the blues with canny ferocity. This new-found flair on his hefty Gibson guitar and the flinty sophistication of his bottle-slide playing left Charley Patton, Willie Brown, and Son House stupefied. Rumors circulated that Johnson had struck a bargain with Satan. This belief would be supplemented by eerie testimony from Johnny Shines, another esteemed country stalwart out of Memphis and a frequent traveling companion of Johnson's. Shines maintained that no matter what godforsaken sleeping arrangements they would make on the road, Johnson would somehow arise from every dusty ditch or straw-strewn boxcar "looking like he's just stepped out of church! Never did nothing to himself any more than me, neither...."

Some of Johnson's relatives later allowed as to how the whole Faustian deal had gone down in 1930, just after nightfall, at a certain rural crossroads: Robert had accepted his talent in exchange for his soul, payment due eight years hence. The supernatural menace of a night-engulfed crossroads looms large in folklore in the deep South; one of the few prominent landmarks in the blunt tableland of the delta, the crossroads epitomizes the vulnerability of the black in a hostile world. To find oneself at a crossroads after dark is to be stranded on open ground, an easy mark for whites who don't like the idea of a black man on the move. Hard choices are the consequences for blacks who "ain't where they supposed to be," and in blues circles, the devil is your only friend when you need to arrive at your next destination in a hurry.

The ambition of most every bluesman was to get onto records. It was common in the late 1920s for field scouts to move through the major cities of the deep South seeking more grist for the lucrative "race records" mill. Portable recording units captured the performances of Charley Patton and Son House, and these sides were sizable hits locally; but few delta blues stylists had significant commercial impact in big markets like St. Louis, Chicago, and New York, where their sound was considered too rustic. Moreover, many of the best delta bluesmen saw themselves primarily as entertainers whose surest grub stake was their local following.

Robert Johnson, however, perceived himself as a recording artist and tailored the solo presentation of his material with such meticulousness that it scarcely varied from night to night. Rather than hold fast to the small-town hegemony that lordly tyrants like Charley Patton thrived on, Johnson was consumed with the idea of projecting his tortured perspective to the largest possible audience. This broader world view was reflected in the mongrel qualities of his sound. His songs do possess the earthy verve of the delta; but the tense single-string guitar attack favored in Chicago and the melodic strength of the best blues emerging from the East are also apparent. Johnson's material didn't ramble on discursively or strive to evoke the harsh idioms and multihued landscape that first inspired it. On the contrary, it was tight and searing in its stark compactness, and it rocked the blues with voodoo abandon.

Most of all, his repertoire was a litany of widening mental and spiritual wounds: heaving, throbbing, scarlet patches of rent muscle and tissue, coupled with the shrieking horror that greets such sights. His recordings of "Stones in My Passway" and "Love in Vain" were you-are-there utterances of the resounding victory of despair over faith.

> *I got stones in my passway*
> *An' my road seem dark as night!*
> *I have pains in my heart*
> *They have taken my appetite.*

The appetite in question is sex, but even as he and his latest conquest rise to ravage each other, the oxygen needed to fuel it is seemingly sucked from their bedchamber, their quivering torsos near to imploding. "I got a woman that I'm lovin', boy," Johnson gasps, as the desolate two-minute confessional culminates in a harrowing carnival of psychic dismemberment, "but she don't mean a thing." Like virtually all of the existing Johnson guitar-and-voice tracks—maybe thirty-two solo songs—"Stones in My Passway" is the sound of a doomed man thinking out loud, feeling with each cutting tug of the frets that he'll never get out of his blues alive.

One can only speculate on the cruel forces that were laying waste to Johnson, but it's clear that he ran toward, rather than from them. Even as he was copping and honing exuberant rhythmic conceits, Johnson was also being influenced by one elder statesman's grotesque sense of etiquette. Charley Patton was a short, brutish son of a preacher whose motley bloodlines allowed him to pass for white, black, or Indian as circumstances dictated. He bullied his way through Mississippi while managing to avoid a single incident of manual labor. Perpetually drunk and abusive, no loggers' barbeque or cutthroats' convention was too rowdy for his tastes, and he took considerable pleasure in beating his eight common-law wives.

For Johnson's part, he never ceased his own wanton womanizing. He even concocted bizarre, misogynous ditties like "Dead Shrimp Blues" to commemorate it. After he remarried, to sweetnatured Calletta Craft, in 1931, the slender, handsome bluesman supposedly demanded that the union be kept secret, lest it cramp his lecherous style. Johnson eventually deserted Calletta. She suffered a complete nervous collapse and, by all accounts, Johnson was unmoved. He cared as little for friendship as he did for lasting love. He was known to drop out of sight on a moment's notice—sometimes in the middle of a show—and not turn up again until weeks or months afterward. His reputation for communion with the supernatural was enhanced by his habit of frequently altering his appearance and manner and adopting a host of aliases. Contemporaries who are still living are said to wonder if they had actually met the real Robert Johnson or only an impersonator. A half-dozen photos of the man allegedly exist, but as of this writing not one has been published.

One thing disciples as diverse as Muddy Waters, Elmore James, John Lee "Sonny Boy" Williamson, and Junior Parker could be certain of was the veracity of Johnson's talent. Robert Johnson's first recording session was in San Antonio, Texas, on November 23, 1936. He'd been introduced to Ernie Oertle, a scout for the American Record Company and the Vocalion label, by H.C. Spier, a Jackson, Mississippi, music shop owner. The Johnson Vocalion session, which took place in a hotel room, documented some of the most formidable blues of that or any other era. "Terraplane Blues," his first 78 rpm single, was a lewd composition that compared his woman to an automobile ("When I mash down your little starter / Then your spark plug will give me fire").

While "Terraplane Blues" would rack up sizable sales in the delta and become Johnson's only real hit during his lifetime, the rest of the tunes he cut in his initial sessions did not attain status as classics until they were rediscovered by Muddy Waters et al., in the postwar heyday of electrified Chicago blues.

The most fearsome of all the inaugural tracks Johnson laid down in 1936 was "Crossroad Blues," in which he snarls through gritted teeth of the dire predicament of finally finding himself stuck on a darkened crossroads with Lucifer laughing in the wings.

In June of 1937, Johnson did a session in a Dallas warehouse and recorded more hair-raising anthems of dashed hopes, among them "Hellhound on My Trail" and "Me and the Devil Blues." The latter concludes with Johnson sternly advising, "You may bury my body down by the highway side / So my old evil spirit can catch a Greyhound bus and ride."

ROBERT JOHNSON DIED ON AUGUST 16, 1938, IN GREENWOOD, MISSISSIPPI, after being poisoned at a house party he'd been hired to play at. The story is told that he got himself pie-eyed—Johnson would guzzle any form of white lightning or grain alcohol—and flirted with his employer's wife. His jealous host retaliated by serving him tainted rye. Johnson is said to have lingered on in agony for several days before expiring. His remains were laid in a pine box supplied by the county; burial was in an unmarked grave. Rumors persist that the site is somewhere just off Mississippi Highway 7—where his evil spirit could indeed board a passing Greyhound and continue to haunt the turnpikes.

H E HAD THE GUMPTION OF A FARMBOY, RUNNING BACK TO HIS roots in rural east Texas, and the flashy savvy of a cowboy, tied to an adolescence spent in the ranch country of west Texas. So it's hardly surprising that, on a dare, he took up the fiddle, that lyric frontier lathe, and went on to become one of the best players in the world.

Born in Hall County, Texas, on March 6, 1905, ten-year-old James Robert Wills was thought to be a damn sight better at handling a horse than a bow made from its tail. But he told his cousin he was sick and tired of hearing him saw out the same sluggish old ditty on his violin. Well, could little James Robert do better? Better and *faster*, came the reply. Wills figured out the melody and a snappy technique in short order and won the dare. After dawn-to-dusk rounds of cotton picking, he would borrow the fiddle and expand his repertoire with frontier tunes like "Gone Indian."

As the stock market was crashing and gangsters were suffering wholesale slaughter in the St. Valentine's Day Massacre, Bob Wills was beginning his professional fiddling career around Fort Worth with guitarist Herman Arn-spiger. They called themselves the Wills Fiddle Band. A standard barn-dance twosome, they were committed to satisfying the old folks with a mid-tempo "Cotton-Eyed Joe" and "Old Dan Tucker," but they also drew in the young folk with a saucy "La Cucaracha" and risky bits of Bessie Smith or W.C. Handy.

T EXAS IN THE LATE DEPRESSION ERA WAS A LAND UNDERGOING A DRA-matic transition as the ravages of the boll weevil were offset by the oil boom of the 1930s, drawing migrants from throughout the South, along with their agriculture-steeped traditions of song and story. Blacks, Chicanos, Cajuns, and white Protestants commingled in a stark new world being built on the old foundations of southern ruralism, and the music they played and shared in their free time became as pluralistic as the state's exploding population.

The cardinal rule of any touring group in the region was to have a fiddler above reproach, one who could approximate, with alacrity, songs called out from the crowd. Wills had that requirement more than fulfilled. While a collector of rhythms, styles, and songs, he was no common folklorist or slick popularizer but rather a canny enthusiast who would blossom into one of the greatest innovators in all of popular music. If country & western can be considered a valid offshoot from the country lifeline, it was Bob Wills who put the "western" into the term, and he taught it how to *swing*.

By 1930, the Wills Fiddle Band had become the larger Aladdin Laddies, and then—under the sponsorship of the Burrus Mill and Elevator Company (whence came fat sacks of Light Crust Flour)—the Light Crust Doughboys. The group performed manual labor at the mill by day and then broke at noon to play live on KFJZ or WBAP, and they prospered under the management of

OKeh

Use Columbia

or Okeh Needles

6692

(H 849)

LET'S RIDE WITH BOB

(Theme Song)   Instrumental

-Wills-

BOB WILLS & his TEXAS PLAYBOYS

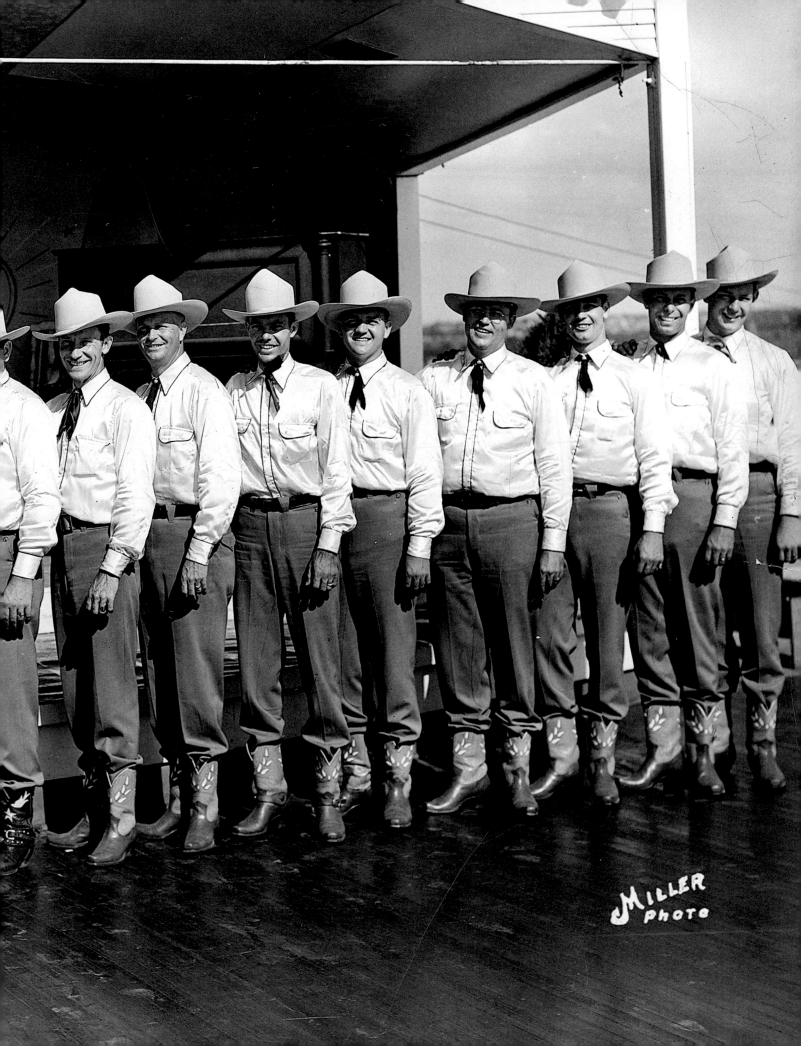

Miller Photo

W. Lee "Pappy" O'Daniel. Bob himself was a star fiddler on no less than three radio stations in the area. But the Doughboys were weakened when Milton Brown, their featured singer, broke off to form the Musical Brownies. Then, in 1933, Wills was bounced from the band by Pappy O'Daniel, who disliked his immoderate drinking habits and the loutish behavior they precipitated. Wills took his banjoist brother Johnnie Lee Wills with him, and they secured a radio show in Waco, Texas.

Forming Bob Wills and His Texas Playboys (in the Doughboys mold), he settled in Tulsa, Oklahoma, and signed a contract in 1935 with Brunswick Records. The Playboys were the premier act in the Southwest; their noontime show on KVOO was the rage, 50,000 watts beaming it out to every cow town and county seat in the region. Wills earned the respect and affection of his fellow musicians for never turning an auditioning picker down. What made him a virtual folk hero, however, was the majestic band he ultimately assembled and the unprecedented dimensionality of their fiddle-based sound. Thrilled by the Big Band swing, New Orleans jazz, and bayou bluegrass of the day, and touched by the wistful sweetness of mariachi and the sprightly uplift of *nortena* polkas, Wills put horns and reeds into his thirteen-piece Playboys. What's more, he gave them a freedom to experiment as vast as the territory in which they toured.

After Prohibition was repealed in 1933, the Playboys had a helluva lot more new dancehalls and roadhouses begging to book them. The sight of their tour bus, with its Longhorn hood ornament fastened above the gleaming grill-work, quickened the pulse of many a rural farmworker, and its very arrival always drew sizable crowds. Entire families would travel as far as 200 miles to see Wills—a beefy, solidly built man with a broad face, high forehead, bushy eyebrows, and warm eyes—in his $200 suits and custom-made boots, a wide-brimmed fedora tilted raffishly on his head, puffing on a fat Corona Corona and greeting every plowhand with the affectionate good cheer of a Dutch uncle. He was one of them, a product of the red dust that mottled their knees and wrinkled their brows, the kind of man who could tell a good joke, take a stiff drink, and hook a woman with the horny twinkle in his gaze.

The band members were no slouches either, dressed in crisp, lordly western outfits and possessing some of the best musical chops in the wild new West. Leon McAuliffe was a master of the steel guitar, his speed and richness of tone unmatched; Eldon Shamblin was a crack rhythm guitarist and arranger whose duets with McAuliffe were seamless; Cecil Brower and Jesse Ashlock were formidable fiddling companions for Wills; and lead vocalist Tommy Duncan's agile country blues tack was one of the most imitated of its day. As for the horn section, it was a heart-stopping drill team, as colorful as it was controversial. When the Playboys moved their base from Tulsa back to Fort Worth, the local musicians' union initially refused to allow them to play, so flabbergasted were they by the rebellious presence of drums and brass in a country & western dance band. Before too long, electric guitars also became part of the equation, and the Playboys' ranks swelled to eighteen. Pop music had never seen such an anomalous musical amalgam, but early rockers understood and were profoundly affected by Wills's iconoclastic tastes.

If Bob Wills was a maverick, he was also a benevolent taskmaster, his gleeful cries of "Ahhh-ha!" and "Take it away, Leon!" a genuine expression of the pride he took in the musical prowess of his team. He toured as far as California, taking what came to be dubbed "Okie jazz" to homesick servicemen training in the lengthening shadows of war, reviving their drive with renditions of "Steel Guitar Rag," "Take Me Back to Tulsa," "Sitting on Top of the World," "Mexicali Rose," "My Confession." But when Pearl Harbor was bombed on December 7, 1941, the band answered the call to avenge the infamous deed, and the Playboys were scattered.

After the war, Wills reunited the Playboys. They decided to deemphasize the brass section somewhat, and they became better known nationally—even breaking some of Benny Goodman's attendance records as they brought their exotic western swing into major cities in the Northeast and Midwest.

In 1964, after a second heart attack, Wills broke up the Playboys, and they passed into legend as the best two-fisted cowboy tavern band that ever set "Sally Goodin" to a swinging beat. Wills had the first of several strokes in 1969, his health and mobility severely curtailed; but in 1973, he went up to Dallas to supervise the recording of a memorial Playboys album for United Artists Records. When Wills took sick again, devoted fan Merle Haggard flew in to help out. It was the last studio session for the original Texas Playboys.

A massive stroke took seventy-year-old Bob Wills on May 12, 1975, while he was being cared for at the Kent Nursing Home in Fort Worth. A true musical outlaw and beloved pioneer, he was a hero to the working poor he devoted much of his life to entertaining, and he was eulogized on country stations from the Panhandle to the Rockies. Men and women who would never forget his fond whoops and his hell-for-leather fiddle breaks wept softly as the bright strains of one of his loveliest ranch dance sonnets swirled out of their radios:

> *Stay all night, stay a little longer,*
> *Dance all night, dance a little longer,*
> *Pull off your coat, throw it in the corner,*
> *Don't see why you don't stay a little longer.*

C H U C K   B E R R Y

I T WAS 1910. THE BOY SCOUTS WERE INCORPORATED, VICTOR HERBERT HAD a big hit with "Ah! Sweet Mystery of Life," and Congressman James R. Mann had a federal statute placed on the books, a statute that would later put a considerable crimp in at least one fellow's rock and roll proclivities. The White Slave Traffic Act and its amendments made it unlawful for anyone to coerce, entice, or transport females across state lines "for the purpose of prostitution or debauchery, or for any other immoral purpose." In other words—in the minds of many noxious, reprobate rockers—"There goes the weekend!"

O N DECEMBER 23, 1959, CHARLES EDWARD ANDERSON BERRY OF ST. Louis, Missouri, was charged with running afoul of the Mann Act. The guitarist and singer, who'd had three singles on the charts in 1958 ("Sweet Little Sixteen," "Johnny B. Goode," and "Carol"), was riding out a fallow year by barnstorming the Southwest, his three-piece band and himself piled into his Cadillac. On December 1, 1959, they performed in El Paso, Texas. Here Berry had the dubious good fortune to encounter one Janice Norine Escalanti, a fourteen-year-old Apache girl with an eighth-grade education, who toiled in the town as a waitress/prostitute. Berry offered her a job as a hatcheck girl in his St. Louis nightspot and invited her to join the tour for the duration, selling souvenir photographs at each show. There was just enough room in the Cadillac's front seat, next to its owner-operator, to make the proposition appealing. So the five took off, scattering the tumbleweed behind them.

They reached Tucson, Arizona, under cover of darkness on December 2, and Berry procured two adjoining rooms at a motel—one for the band, the other for himself and Janice. From Tucson, the party proceeded to Phoenix, then Santa Fe, New Mexico, and Denver, Colorado, where Berry registered Janice and himself at the Drexel Hotel under the names "Mr. and Mrs. Janet Johnson." The room had one bed. Soon they were on to Pueblo, then Kansas City, Missouri. From Kansas City, Chuck flew to St. Louis; the band and the girl hit town in the Cadillac hours later.

After taking Escalanti to his house, Berry escorted her to his night club, where he introduced her to manager Francine Gillium, at whose home Janice was to stay. Smiles were exchanged all around. Then, on or about December 18, Chuck informed Janice that her execution of the delicate art of hatchecking was unsatisfactory, and he discharged her. Janice collected her things in a brown paper bag, and Berry drove her to the bus depot. He bought her a one-way ticket to El Paso (she'd wanted one to Yuma, Arizona), and gave her $5 before he sped off. Changing her mind about leaving town, she showed up back at the night club. A disapproving Berry seized the semiprecious bus ticket from her purse, leaving her to her own meager resources.

On December 22, police in Yuma got an informative phone call from Janice Escalanti. They told her to sit tight and expect the St. Louis police to

pick her up. Berry and Escalanti were taken into custody and brought to a St. Louis station house. In the trial that transpired, she testified that Berry had had sexual intercourse with her in numerous locations—in the Tucson motel, twice in the back seat of the speeding Cadillac (en route to Denver), in the Drexel Hotel, in the home of Francine Gillium.

Berry entered a plea of not guilty. The jury thought otherwise. On March 11, 1960, Berry was sentenced to five years imprisonment and ordered to pay a fine of $5,000. He appealed, asserting that the evidence was insufficient to establish the intent necessary to make his admitted transportation of the girl a criminal offense. He also felt that the "hostile and prejudicial conduct and remarks of the trial court" and of Judge George H. Moore, Jr., concerning his race made the trial unfair. The appeals court concurred on the latter point and set a new trial.

At the second trial, Berry—who testified on his own behalf—was asked, "What was your purpose in bringing Janice from Texas to Missouri?" His answer: "She needed a job, and I had a job for her at the club." The jury returned a verdict of guilty, and Berry was sentenced to three years and a $5,000 fine. He spent two years in prison in Terre Haute, Indiana.

Shortly before his release in 1964, he had a Top 10 record in England with a reissue of "Let It Rock/Memphis, Tennessee." Berry's preprison recordings, including his 1950s hits—"Maybellene," "Roll Over Beethoven," "School Days," "Rock and Roll Music"—had made him a favorite and strong influence of the bands who were mounting the first British Invasion. Both the Beatles and the Rolling Stones sang his praises and covered his songs on their first few LPs. Their ebullient support helped create the environment in which Berry regained his former status as the foremost black rock and roll star, scoring with songs like "You Can Never Tell." His best material—"Round and Round," "Nadine," "Little Queenie," "You Can't Catch Me," "Sweet Little Rock and Roll," and "Living in the U.S.A."—would continue to be recorded. The leading talents of rock and roll rightfully identified with Berry's witty, slyly vulgar sendups of teenage social mores and aspirations and admired the peerless, percolating meld of country & western and blues strains.

But Berry himself would achieve his greatest commercial success with an outtake from his writing files. "My Ding-a-Ling" was a tacky fragment of bathroom humor at its most puerile, but Berry fashioned it into a festive live sing-a-long, and a nation with nothing better to do in 1972 bought enough copies to make it Berry's first million-selling No. 1 single. Whether his audience had sunk to his level or he'd risen to their new low-water mark is a nonburning question of the "chicken or the egg" variety; history will chronicle that Berry crossed state lines to dispense juvenile smut.

CHUCK WAS BORN TO MARTHA AND HENRY BERRY IN SAN JOSE, A TOWN in California's Santa Clara Valley. The date was October 18 or January 15, 1926 or 1931; nobody has ever given a straight answer. At the height of the Depression, Henry Berry took his wife and six children to St. Louis, settling in the suburb of Elleadsville. At the age of six, young Chuck began singing in the choir of the Antioch Baptist Church, but his thoughts were elsewhere. In his teens, he excelled in both hairdressing and attempted robbery. He earned a stretch in reform school (1944 to 1947) for the latter and a Poro School of Beauty Culture degree in cosmetology and tonsorial

PRECEDING PAGE
Chuck Berry, backseat Romeo (Frank Driggs Collection).

FACING PAGE
Jailbait rock, 1958 (Frank Driggs Collection).

skills for the former. While at Sumner High, he learned to play guitar on a secondhand Kay model given to him by St. Louis blues shouter Joe Sherman. St. Louis was a hotbed of rhythm and blues experimentation, and Chuck counted Billy Eckstine and Nat "King" Cole as his chief vocal influences, while Aaron "T-Bone" Walker, Charlie Christian, and Muddy Waters helped forge his cheerfully repetitive chord and riffing patterns. He supplemented his earnings from playing in the Cosmopolitan Club in East St. Louis by laboring on the assembly line of a General Motors Fisher Body plant.

In 1952, he transformed the Johnny Johnson Trio, which he'd often sat in with, into the Chuck Berry Trio, which featured Ebby Harding on drums and Johnson on piano. By 1954, Berry had a wife and two kids to support. He accepted an invitation from Muddy Waters, who'd caught him at the Cosmopolitan Club, to come to Chicago and meet Leonard Chess of Chess Records. Chuck played him two songs the trio had set down on a borrowed portable tape recorder, a blues number called "Wee Wee Hours" and "Ida Red," a traditional country tune popularized by Bob Wills. Chess took him into the studio in May of 1955, and he cut a new version of "Ida Red" which Leonard Chess renamed "Maybellene" (inspired by a hair cream of the same name). The record was sent to disk jockey Alan Freed, who accepted the payola perk of a credit as coauthor and added "Maybellene" to his playlist. The single clicked, and the rock gospel according to Chuck Berry was born; its Old Testament was fleshed out with "Roll Over Beethoven" in 1956, while the New Testament had to wait until the postprison days, with 1964's "No Particular Place to Go."

The world was presented with his impishly angular features, pencil moustache, conked curls, two-string guitar lick, and skinny-legged duck walk in a succession of rock and roll films, *Rock, Rock, Rock* (1956), *Mister Rock and Roll* (1957), and *Go, Johnny, Go* (1959). In 1966, Mercury Records lured Berry away from Chess with an advance of $150,000. But after three fruitless years, Chuck was back in the Chess stable. His greatest songs—roughly forty lightly lurid gems about the inability of modern youth to conform to parental strictures, the speed limit, and the bent arm of the law—have become so ubiquitous in western culture that Chuck Berry is one of the few living rock and roll legends who can travel to any town on the map, carrying only his guitar, and within hours locate a young group of musicians who can back him up (on the cheap) with minimum coaching and scant rehearsal. The fat twang of his guitar and the swaggering cant of his lyrics epitomize rock and roll; they are its universal calling card...and then some. In 1977, when the Voyager 1 and 2 space probes were hurtled into the uncharted heavens, they carried audio equipment designed to last a billion years and a gold-plated copper record containing, among other things, the music of Chuck Berry.

Berry tours tirelessly, or holes up at his house on the grounds of Berry Park (his amusement park in Wentzville, Missouri), often chasing nosy press off the property. His recording activity has been slight, but a 1972 reissue of "Reelin' and Rockin' " did well. In 1979, he had an especially momentous year, with the release of the well-received *Rockit* album (his first LP in five years), an invitation to duck walk at the White House, and a 120-day prison term after being convicted of tax evasion by the Internal Revenue Service. A few waggish disk jockeys in the Midwest, loyal to the rock and roll Pied Piper, dug out a 1956 hit. The lyrics ran,"...free that *brown-eyed handsome man!*"

FACING PAGE
Berry in 1970, a paisley Pied Piper (Frank Driggs Collection).

R A Y   C H A R L E S

I T TOOK HIM ALMOST TWO YEARS TO LOSE HIS VISION, A SLOW-MOUNTING blur culminating in utter blackness. Among the sights he had to bid goodbye to were his mother Aretha's lustrous ebony hair, which ran down to her rump; the sawmill in Greenville, Florida, where honorary second mother Mary Jane Charles (his father's burly first wife) pulled water-coated planks away from the screech of the saw blade; the seasonal hog slaughter, which began with a gun muzzle jammed inside the ear, the bark of a single bullet, a slit throat, and a splash of red on the grass; wizened old Mr. Wylie Pittman approximating boogie-woogie "pie-ano" in the Red Wing general store and café. One last tableau captured in his mind's eye was that of his four-year-old brother George kicking, gasping, and ultimately drowning in the rinse water of a No. 4 washtub that his mother used for take-in laundry.

Puny five-year-old Ray had tried to pull his brother out of the water, but he couldn't and ran screaming for his mother. A few months after the funeral, his eyes began to secrete mucus and had to be pried open each morning after being daubed with a damp cloth. By the age of seven, glaucoma had taken its ultimate toll.

R AY CHARLES ROBINSON WAS BORN IN ALBANY, GEORGIA, ON SEPTEMBER 23, 1930, the son of Bailey Robinson, a roaming railworker he never knew. Ray's mother and Mary Jane took the child across the border into Florida in the first months of his life. The first piano he ever touched was Wylie Pittman's upright. He learned to read Braille in a segregated state boarding school for the blind ("Imagine the nonsense of segregating *blind* kids!") in St. Augustine, Florida, and delighted in *Tom Sawyer* and *Huckleberry Finn*. In 1937, near the end of his first year in school, he had to have his festering right eye removed. In 1940, word reached the family that his father had died. That same year, Ray began riding a bicycle and was able to do so freely and without need of supervision.

While in St. Augustine, he learned to compose, writing music in Braille, and to play clarinet, trumpet, saxophone, and keyboards. One of the first songs he learned to sing by heart was Lil Green's "Romance in the Dark." At the age of twelve, he lost his virginity in the restroom of a night club in Tallahassee, after a stint singing and playing with a combo led by a man named Lawyer Smith. Ray was fifteen and away at school when he learned that his mother had died. Leaving school, he began playing with various dance bands in the state (including an otherwise all-white hillbilly band called the Florida Playboys). He recorded his first original song, "Found My Baby There," on a wire recorder. Another similar session in Tampa produced "Walkin' and Talkin'," "Wonderin' and Wonderin'," and "Why Did You Go?"

Bored, and longing for a drastic change in his lonely life, he took his entire savings of $600 and traveled until he reached Seattle, Washington. Commandeering the piano in local cabarets like the Rocking Chair, the 908 Club, the

Washington Social Club, and the Black and Tan, he'd accompany himself in imitations of Nat "King" Cole. Eventually he formed a guitar, bass, and piano act called the McSon Trio, and he adopted Charles as his last name to prevent confusion with boxer Sugar Ray Robinson. At eighteen, he smoked his first jive and shot his first smack. In 1950, he had an illegitimate daughter with a woman named Louise. A block-jawed, square-shouldered youth with a well-knit physique and a bantering zest for seduction, he had a beguiling effect on women. They liked the brash confidence of his approach and the titillating mystery of his sunglassed glare.

Charles got to know Jack Lauderdale, owner of the small Swingtime label, from bumping into him constantly in the upstairs gambling parlor of the Rocking Chair, and in 1948, they cut a song Ray had written back in Florida, "Confession Blues." A year later, they went down to Los Angeles to do "Baby, Let Me Hold Your Hand"—Ray imitating the mellow, spooky delivery of blues balladeer Charles Brown—and it reached the Top 10 on the national R&B charts in 1951. He toured with blues singer Lowell Fulsom, who was doing well with "Everyday I Have the Blues," and became the pianist in Fulsom's band.

Ahmet Ertegun, Herb Abramson, and Jerry Wexler of Atlantic Records courted Charles when they heard the enormous potential in his brusque baritone, and they bought his contract from Swingtime in 1952 for $2,000. New York sessions in 1952 and 1953 resulted in the wry boogie-woogie of "Mess Around" and the vigorous, droll novelty single "It Should've Been Me." But Ray was to discover his own special direction down in New Orleans.

Wexler and Ertegun were in the Crescent City working with Big Joe Turner at producer Cosimo Matassa's studio when they bumped into Charles, who'd just gotten divorced after being married some sixteen months to a beautician named Eileen. He was hot to do some more recording, and they eventually got two exceptional sides: a Charles original, "Don't You Know," and a cover of the Guitar Slim sobber "Feelin' Sad."

The watershed session took place in an Atlanta radio station in 1954, shortly after he'd remarried, to a woman named Della, and attended the funeral of Mary Jane Charles. It was the first studio work since his formal signing with Atlantic, and it resulted in a rollicking gospel-blues exhortation written by Charles. Gone was the polite pose of a Nat Cole impersonator. In its place was a grinning growl that shot into falsetto flights. Backed by a seven-piece band, Charles's crowing bonhomie combined the splendid degeneracy of the chitlin circuit with the whooping sanctification of a church stomp. "I Got a Woman" rose to No. 2 on the national R&B survey in 1955 and created a new market for musical sacrilege. Ray promptly bought a new Cadillac, organized his own big band, and hired the Raelettes, a call-and-response female singing trio added to keep things nicely frenzied. The gritty gospel-blues hits kept on coming ("This Little Girl of Mine," "Blackjack," "Drown in My Own Tears," "Hallelujah I Love Her So," "Lonely Avenue," "Ain't That Love"), and Ray capped the decade with "What'd I Say," an unhinged ode to saturnalia that became a million-seller.

The word in the street was that Ray Charles was a flatout genius, able to hammer out show tunes, country & western, Latin rhythms, jazz jumps, and old standards with stunning finesse and a corrosive, soul-piercing rasp. And he was no stranger to classic rhythm and blues ostentation, riding around in a new

Caddy every year, then a DeSoto Firedome, and eventually a Wiener—a customized, four-door, four-seat number made from the bodies of two Chevrolet sedans! What the bloods on the corner weren't hip to was that the brother was easing into his twelfth straight year of heroin addiction.

After a final three-song session for Atlantic, which included the wrenching "I Believe to My Soul," he jumped to ABC Records in November of 1959. Raelette Margie Hendrix took him aside to tell she was pregnant by him, and he encouraged her to have the child, a boy she named Charles Wayne. Ray conquered the pop crowd in 1960 with "Georgia on My Mind" and "Hit the Road, Jack" in 1961. In 1962, he released *Modern Sounds of Country and Western Music* and triumphed again. A single off the album, "I Can't Stop Loving You," sold a staggering three million copies. "Busted" was his biggest song of 1963, and it became a physical reality in 1964 when Federal agents cornered him at Boston's Logan Field and arrested him for possession of heroin and marijuana. Prior to his trial, he resolved to kick his habit, and he checked himself into St. Francis Hospital in Lynwood, California, going cold turkey in ninety-six hours. After a one-year postponement in sentencing, he was given five years probation.

From the mid-1960s on, Ray Charles concentrated on a slightly slicker, at times rather bland blend of commerical pop and recycled Tin Pan Alley. Exceptions included "Crying Time" and "Let's Go Get Stoned" in 1966. His versions of "Yesterday," in 1967, and "Eleanor Rigby," in 1968, were distinctive blues-accented treatments of the Beatles' hits, an affectionate homage to the group that had played an intermission during one of Charles's early 1960s concerts in Hamburg, Germany.

In the late 1970s, Charles's twenty-year marriage to Della Robinson was dissolved. He blamed the breakup on his frequent absenteeism and two ugly paternity suits that he'd lost. Charles stated he'd never denied fathership or support; "I was just denying I was the Bank of America." He acknowledges nine offspring, three by Della and six out of wedlock. Charles has pronounced himself finished with marriage and says he prefers to confine his sexual activities to all-night trysts with select groups of three or four women.

LITTLE RICHARD

HE HAD CONFRONTED "THE UGLY STRAIN OF HIS OWN DAMNA-tion" back in October of 1957. "I gave up rock and roll for the rock of ages! I used to be a glaring homosexual until God changed me!" Such were the homilies of Richard Penniman in the late 1970s as he recalled his sweeping transformation from gay dissolute into—well, he's never made that entirely clear. He did become an evangelist. The Soviet launching of Sputnik had been a sign that a change had to come; this became clearer in a dream in which Richard saw "the world burning up and the sky melting with the heat." These visions occurred while he was on a tour of Australia with rockabilly stars Eddie Cochran and Gene Vincent—although, just prior to the visions, there had been the little matter of a dicey plane trip during which the fusilage caught fire. Regardless, when Little Richard reached Sydney, he cast thousands of dollars worth of jewelry into the Tasman Sea to seal his pious pact with heaven. "If you want to live with the Lord, you can't rock and roll it, too," he sermonized. "God don't like it."

Whether this fickle Supreme Being frowned on rock and roll in the 1950s but only winked at homosexuality until the 1970s goes unrecorded. This much is plain: this particular man of the cloth is a cocky ex-heathen if ever there was one. How many clerics, however convulsionary, can also claim to be *Little Richard*, the most monomaniacal screaming meemie to ever roll a congregation like he rocked the league of nations!

RICHARD WAYNE PENNIMAN'S ACTUAL BIRTH DATE IS UP FOR GRABS. Some mark it as Christmas Day, 1932, others claim 1935, a few prefer the latter year but opt for a December 5 delivery date; but all agree on Macon, Georgia, as the site. The family was devout Seventh Day Adventist, but his father set an iffy example for his brood of seven boys and five girls by hatching a little "scrum" (sourmash whiskey) on the sly. The squeaky-voiced Richard attempted to amble in the footsteps of his grandfather and two uncles, who were ministers, by warbling in a gospel group and playing piano at prayer meetings, but he soon strayed. He ran away from home as a boy to tap-dance and sing in Doctor Hudson's Travelling Medicine Show. Returning home attired like a "sender," sporting loud zoot suits and *lah-de-dah* lingo, he quickly earned his father's outrage. This turned to contempt when Dad found out he was gay. The diminutive Richard was disowned and took refuge in a Macon dive called the Tick Tock Club; his protectors were the white proprietors, Enotris "Johnny" Johnson and wife Ann. The couple sent him to school, encouraged his interest in race music, and permitted him to perform at the Tick Tock Club—scandalizing his family.

At the age of sixteen, Richard answered a talent call for an amateur hour, run by "Daddy" Zenas Sears of WGST radio, at the Eighty-One Theater in Atlanta. He won, and the prize was a recording contract with RCA Victor. He cut eight undistinguished jump blues sides, but his pendulous pitch and slippery phrasing were in crude evidence on "Ain't Nothing Happening," "Get Rich Quick," and "I Brought It All on Myself." In the mid-1950s, he moved to Houston and was signed to Peacock Records by owner Don Robey. Backed by two instrumental vocal groups, the Deuces of Rhythm and the Tempo Toppers, Little Richard offered some breezy rhythm and blues vamping on entertaining tracks like "Rice, Red Beans and Turnip Greens." He also cut some material with the orchestra of Johnny Otis. The label did poorly with all his records, however, so Little Richard got canned.

Bloodied but unbowed, he took a job as a dishwasher in a Greyhound bus station, moonlighted as a professional drag queen, and mailed demos to Art Rupe of Specialty Records. Rupe admired the freaky abandon in the songs, and on September 14, 1955, Rupe took Little Richard into Cosimo Matassa's J&M Studios in New Orleans with producer Bumps Blackwell and an itching-to-go rhythm section. Everybody was eager, but nothing caught fire until Richard, according to Richard, became exasperated and broke into a filthy little aria he'd howl back in the kitchen of the Greyhound station. He tapped it with the nonsense pots-and-pans curseout he'd showered the cook with when he quit—"A-wop-bop-a-lu-bop-a-wop-bam-boom! Take 'em out!"

In that vociferous outcry was the germ of a new golden era in rock and roll. New Orleans writer Dorothy La Bostrie cleaned up the whole obscene yammer, and the tape rolled on "Tutti-Frutti," a crazy-brilliant rush of piano, drums, saxophones, guitars, with Little Richard leading the way with grandiloquent glee. The words, when you could make them out over the riotous discord of "*Whoooooo*'s" and barnyard calls, concerned a gal, named Daisy, who had the singer—if not the world—crazy. One of the biggest and most sound-shaping explosions in the history of rock and roll, this song created a mayhem that was irresistible. "Tutti-Frutti" sold to black and white alike when released in 1955. And it was the first of a string of seven million-selling records of similar breakneck tempo: "Long Tall Sally," "Rip It Up," "Lucille," "Jenny, Jenny," "Keep a Knockin'," and "Good Golly, Miss Molly."

Torrents of sexual hoopla and frenzy, whipped up by an effeminate, pixilated black man with a double-dip pompadour and a $1,000-a-day drug habit, these singles were an unbridled semaphore to the straight music community that rock and roll was staging a new offensive and taking no prisoners. That Little Richard chose to quit the battlefield with "Good Golly, Miss Molly" mattered little. The scorched-earth policies he advocated continued unabated.

Settling down to life as a Bible student at Oakwood College in Huntsville, Alabama, he raged against what he had wrought, but he did it with such fervor and facility that it came off as a different side of the same coin: "I'm quittin' show business; I want to go straight. / I'm going to serve my Lord, before it's too late."

Of course, he never really packed it in. There were constant furtive comebacks under a gospel cloak, and "I Don't Know What You've Got but It's Got Me" satisfied his latent rock and roll urges. His last major contract (with Reprise in the early 1970s), produced three often-rewarding albums: *The Rill Thing, King of Rock and Roll,* and *Second Coming.* The Reverend Little Richard Penniman has clambered in and out of the lion-infested rock and roll arena during the late 1970s and early 1980s, appearing at the Toronto Pop Festival in 1970 and on the 1982 Grammy Awards. His immortal soul may be in Limbo, but his heart's still in rock and roll.

OVERLEAF
Little Richard, one leg up on the Lord (Frank Driggs Collection).

ELVIS PRESLEY

IN JULY OF 1954, TWO HISTORIC, DISPARATE, AND HIGHLY CONTROVERSIAL lines of demarcation were being drawn. One was political in nature: agreements reached in Geneva provided for a demilitarized zone between North and South Vietnam—the DMZ. The opposing sides would withdraw pending unification elections. Such elections were never held, and a monumental global trauma had taken root.

Regardless, a momentous cultural schism was in the works. The long rehearsals of two parttime Tennessee-based musicians—Scotty Moore and Bill Black—and local truckdriver/singer Elvis Presley were culminating in a trial-and-error taping session at the Memphis Recording Service studio at 706 Union Avenue. During a break, young Elvis brashly toyed with a rural blues song by Arthur "Big Boy" Crudup called "That's All Right," and his cohorts joined in. The rough-hewn syncopation of their outburst was so peculiar that the studio proprietor, Sam Phillips, interrupted the trio to ask, "What are you doing?" No one had an adequate answer for him—beyond the music itself—so they revved up again while Phillips rolled the tape. When Moore, the lead guitarist, heard the playback, he was shocked; he told bassist Bill Black that he feared the racially ambiguous sound slamming out of the loudspeakers would spark local outrage in the segregated city of 300,000 and possibly generate enough personal denunciation to drive the group out of town. Sam Phillips's reaction was well-documented: he prevailed upon WHBQ disc jockey Dewey Phillips (no relation) to spin a pressed single of the song, backed by an agitated version of the bluegrass standard, "Blue Moon of Kentucky," on his "Red Hot and Blue" R&B program. On Wednesday, July 7, 1954, Dewey aired "That's All Right" and the WHBQ switchboard was deluged with calls demanding replays and clarification. The largely white audience was accustomed, of course, to hearing black artists on the show, and even some white performers adapting the current black fare to their own discreet idioms. But the lean, shiversome energy of "That's All Right" was unnerving in its newness, and it induced a sense of disorientation verging on vertigo. Was the singer black or white? Was his music blues? rhythm and blues? the resurrection of some sort of prehistoric country pop? The controversy stemmed solely from the deep visceral confusion gripping the listeners, the sensation that a cocky? criminal?—no, *cancerous*—hybrid had arisen to decimate their drowsy, strictly delineated existences. Their instincts derived not from any syllable of the song's lyrics but from the threatening *feeling* pouring from the singer, the sensual emotion addressing the galloping beat.

Some music critics and social observers would later see the record and its reception as the birth of rockabilly—that frenetic fusion of white hillbilly blues and country & western brio—or even of rock and roll itself. It was also considered the death knell of southern segregation and the seed of an agonized orgy of national self-hatred and cultural shame. Yes, no, maybe, perhaps. Most assuredly, it was the belated birth of Elvis Presley, the pale, shy, pimpled poorboy crooner who had retreated to a Memphis movie house on the Wednesday

night the song broke rather than face the possible embarrassment of its being mocked in the marketplace.

LEGEND HAS IT THAT ELVIS MADE HIS FIRST RECORD—A COVER OF TWO Ink Spots' ballads, "My Happiness" and "That's When Your Heartaches Begin"—at the Sun studio on Union Avenue in Memphis as a birthday present for his mother. That's highly unlikely; the session took place in the late summer or early autumn of 1953, long after Gladys Presley's April birth date. More probably, this four-buck recording experiment reflected a deeply rooted longing on Elvis's part. At the age of ten, he took second prize in a talent contest at the Mississippi-Alabama Fair and Dairy Show, singing the cornpone boy-and-his-dog ditty, "Old Shep." On his next birthday, his father, Vernon, gave him an acoustic guitar. Other talent shows would follow, and with them a reputation that flowered at L.C. Hume High School in Memphis. His skills were fed not from woodshedding sessions with schoolboy chums, but from nocturnal meanderings down along Beale Street, storied main drag for the black denizens of the blues. After graduation, Elvis slipped down there to spend his $1.25-an-hour salary as a driver and warehouseman at the Crown Electric Company, the money going mostly for race records and for the peacock apparel to be had at Lansky Brothers, clothiers to Beale Street's top honkers and shouters. At night, he listened to WDIA, a flagship blues station of the South that featured such flamboyant black disk jockeys as Rufus Thomas and B.B. King (both of whom also sang live on the air).

These interests and involvements eventually led Elvis back to the Sun studios. Sam Phillips had summoned him for a formal audition as a balladeer after recalling a tape of the Ink Spots session, which an engineer had had the curious prescience to make. (In those days, such vanity recordings were usually cut directly onto an acetate disk, with no copies kept.) Phillips had run across an impressive demo by an anonymous black kid, who'd turned in a stunning performance on a love song entitled "Without You." Unable to locate the song's originator, and sensing that the material had commercial potential beyond the black audience he usually catered to, the producer was eager to find a young white singer who could duplicate the nameless performer's work.

Elvis had jumped at Phillips's invitation and arrived immediately after his phone call, boasting that he could sing anything. He couldn't. The unique vocal facility demonstrated on the nuance-laden "Without You" demo was beyond the green Elvis's grasp, and he could hardly match, much less rival, the black singer's style. In a show of vulnerability unmatched in his entire career, Elvis burst into tears after repeated, deteriorating attempts, and he began denouncing his unknown opponent. "I hate him!" he shrieked. "I hate him! I hate him!"

If Elvis hadn't had uncommon reserves still in store in the tritely tragic aftermath of the "Without You" episode, he might have remained a truckdriver. But he did, and he told a bored Phillips that he could *still* sing anything—any damned thing at all. Then *do it* fella, he was dared, and something inside the Tupelo shitkicker exploded. Stepping up to the microphone once more, he unleashed a blistering barrage composed of every sound he held in his musical memory bank, a thorny torrent of choirboy couplets, Beale Street blues snarls, rude hunks of the Hit Parade and the Grand Ole Opry. It wasn't a song, it wasn't a medley, it wasn't an audition. It was a force of nature. In that

instant, a phantom leapt out of the mouth of Elvis Presley and assumed proportions that easily eclipsed conventional alter-ego status. In the decades that followed, Sam Phillips, The Grand Ole Opry, WSM's Louisiana Hayride, RCA Records, Las Vegas, Colonel Parker, Steve Allen, Tommy and Jimmy Dorsey, Ed Sullivan, Hollywood, the White House, and the uncounted multimillions who were dumbstruck by his talent all tried to wrestle some sense of self-recognition out of the gleaming ghost looming before them. For the rest of Presley's short life, the frustrated, fascinated outside world would strain to locate some trace of themselves in this wraith's eyes. They couldn't. But none would fight more expectantly, more furiously, than Elvis for a closer look. And Elvis himself was thwarted, utterly, in the end.

ELVIS AARON PRESLEY CAME INTO THE WORLD ON JANUARY 8, 1935, IN Tupelo, Mississippi; his twin, Jesse Garon, was born dead. His father and mother were of sharecropper stock, but they left the land behind before the twins' birth to labor as journeyman truckdriver and sewing-machine operator, respectively. They were always just a hope away from the poorhouse, drifting on and off the relief rolls, relocating when the promise of better wages beckoned. They made several more moves (usually under cover of darkness), after giving up the two-room shack Elvis had been born in, finally renting rooms above a rabbi in a house at 462 Alabama Street, Memphis.

In retrospect, the facts attending Elvis Presley's instant fame seem feeble. Elvis, Scotty, and Bill toured the South and Southwest during 1954 and 1955 on the strength of their Sun singles, among them a cover of Roy Brown's "Good Rockin' Tonight," as well as "Milkcow Blues Boogie" and "Baby, Let's Play House." In concert, well-bred southern belles ripped Elvis's clothes from his supple body; one young lady appeared on "I've Got a Secret" with a pair of pants that Elvis had split in an ecstatic recording session. He purchased a pink Ford and a pink Cadillac.

In 1955, Presley met "Colonel" Tom Parker, former manager of country & western singers Eddy Arnold and Hank Snow. Parker shrewdly eased Sun-affiliated manager Bob Neal out of the picture by telling Elvis's mother that Neal was working the lad too hard. The same year, Parker orchestrated the Presley contract with RCA. Elvis went into RCA's Nashville studios on January 10, 1956 to cut "Heartbreak Hotel." Weeks later, it was at the top of the national charts. Steve Allen booked Elvis on his Sunday evening TV variety show, dressing him in tails and having him sing "Hound Dog" to a basset hound perched on a pedestal. Ed Sullivan showcased him on the tube—but from the waist up, to avoid scandalizing home viewers with Elvis's goading crotch and heaving hips.

The Army drafted Elvis in December 1957. While overseas, he maintained a close relationship with a fourteen-year-old named Priscilla Beaulieu, later to become his bride; he also corralled chorus girls from a Paris night club for wild parties. When his mother died, he was disconsolate, crying at the funeral, "Oh God, everything I have is gone!" During his two-year stint in Europe, he enjoyed another seven chart-toppers. His subsequent hits were increasingly tied to what would be a string of thirty-one movies in which he starred, each of them doing handsomely at the box office. He and his entourage—a group dubbed the Memphis Mafia—were thrown out of some of the country's best hotels for extreme rowdiness. His cronies procured women for perverse parties in a Bel Air mansion, occasions during which the singer threw a pool cue at one woman and dragged another across a table and through several rooms by her hair. After seven years away from the concert stage, Elvis did a 1968 Christmas special for ABC-TV, an electrifying portion of which was before a live audience, with Elvis looking lean and limber in black leather.

Elvis loved karate. He gorged himself on gooey junk food. He dated Tuesday Weld and Natalie Wood. He never granted a single in-depth interview. He named his Convair 880 jet after his daughter, Lisa Marie. He got fat. He sold some 300 million records worldwide by the late 1970s. He wrote none of his songs. He had a bad temper. He once fired a gun at a television during a performance by singer Robert Goulet. He became a virtual recluse in Graceland, his mansion in Memphis. He memorized all of James Dean's dialogue in *Rebel Without a Cause* and cornered the film's director to recite it. He had bouts of dependence on pharmaceutical drugs. He was appointed an honorary narcotics agent for an antidrug campaign by President Nixon. He was briefly a disciple of Yogi Paramahansa Yogananda. He got fatter.

At 2:30 P.M. on Tuesday, August 16, 1977, Elvis was found in his blue pajamas, passed out in an upstairs bathroom at Graceland. He'd been seated on the toilet, thumbing through a book entitled *The Scientific Search for the Face of Jesus*. He was rushed to Baptist Memorial Hospital in Memphis, and, an hour after he was found, Elvis was dead of heart failure. He was still wearing his blue pajamas. A hospital employee told reporters, "Elvis had the arteries of an eighty-year-old man. His body was just worn out." The *Memphis Press Scimitar* hit the streets the day of his funeral with the banner headline: A LONELY LIFE ENDS ON ELVIS PRESLEY BOULEVARD. Air National Guardsmen formed his final honor guard. Even the Soviet Union sent a floral wreath. His fans adored him beyond the end.

The opinions of Elvis grow petty with time. He was a man's man. A mama's boy. A native genius of the spirit. A tentative step above white trash. A vain hick. A valiant hero. The maker of some of the finest gospel and spiritual records ever released. A sacrilegious church truant. A loyal friend. A loutish bully. An archetypal southern gentleman. A lowliving letch. A princely appreciator of his fans. A pasty-faced pillhead. The rock voice without peer. The rock enigma without equal. The King.

One thing is certain. The sudden appearance of Elvis Presley on the scene was nothing less than the full-blown arrival of modern rock and roll. By virtue of the white-hot urgency of that arrival, Elvis Presley became the "Mystery Train" he sang about in one of his early Sun sessions, an unmarked locomotive rocketing down a jet-black track, piloted by a specter, making only unscheduled stops. It was not the kind of train that brought things back.

BUDDY HOLLY

THE STATEMENT WAS UNEQUIVOCAL: "WITHOUT ELVIS, NONE of us could have made it." Buddy Holly's words were full of characteristically open-hearted gratitude for the fella who made rock and roll a nearly legitimate profession for a boy to try his hand at. Elvis Presley helped many a skinny high school hayseed dream big dreams and encouraged them to pick up guitars and put a hard edge on the country & western dance music that whistled out of the battered cathedral radio in the general store. In fact, the guitar had not been an especially popular instrument before Elvis transformed it into a symbol of masculine verve and power, sending sales of both acoustic and electric models up into the stratosphere.

As a boy growing up in west Texas, Holly would have had considerable exposure to the country dance rhythms so popular to the region—popular, that is, with the lower and lower middle classes who would concede their interest in the music and who felt no shame about taking wife, girlfriend, and kin to the live "jamboree" concerts held on Saturday nights from the 1930s onward in small towns throughout the area. Unlike in Mississippi, where country music enjoyed a sit-down-and-pay-attention tradition, west Texans associated the crackling strum of a tenor banjo and the lusty skip of a fiddle with a well-waxed dance floor. Thanks to Bob Wills—who had had to bully the Grand Ole Opry into allowing his drummer onstage in 1945!—and other broad-shouldered country swing bandleaders, a Texas man who couldn't execute at least a confident two-step was something less than he oughta be, and unlike the stiff-necked custodians of the Opry, the dancer liked some assertive slapbass *and* snare drums to fill in the blanks.

What Holly would have known little of were the hoodang honky-tonks and randy rites of the black blues. Lubbock, Texas, was the very buckle of the blue-eyed Bible Belt. It was a community of innumerable churches and zero barrooms. No liquor was served or sold inside the town line. Blacks and Chicanos were seldom seen, never heard. There was plenty of hell-raising and mischief available, but it was the sort that one had to sally out through the screen door and go a-hunting for—usually along the state roads beyond the city limits.

That even in manhood a first-rate rock and roller like Buddy Holly would never go on such excursions in the service of his art says something quietly compelling about his own vision and the brief, poignant passage it prepared him for. His intensely innovative music (he was the first to use strings and vocal double-tracking, and he popularized the now-standard rock lineup of two guitars, bass, drums) was more apt to be punctuated by cheerful handclaps and tinkling cymbals than the raucous pansexual percussion of his iconoclastic, noncomposing hero. An unimposing beanpole, the soft-spoken, bespectacled Holly was thankful to Elvis for giving him the stubborn pride to keep his horn-rims on when he plunked his Stratocaster at the sock hop—Buddy was unaware that Elvis had discarded his own eyeglasses for his first amateur stage appearance. Holly thanked him for giving him the moxie to throw his towhead back and sing his untempered heart out, even though his best and boldest songs were as pristine, sweetnatured, and unjadedly childlike as Elvis's were taunting, worldly, and erotic. Holly thanked Elvis for galvanizing him with the notion that the living musical heritage of the common people was a thing of wonder, capable of being augmented by the big beat that pounded in his own chest. Buddy Holly celebrated time-honored American values, speaking with a sober honesty to the trusting, impatient heart and the risks it takes. Elvis Presley questioned time-withered American values that conspired to curb his urges and prematurely sate his wants. Only in rock and roll could a man such as Buddy Holly see a man such as Elvis Presley as his mirror image—and only through Buddy Holly's eyes.

HE WAS BORN CHARLES HARDIN HOLLEY ON SEPTEMBER 7, 1936, THE third son of Lawrence and Ella Holley. Mr. Holley was a farmboy out of northeastern Texas who had met his wife while he was working as a short-order cook. They married and moved to Lubbock in the mid-1920s, when west Texas began to experience an economic boom occasioned by the advent of cotton farming. The Holleys were a highly musical brood; Buddy's eldest brother, Larry, was proficient on violin and guitar, while his brother Travis played accordion, piano, and guitar. And sister Pat liked to sing along with her mother when the boys held forth at family get-togethers. Buddy's musical debut was something of a gentle hoax; his mother had insisted that his brothers take five-year-old Buddy along with them to a talent contest they'd entered in the nearby town of County Line. They greased the strings of his toy fiddle so he couldn't sour their sound and used him as a prop. But it was Buddy who took home a $5 prize for singing a number his mom taught him, "Down the River of Memories."

After brief passes at piano and steel guitar lessons, Buddy settled on straight acoustic guitar and began to teach himself Hank Williams songs like "Lovesick Blues." By the early 1950's, he had formed a country-oriented combo called the Western and Bop Band with school friends Bob Montgomery and Larry Welborn. The group was good enough to land a half-hour Sunday afternoon segment on local radio station KDAV. In 1956, Buddy and Bob, as the act was known on KDAV, replaced Welborn with Don Guess and the backup band became the Three Tunes. That year, Buddy was signed to Decca Records and lost the "e" in his name due to a misspelling in the contract. Holly's first release was a straight country outing, "Blue Days, Blue Nights." The Decca deal was uneventful but for another country song Buddy issued, a tune called "That'll Be the Day."

Back in Lubbock, Buddy and drummer Jerry Allison crossed over into rock and roll after opening for Elvis Presley at the Lubbock Youth Center. The next day, Holly talked Elvis into accompanying him to Lubbock High to meet some of his friends and teachers. Forming the Crickets (Joe Mauldin on bass, Jerry Allison on drums, Niki Sullivan on guitar), Buddy recut "That'll Be the Day" with a rock edge, and it got picked up by the New York–based Coral-Brunswick label, which made it a Top 5 hit in 1957.

Buddy was unfazed by the negativity and fatalistic gaiety in the world around him, and the hit records that he would create both with the Crickets and solo in the next two years had a blushing tenderness and a rollicking brand

ROCK STARS

of good will unlike any rock has enjoyed before or since. "Peggy Sue," "Maybe Baby," "Oh Boy!" "Rave On," "Think It Over," "Heartbeat"—each were sung with a straightforward zeal that never wavered and a bright outlook that never turned mawkish or hackneyed.

"Peggy Sue," Holly's ode to the eternal adolescent crush and the marvelous sense of belonging it provides, is an astonishing case in point. His trademark staggered-hiccup vocals alternate with a dignified expression of fondness and some remarkably uncloying babytalk and nasal cooing, a boy wondering what it sounds like to be a man, amused he's no longer a child, happiest living in the present. The metallic vibrato rhythm guitar break, a cold shower of spunky electricity, defines in one neat downpour what it feels like to be the leader of a teenage garage band, the peek-a-boo might of your emerging personality ricocheting off concrete walls, the entire neighborhood at your feet.

Holly himself was unchanged by the acclaim that touring and recording brought him, usually appearing onstage attired like an accountant in a neat black suit or a tweed blazer, a bowtie, his hornrims gleaming in the footlights. Holly was too sure and purposeful to ever be mistaken for a wimp, and his anachronistic appearance became so popular that fans began sporting hornrims fitted with ordinary glass. Offstage, he rarely drank. His forays into the wild side of paradise were occasional back-of-the-bus crapshoots with roustabout Chuck Berry. But he increasingly became victimized by the depth of his trusting nature. After his marriage in the summer of 1958 to Maria Elena Santiago, a Puerto Rican girl from New York, he began to scrutinize his business agreements of the recent past. At the urging of a knowledgeable, suspicious Elena, he confronted manager Norman Petty about the presence of Petty's name in the writing credits of several songs and the purportedly slipshod way in which Petty promoted both the group and Holly, for whom he held separate contracts. Sick at heart, Holly left the Crickets, whom Petty convinced to stay behind in Texas, and moved with his wife to New York's Greenwich Village. Money was tight, so he took a new group, consisting of guitarist Tommy Allsup, drummer Charlie Bunch, and green young bassist Waylon Jennings, on the road to raise seed money for his fledgling publishing company.

In the midst of a bus tour in the winter of 1959, twenty-two-year-old Holly chartered a private plane with costars the Big Bopper (J.P. Richardson) and Richie Valens in order to buy some time to get his laundry done before the next gig. The small Beechcraft Bonanza crashed shortly after 2 A.M. on February 3, disintegrating in a field nine miles from Iowa's Mason City Airport, killing all on board. Singer Don McLean immortalized the tragedy in his 1972 "American Pie" as "the day the music died." It was more accurately the death of innocence for rock and roll.

FACING PAGE
Buddy Holly's grave-side granite guitar (Martin Benjamin).

NOBODY IN FERRIDAY, LOUISIANA, HAD EVER SEEN THE MAD dog that lingered outside the window of Elmo and Mamie Lewis's frame house on the morning Jerry Lee was born, and that cur howled like one of Satan's prize hounds at the moment the babe's first cries were heard.

Old-time Louisiana stock will tell you that it's bad business to allow children out of the state before they come of age. There's something otherworldly about Louisiana air—moist, still, so dense an infant has to swallow it like porridge to get it down. Babies get dependent on that air, come to need it like mother's milk. An unripe intellect bred on the even heavier oxygen found upwind of New Orleans, in the low-lying cotton country of Concordia County, that's an especially delicate case. Louisiana offspring can't be weaned in the thin atmosphere found in the rest of the South. The foolhardy, those rash enough to move a child, can expect beastly consequences not unlike the bends. Even a *medical* doctor will advise parents to proceed with extreme caution. Thoroughly confounded by the phenomenon, they nonetheless affirm that a sudden change of air can shrivel a child's brain stem. Still, even the wisest parents sometimes fail to take heed, and their offspring pay the price.

In order for the stricken to get proper care, they must be brought to gris-gris men out in the Cajun swamp basins. The gris-gris will tell you the baleful condition is the hex of Baron Samedi, Guardian of the Graveyards. It leaves a victim ravaged. The worst victims are those whose birth is marked by a bad sign.

By the fruits of their malady shall ye know them.

ONE MUGGY, STARLESS NIGHT IN NOVEMBER 1976, ROBERT LOYD, security guard at Graceland, Elvis Presley's mansion, was forced to confront one of the stricken. He came by automobile, a brand new Lincoln Continental with an evil gleam. The Lincoln ripped up the gravel driveway and planted a cold chrome kiss on the iron quarter and eighth notes soldered to the webbed front gate. "I wanna see Elvis!" hollered the curly blond hooligan at the wheel. "You just tell him the Killer's here! Git on that damn house phone and call him! Who the hell does that sonofabitch think he is? Doesn't wanna be disturbed! He ain't no damn better'n anybody else!"

He was too drunk to ball, as the saying goes, but the .38 derringer in Jerry Lee Lewis's unsteady grip spoke louder than words, and Loyd felt obliged to do as he was told. Word came back from the inner sanctum to call the cops. The King would not receive the Killer. Officer B.J. Kirkpatrick of the Memphis police force led the flying wedge of patrol cars that converged on the scene. He disarmed the Killer and escorted him back to the station house as Jerry Lee vowed, "I'll have your fucking job, boy!"

But Jerry Lee's own profession was clearly keeping his hands too full for

BREATHLESS

Words and Music by OTIS BLACKWELL

Recorded by
JERRY LEE LEWIS
on Sun Records

PRICE
50¢
(In U.S.A.)

HOME FOLKS MUSIC, INC. AND OBIE MUSIC, INC.
Sole Selling Agent:
HILL AND RANGE SONGS, INC.
1650 Broadway   New York 19, N. Y.

2

BREATHLESS

Bright Rock Tempo

Words and Music by
OTIS BLACKWELL

CHORUS

Now, if you love me, let's please don't tease. If I can hold you then
shake all o-ver and you know why. I'm sure it's love___ and

let me squeeze. My heart goes 'round and 'round; my love comes
that's no lie.___ 'Cause when you call my name, I burn like

tum - blin' down. You leave me (breathe out . . . .)
wood in - flamed.

HF 130

(whisper) Breath-less! Oh, I (spoken) Oh, ba-by!

Mm - mm. Cra - zy! You're

much too much. I can't love you e-nough. Now it's all right to
(sing)

hold me tight, but when you love me, love me right.

any sort of moonlighting. He was a fallen evangelist of the rock and roll persuasion, a rambling, gambling shill for the lead Horseman of the Apocalypse. Like Buddy Holly, Jerry Lee owed a debt. Elvis had paved the way at Sun Records for the rockabilly machinations of Lewis's first hit, "Whole Lot of Shakin' Going On." Their close proximity in the early days, followed by the high road handed Elvis and the dank crawlspace accorded Jerry Lee, had slowly pushed an already fevered brain into acute inflammation. Even on the fabled afternoon they'd gotten along best—December 4, 1956—when he, Elvis, Carl "Blue Suede Shoes" Perkins, and Johnny Cash crowded around the piano in the Sun studios for a little joviality on "Keeper of the Key" and "Just a Little Walk with Jesus," Jerry Lee found himself well-nigh asphyxiated, his lungs aching. Elvis seemed to draw every breath of air from the room.

Buddy Holly had willingly chosen to bask in the King's reflected glow, but Jerry Lee coveted both the throne and the light that shone down upon it. "I never considered myself the greatest," he hissed, "but I'm the best."

JERRY GREW UP AN UNTAMEABLE RASCAL WHO LIKED TO TURN CHURCH hymns into saloon harangues, but the family thought he might settle down some after he got married. In his sixteenth year (he lied that he was twenty-one), Jerry Lee plighted his troth to comely seventeen-year-old Dorothy Barton, daughter of a Pentecostal preacher. For a brief spell, Jerry Lee even took to preaching himself at the Church of God on Mississippi Avenue in Ferriday. But by 1953, the whole association was history, Dorothy back home, the marriage in the wind, the devil on the wing.

From then on, you'd find Jerry Lee down on Highway 61 outside of Natchez, Mississippi, playing piano, winking at the barmaid, and breathing the fumes of bad whiskey and worse perfume in the Dixie Club. Although some nights he was a latecomer: sometimes he got sidetracked at Nellie Jackson's cathouse on North Rankin Street.

His reputation for rocking began to grow, and Lewis wrangled a twenty-minute radio spot on WNAT radio. Jerry Lee got himself hitched again in the summer of 1953 to Jane Mitcham, another eye-catching teen queen, and the sin of bigamy besmirched his seventeen-year-old soul. In 1954, they had a fair-haired son, Jerry Lee, Jr. In 1955, Jane gave Jerry Lee a dark-haired lad, Ronnie Guy. Jerry Lee declined to call this child his own, and he issued Jane her walking papers. In December 1957, Lewis secretly married thirteen-year-old Myra Brown. Double bigamy. At this point, Jerry was a full-fledged star with a catalogue of million-sellers: "Whole Lot of Shakin' Going On," "Great Balls of Fire," "Breathless," "High School Confidential." Jerry Lee made the mistake of taking Myra with him for his 1958 tour of England. The British press quickly tired of the lame line about Myra being Jerry Lee's sister, and the public outcry about his robbing the cradle pushed him into exile most foul.

Reduced to playing county fairs and the gin mill grind, he adopted Benzedrine and bourbon as his favorite repast. In 1962, his three-year-old son by Myra, Steve Allen Lewis, drowned in the family pool. In 1970, Myra left Jerry Lee after she caught him cheating on her. In their thirteen years together, she claimed she'd spent only three evenings alone with him, but they were memorable ones: "He usually arrived unannounced in the middle of the night, wanting a hot meal and hot sex." And he was not adverse to cuffing and thumping his wife into submission.

In October 1971, Jerry Lee wed Jaren Elizabeth Gunn Pate, twenty-nine, of Memphis. They separated two weeks later. In November 1973, his beloved son, Jerry Lee, Jr., was killed in an auto accident. That's when Jerry Lee's rock and roll lifestyle really accelerated. In September 1976, he shot his bassist, Butch Owens, square in the belly with a .357 Magnum, after beckoning him to "look down the barrel of this." A few months later, Lewis's Rolls Royce somersaulted on a lonely road near Collierville, Tennessee. Hot on the heels of his pistol-packing social call to Elvis, Jerry Lee stopped into a Memphis hospital to give up his gall bladder and let doctors have a gander at his collapsed right lung and his pleurisy; the doctors also probed his lower back, which was still paining him from the tumble in the Rolls.

In 1979, an Australian tour was cancelled after Jerry Lee picked a fight onstage with a fan, suffering fractured ribs in the fracas. In February of that year, the Internal Revenue Service confiscated his numerous flashy cars—for the second time—for nonpayment of taxes, busting him in the process for possession of cocaine and marijuana. A month later, Jerry Lee ran a leased white Corvette, brand new and with plenty of horsepower, into a ditch in DeSoto County, Mississippi. To close out the year, he sued Jaren, his long-estranged spouse, for divorce. She countersued, charging him with "cruel and inhuman treatment, adultery, habitual drunkenness, and habitual use of drugs." One might ruminate as to what her allegations would have been had they stayed together for say, *three* weeks. She later drowned, not long before the final divorce settlement.

The man kept on making records, many of them pretty incendiary. And he outlasted Elvis—although he almost succumbed due to a ruptured appendix in the early 1980s. A fifth wife, the former Shawn Stevens, was less lucky. She perished in 1983 at the age of twenty-five from what a Mississippi grand jury determined to be a self-inflicted overdose of methadone pills. While the grand jury cleared Jerry Lee of any wrongdoing—without having questioned him directly—others had misgivings. Mortician Danny Phillips, for one, was perplexed. The body was bruised; there was blood under the fingernails. In February 1984, a rather glassy-eyed Jerry Lee told ABC News that he'd never hit a woman in his life. In April 1984, he married Kerrie Lynn McCarver.

Jerry Lee Lewis attributes his staying power to a diet of malted milk, shrimp, Scotch—and "almighty rock and roll." This was once the black man's euphemism for sex, sinful magic, and moderation-scorning music; now it's a modest description of one Louisiana profligate's waking hours on this planet.

S A M   C O O K E

HE DIDN'T LIKE TO BE DENIED, AND HE TOOK PERSONALLY any attempts by anyone to do so. The son of a Baptist minister, his willful nature acquired an almost religious intensity once he achieved recognition as a singer. In June of 1964, he created a minor sensation in New York City by spending $10,000 of his own money to erect a 20-by-100-foot billboard in Times Square emblazoned with the question, "Who's the biggest Cook in Town?"

Several days later, the sign was enlarged and a 45-foot, 1,500-pound photograph added, along with a new message: "Sam's the biggest Cooke in town." And so he was, his smooth features and rakish crescent smile beaming down on the Great White Way—much to the embarrassment of his press agent, who had to explain the motives behind the insolent display when Cooke would not. "In short," the agent told the *New York Times*, "he's bothered that he hasn't been able to make it big in a New York night spot and wants people to know he's here."

Cooke was scheduled to open at the Copacabana. This splashy saloon had given him a cool reception four years earlier, despite the fact that he'd been at the top of the charts with the R&B record "Chain Gang," whose huff-and-puff male chorus and gandydancer sound effects strained the bounds of novel artificiality. The experience left the edgy, calculating former gospel singer with a permanent grudge against New York and its leading night club. The Times Square billboard announced the dimensions of that enmity.

Born in Chicago on January 22, 1931, he pleased his demanding father with his featured-performer status in the church choir as well as his presence in a family quartet called the Singing Children. While attending Wendell Phillips High School, he became interested in the local gospel circuit and hooked up with the house group at the Highway Baptist Church, the Highway QCs. They were managed by R.B. Robinson, baritone in the Soul Stirrers (the group generally regarded as having conceived the modern quartet sound). In 1951, Cooke replaced renowned tenor Rebert H. Harris as the lead singer of the Soul Stirrers and suddenly found himself with a sizable national following. Boasting a crisp, sonorous voice as unblemished as his complexion, and an assiduously controlled delivery, he won over diehard gospel fans accustomed to the growly vocal vaulting of his contemporaries. He also attracted a young audience, his matinee idol looks, suave demeanor, and flirtatious melismatic crooning making him a sepia Sinatra; according to gospel historian Tony Heilbut, Cooke was "the greatest sex symbol in gospel history." Signed to the Specialty label (whose name indicated their exclusive interest in black performers, especially gospel acts), the Soul Stirrers had a prosperous seven years behind Cooke's charisma. Art Rupe, Specialty's white owner, took umbrage, however, when Cooke told him that he wanted to test the waters in the R&B market; Rupe saw Cooke's interest in "worldly" music as the seeds of artistic suicide.

After a series of arguments with Cooke and his manager J.W. Alexander,

Rupe relented and took Sam into the studio with some rhythm and blues and pop material, but he resisted releasing any of it. A compromise was worked out in which the pop song "Lovable" was issued under the pseudonym of Dale Cooke. When Cooke's pop ambitions failed to abate, Rupe sold the rights to Sam's pop career to Specialty producer Bumps Blackwell, who departed to start Keen Records. Blackwell's first release was Sam Cooke's "You Send Me," a breathy pop ballad written by L.C. Cooke, Sam's brother. It sold 1.7 million copies in 1957 and reached the No. 1 spot on the R&B charts. Despite such massive sales, and even though it handily outsold Teresa Brewer's cover version, it did not appear on the mainstream pop charts; such were the tyrannies of the white-dominated pop world. Specialty responded to "You Send Me" by rush-releasing one of its shelved Cooke R&B tracks, "I'll Come Running Back to You," which made the Top 10 on the R&B charts but didn't approach the mainstream appeal of "You Send Me." Subsequent Keen hits like "Win Your Love for Me," "Only Sixteen," and "Everybody Likes to Cha Cha Cha" paved the way for Cooke's signing with RCA in 1960. His last Keen single was "Wonderful World," a lovely pledge of devotion written by Barbara Campbell, Lou Adler, and Herb Alpert.

RCA saw Cooke as the only black pop contender capable of eclipsing Columbia's Johnny Mathis, but he was much more than that. Cooke's effortless interbreed of gospel, rhythm and blues, and pop argots was the bedrock of soul music. His deft, absorbing execution of the new sound, glistening with an articulate vocal clarity unlike any of the age, gave RCA a string of huge hits between 1960 and 1964: "Sad Mood," "That's It—I Quit—I'm Movin' On," "Cupid," "Twistin' the Night Away," "Nothing Can Change This Love," "Somebody Have Mercy," "Send Me Some Lovin'," "Another Saturday Night," "Frankie and Johnny," "Good News," "Good Times," "Tennessee Waltz," "Cousin of Mine."

But Cooke would never gain the mass acceptance of Johnny Mathis—the compromises required were too great. Cooke's polish was more a matter of instinct than strategy, and he essentially avoided the vaporous, homogeneous themes Mathis favored, selecting and even writing hits that heralded the black urban experience with an emotional colloquial recipe ("That's Where It's At," "Having a Party," "Bring It on Home to Me"). Although a shrewd businessman, eventually owning his own management firm and music publishing and record companies, he did not take the racial indignities of the era lightly.

In 1963, Cooke and his wife, former high school sweetheart Barbara Campbell, were arrested in Shreveport, Louisiana, on charges of disturbing the peace; the couple and two of their friends had attempted to register at a whites-only hotel. A year later, Cooke died in a bizarre shooting incident at a Los Angeles motel. Rumors in the record industry were that Cooke had been set up for a rubout by mob figures trying to gain control of his publishing interests, but the accounts given by newspapers at the time make no mention of any such allegations.

According to the principals involved, Cooke had picked up a Eurasian girl named Elisa Boyer at a bar on the evening of December 10, 1964, and she had accepted his offer of a ride home. Instead, he drove them to a motel on South Figueroa in Los Angeles and registered as "Mr. and Mrs. Cooke." Boyer told police that she insisted he take her home, but that Cooke refused and forced her into the motel room. She testified that he "began to rip my clothes off."

PRECEDING PAGE
Sam Cooke, the gospel Sir Galahad (Frank Driggs Collection).

When Cooke went into the bathroom, she fled on foot with her clothes and most of Cooke's. Clad only in a sports jacket and his shoes, he pursued her. The manager of the motel, Mrs. Bertha Lee Franklin, told police that Cooke kicked in the door of her apartment and accused her of harboring the girl (who was actually in a nearby telephone booth, calling the police). Franklin testified that Cooke struck her twice with his fist. She responded by producing a .22 caliber pistol and firing three shots; one hit Cooke in the chest.

Mortally wounded, he continued to charge her, she said, so she bludgeoned him with a stick. When the police arrived, they found him dead on the floor.

His wife, Barbara, became hysterical when police notified her at their Hollywood home; with her were two of their children, a third child having drowned in their swimming pool that summer.

Thousands of anguished fans stormed the twin chapel at the A.R. Leak Funeral Home at 7838 Cottage Grove in Chicago during the public wake, breaking glass and splintering wood. One woman screamed, "Please let me in! I've never seen anything like this in my life!"

SHORTLY BEFORE COOKE'S DEATH, HE HAD BEEN A GUEST VOCALIST WITH the Soul Stirrers at an anniversary concert in Chicago. When he took the microphone to raise his pure, sweet voice in Stirrers standards like "Jesus Wash Away My Troubles" and "Nearer to Thee," the crowd fell silent and then began to castigate him. "Get that blues singer down!" they yelled angrily. "This is a Christian program! Get that no good so-and-so down!"

Cooke walked off the stage in tears.

Tawdry demise of a major talent (Don Hamerman).

DEC 12 1964   THE

SAM COOKE SLAIN IN COAST MOTEL

N.Y.T.

Singing Star Shot to Death in Los Angeles Incident

LOS ANGELES, Dec. 11 (AP) —Sam Cooke, Negro singing star, was shot to death early today by a woman motel manager after he burst into her apartment in pursuit of a Eurasian girl he had met in a bar. Mr. Cooke, 32 years old, whose

J A M E S   B R O W N

HITTING THE STAGE OF HARLEM'S APOLLO THEATRE IN THE early 1960s, shimmy-shuffling sideways in triple-time, balanced on one patent leather heel-and-toe propeller while the other foot was hiked up against his knee like the rudder of some runaway flamingo—*Bop!*—he'd stop, center stage, in sync with the rimshot metronome. *Bop! Bop!* He'd drop, halfway to his knees, his brutish head turned back from the fans, as he seized the mike stand by the throat and tipped it outward at arm's length. *Bop! Bop! Bop!* And he'd be back on top, slaying the crowd with "Please, Please, Please."

The band fell in behind him, splintering bass patterns and punching out horn riffs as they progressed, the rhythm guitar chopping away in twiddled time, as Mr. James Brown pleaded and bleated, giving off keening shrieks that peaked past the speedbump of human hearing, disappearing into the ultra-pitched domain of a dog whistle.

The footlights would wash over his clothes. These could be citrus-colored suits with matching toreador vests and cutaway jackets, contrasting ruffle-drenched shirts with broad collars that hung down to his belt, or any number of other eye-inflaming satin or stretch-knit getups that would cling to his stumpy frame like a bad debt. On his album covers, he often included the unsurprising credit: "Clothes designed by Mr. Brown." As if these outfits, indeed *anything* about Mr. James Brown, could have been the work of anyone else.

He was ugly, uncourtly, a low piece of trumpery whose antics embarrassed everyone, but in the end even those properly repulsed would be converted, their critical appraisals short-circuited by the acrobatic might of a man so completely into himself.

At the close of "Please, Please, Please," Brown would sink to the floor, despondent, unable to regain the precious love interest who he had driven away. Aides would take the stage to coddle and collect him, one settling a purple cape on his shoulders as they helped him up, shaking their heads as they led the pathetic, slack-jawed shell toward the wings. Halfway there, Brown would break free and shake off the cape; he would scamper, then slide back across the stage on one knee, topple the mike stand and catch the microphone as it fell, and belt "Please!" once more as the Famous Flames augmented his anguish with halting thrusts of the chorus. Again, aides would come to the sad rescue, this time draping a gold cape upon his twisted form before ushering him away. Again, he'd spin away from their grasp, rushing to the only lifeline left between him and his heart's desire. "Baaay-beeee *please!*" Finally enervated, his clothes sopping wet (he was said to sweat off seven pounds a show), he would be helped off—amidst torrential cheers—in a flowing black cape.

Minutes later, Brown would appear for an up-tempo encore, impeccable in a candy-apple red traveling suit, swinging a heavily stickered suitcase, jerking his hitchhiker's thumb with a grin as brilliant as a searchlight. And all the emcee could say was, "LADIES AND GENTLEMEN! MIS-TER JAMES BROWN!..."

BORN IN MACON, GEORGIA, SUPPOSEDLY IN 1933, AND SPENDING HIS EARLY childhood on King Street in Augusta, he and friend Willie Glenn would run alongside sluggish troop trains leaving Fort Gordon, bound for war. They earned what pennies might be tossed to them by bored soldiers: James danced while Willie clapped his hands in accompaniment. Brown became a shoeshine boy. Then a pool-hall attendant. Then a thief. After pillaging four cars in a single night, sixteen-year-old James spent four months in Richmond County Jail while the judge decided what to do with him. He was sentenced to eight to sixteen years at hard labor in a state prison. He served only four before having his sentence commuted for good behavior.

Brown tried his hand at semiprofessional sports, principally boxing and baseball, but gave up the hope of pitching in the minor leagues. He had been in a singing combo in prison with fellow prisoner Johnny Terry, and they formed a gospel group, the Swanees, upon Terry's release. Moving away from gospel during the rise of the black doo-wop sound, the Swanees (which also included Bobby Byrd, Sylvester Keels, and Nafloyd Scott) became the Famous Flames. Each member sang and played an instrument; James was the lead vocalist and drummer. In 1956, Ralph Bass played a Flames demo of "Please, Please, Please" for Syd Nathan, head of the King Records label. Nathan hated it. The song's lyrics consisted of one stretched and knotted word; it was base, unalloyed emotion, leveling all the boundaries between blues, rhythm, and the spontaneous testimony of a ravaged heart, and it was downright scary to hear. Bass prevailed, however, and the record was issued on the Federal label. Promo man Henry Stone worked the single hard on the black jukebox network and got the Flames booked into the Palms in Hallandale, Florida, a leading venue for race acts. The record electrified the deep South, eventually selling a million copies.

When Syd Nathan refused to let the Flames' ever-touring support band duplicate their blistering sound in the studio, an irate Brown rehearsed them on the sly and helped them get the national dance hit "(Do the) Mashed Potatoes" on another label in 1960 under the name Nat Kendrick and the Swans. Nathan saw the error of his ways, and the reunited ensemble, now called the James Brown Revue, had even more hits.

In 1963, Brown was crowned the "King of Soul" at the Apollo. After business disagreements with Nathan, Brown put two singles out on Smash, a subsidiary of Mercury, and one of them sold handsomely in 1964 ("Out of Sight"). Legal hassles with Nathan arose, but Brown would not be intimidated, and a year later a settlement was reached that gave Brown unprecedented control over his artistic and business affairs.

"Papa's Got a Brand New Bag," heralded his dominance of the R&B charts and broadened his base in the white pop surveys. Other big singles of the mid-1960s were "I Got You (I Feel Good)," "Ain't That a Groove," "It's a Man's Man's Man's World," "Don't Be a Drop-Out," "I Can't Stand Myself," "Licking Stick—Licking Stick," "Say It Loud—I'm Black and I'm Proud," "Give It Up or Turnit a Loose," "The Popcorn," "Mother Popcorn (Part 1)," and "Let a Man Come In and Do the Popcorn (Part 1)." Most of the records were atypical in their attention to rhythm to the near exclusion of melody. The "Popcorn" series was little more than screamed exclamations peppering an inert chord structure, as the instrumentation of the new backup crew, the J.B.s, provided a percussive hammering effect.

PRECEDING PAGES
Page 77: Mr. Brown, glad and bad (Frank Christian).
Pages 78–79: James and an early outfit (Frank Driggs Collection).

In 1971, Brown signed with Polydor Records and restructured his organization, selling off his old catalogue and dismissing most of the current J.B.s. Following the release of the film *The Godfather*, Brown appointed himself the "Godfather of Soul" and became immersed in movie scoring. An increasingly controversial black figure with a high public profile, Brown was arrested on December 11, 1972, for disorderly conduct in Knoxville, Tennessee, following a concert. He claimed that he, his manager, and a roadie had been talking with fans about the evils of drugs when two policemen—who were hurt in the ensuing scuffle—accused Brown of trying to start a riot. Charges were later dropped, but the mayor accused Brown of milking the case for publicity.

Working with a revamped J.B.s, his singles output with Polydor was prodigious, and the successes many; some of the biggest were "Talking Loud and Saying Nothing," "Get on the Good Foot," "Make It Funky," and "Papa Don't Take No Mess—Part I."

The Treasury Department poked him in his sequined chest in 1975 and claimed he owed $4.5 million in back taxes for 1969 and 1970. His financial house of cards began to fold inward. He lost three radio stations he owned, as well as a soul-food answer to McDonald's that he'd been franchising. There was mutinous dissension within the ranks of his band, fueled by incidents like one in the mid-1970s in which a Zaïre-bound flight carrying B.B. King, the Spinners, the Crusaders, Lloyd Price, Johnny Pacheco, and Brown to a concert almost failed to take off because the plane was so severely overloaded with Brown's equipment. Personal luggage had to be removed in order to make lift-off just barely possible, and several of the passengers described the stunt as being potentially life-threatening. By the end of the tour, several members of his band had quit.

His son Teddy, nineteen, the eldest of six children from two marriages, perished when the car he was driving struck a tree in upstate New York. Second wife Deidre left their sixty-two-acre ranch in South Carolina one day with her two girls and didn't bother to come back. Brown, his father Joe, and his sons worked the grounds themselves after the staff was let go; even the blue and green private jet plane that was his pride and joy had to be sold to improve cash flow.

Brown mounted a comeback under the banner of "The Original Disco Man" (a.k.a. the "Sex Machine"), sporting a scarlet costume with a huge waistband emblazoned with the word SEX. He eventually parted company with Polydor, his last sizable record sales for the label coming in 1979 with the release of "It's Too Funky in Here," which rose to No. 15 on the R&B charts. His IRS problems endured.

A cameo appearance as a revivalist preacher in *The Blues Brothers* film in 1980 led to increased concert bookings—"It got me going again, got me rediscovered and appreciated"—and he was signed to Island Records. Recording sessions were held, but the project was scrapped due to "artistic disagreements." Brown returned to Jaydee Ranch in South Carolina to cut an album for an obscure local label and to drive his forty various motor vehicles around the lonesome, sprawling property, contemplating the humble renascence of the man once known as "Mr. Dynamite."

C H A P T E R

T H E   D E S C E N D A N T S

FACING PAGE
Rod "the Mod" Stewart, on the town (Brian Avis/Photo Trends).
OVERLEAF
Bob Dylan, in concert (Peter Simon).

B I L L   H A L E Y

ORE THAN ANYTHING ELSE, WILLIAM JOHN CLIFTON Haley, Jr., wanted his lifelong claim to the title "Father of Rock and Roll" to be taken seriously. It never was. "The story has got pretty crowded as to who was the Father of Rock and Roll," commented Haley in a rare public statement from the late 1970s. "I haven't done much in life except that. And I'd like to get credit for it."

He was arguably the first white singer to put a high-energy edge on a black R&B hit when Bill Haley and the Saddlemen covered Jackie Brenston's "Rocket 88" in 1951, but it was Elvis Presley's plenary execution of rock and roll's forbidden pleasures that got the lion's share of the acclaim. Pubescent audiences were more eager to fantasize about a loose-limbed Lothario like Elvis. Yodeling Bill Haley (his original stagename)—a chunky country & western singer from Highland Park, Michigan—looked like a mailman, moved like a lummox, and inspired no wet dreams. He and the Saddlemen sold 75,000 copies of "Rock This Joint," and then, after renaming the group the Comets, became the first identifiable rock and roll band to place a record on the *Billboard* pop charts with "Crazy Man Crazy." Even then, proper recognition for Haley proved elusive.

Swarms of amorous, tight-sweatered nymphets would hug the lip of the stage at an Elvis concert, craving the attentions of the satyr from Tupelo. So Haley tried to spread stories about how he and his band were taken to orgies in a certain small theater by their manager, who then forced them to watch from the balcony while the debauchery unfolded. Rumor had it that such a scene might have transpired in a joint in Philadelphia known as Hound Dog Hill. Haley said that while they were not permitted to participate, the view would get them sufficiently aroused to knock out another vascular rock anthem. Insiders would size up chubby-faced Bill's quaint curly forelock and the pudgy aspect of his homely sidemen, consider the gawky boosterism at the core of the music, and conclude that voyeurism was probably their *only* forte.

BY 1956, HALEY AND THE COMETS HAD SCORED A NUMBER OF HUGE HITS for the Decca label, including a clamorous but sanitized version of Joe Turner's lewd "Shake, Rattle and Roll," "Dim, Dim the Lights (I Want Some Atmosphere)," and "See You Later, Alligator." The biggest was "(We're Gonna) Rock Around the Clock," a song by Jimmy De Knight that sold 22 million copies after it was selected in 1955 for the soundtrack of *Blackboard Jungle,* a Hollywood film that dramatized teen rebellion. When knife fights and bottle-throwing melees started to break out at Comets' concerts, a wave of protest against the music began to rise. This time recognition came Haley's way, all right—he got blamed. A defensive Haley stated, "The music is stimulating enough without creating additional excitement," but he soon vowed to avoid "suggestive lyrics."

Haley starred in his own film, *Rock Around the Clock,* and the nation and world were surprised at what they saw: a balding family man slipping inelegantly into middle age. Could this be the sort of fellow capable of sparking what a psychiatrist told the *New York Times* was a "cannibalistic" trend? When a second Haley film, *Don't Knock the Rock,* appeared in 1957, much of the storm surrounding Haley had passed on, along with his rowdy stateside following. An English trip in February created pandemonium, however, and British fans remained loyal long after his last Top 40 record, "Skinny Minnie," sank from view late in 1958.

ALTHOUGH HALEY CONTINUED TO TOUR AND RECORD WITH VARIOUS incarnations of the Comets, the bulk of his appearances were confined to so-called Rock and Roll Revival shows. Two failed marriages and tragic family deaths clouded his later years, and he eventually became a problem drinker. In 1973, he was arrested twice in one week in Iowa for public drunkenness. Repeatedly stymied in his attempts to put down roots and establish a financially secure home base, his frequent relocations took him to various states and even down to Mexico.

Haley was south of the border in the winter of 1976 when longtime friend and gifted saxophonist Rudy Pompilli died from lung cancer. The death left an already perturbed Haley distraught and hastened his descent into alcoholism.

Haley dropped from sight, declining to perform or record for three years. Unlike Robert Johnson, he was apparently unable to locate a mojo man or necromancer to reverse his musical decline, for when, in 1979, he popped up again to cut a comeback album for Sonet Records at Fame Studios in Muscle Shoals, Alabama, few people cared. The LP, *Everyone Can Rock and Roll,* attracted no significant attention, but it gave Haley a chance to tour Europe once more. Queer reports trailed after him on this sorry sortie, tales of him assaulting fans and disrobing onstage.

In 1980, plans for another European tour were canceled, although he did a few poorly received dates in South Africa at the beginning of the summer. He retreated to his home in Harlingen, Texas, a small town in the Rio Grande Valley, just over the Mexican border, refusing all requests for interviews and sometimes denying his identity. Police would often find him wandering aimlessly after nightfall, lost on some remote country lane, delirious, incoherent, suffering from amnesia. He was pronounced dead of a presumed heart attack on February 9, 1981; a friend found his fully clothed body stretched out on a bed in a room in the garage behind his house. It had been lying there for approximately six hours. According to the birth date, July 6, 1925, listed on his driver's license, Haley was fifty-six, but his various press bios over the years maintained that he was as much as three years younger.

Four months before his death, Haley's eldest son, Jack, described his rock and roll father's mounting dementia in an interview for National Public Radio: "He would talk about his life in the Marine Corps, which he was never in. He was never in the service at all. He said he was a deputy sheriff down there in Texas, which he wasn't. I knew he was lying, but I never dared say it. I didn't wanna make him mad for fear that I would never hear from him again."

To the last, Bill Haley kept his story shady and his rock and roll straight. It was a sadly inverted sense of priorities.

PRECEDING PAGE
Rock Cinema, 1957.
"What's wrong with
this picture?" (Frank
Driggs Collection).

FACING PAGE
Bill Haley, bulky
troubadour (Frank
Driggs Collection).

BRIAN WILSON

THE PLANE WAS FIVE MINUTES OUT OF LOS ANGELES, EN ROUTE to Houston, when the screaming started. The tall, dough-faced young man sitting in the forward section, whose manic stares before takeoff had since given way to white-knuckled catatonia, had suddenly begun crying and then making jagged, high-pitched yowls as he grabbed for his pillow. His traveling companions leaped to his side, trying to pry the pillow from his swollen face.

"Cool it, Brian!" barked Al Jardine.

"My God, what's wrong, Brian?" asked pudgy Carl Wilson. "Brian, please tell me what's wrong!"

By now Brian Wilson had spun out of his seat and was on the cabin floor, sobbing convulsively.

"I can't take it!" hollered Brian, as he rolled and lurched about the plane. "I just can't take it! Don't you understand? I'm not getting off this plane!"

Wilson went on to perform that night, but he woke up at the hotel the next morning with a crippling knot in his stomach. Throughout the day, he burst into tears at half-hour intervals. The group's road manager put Brian on the late plane back to Los Angeles, where he was met by his mother, Audree. She drove her son to his boyhood home at West 119 Street in Hawthorne, California. (The Wilsons had moved to a new house in Whittier, but they'd held on to their previous home.) Once inside his old bedroom, the emotional floodgates burst. Over the next seventeen months, Brian would have two more serious breakdowns. His doctors advised him that continued touring could prove disastrous not only to his psyche but also to his hearing. Since childhood, Brian had been deaf in his right ear, and his left ear was being overtaxed by the escalating decibels at live rock and roll concerts. It was a low blow. The Beach Boys had been his creation, his window to the world. Through them he had been able to break out of his childhood shell, overcome his paralyzing reticence. He loved performing—stepping up to the microphone and singing his lyrics, in his harmonies, set to his music. It was more fun, more satisfaction, and more human contact than he had ever dared hope for.

THE BEACH BOYS WERE THE PRIME PURVEYORS OF THE CALIFORNIA ethos exemplified by the affluent, leisure-obsessed state's top-down, teenage car culture and the exotic sport of surfing. Before the sudden ascension of Brian's Beach Boys in the white-rock hegemony of the early 1960s, Philles Records owner-producer Phil Spector had been the undisputed soothsayer of rock and roll, his towering "Wall of Sound" studiocraft with such girl groups as the Ronettes and the Crystals appearing impervious. Nineteen-year-old Brian Wilson, a bashful guy with minimal professional musical experience, turned the tables on Spector and the L.A. music mafia in 1961 with "Surfin'," a seminal single released on the local X and Candix labels. The Beach Boys were swiftly signed to Capitol Records, and in their first

three years with the label placed eight singles in the national Top 20. Among their sunny, highly polished hits were "Surfin' Safari," "Surfer Girl," "Fun Fun Fun," "I Get Around," and their quintessential smash, "Surfin' U.S.A." (which sounded so much like Chuck Berry's "Sweet Little Sixteen" that the lawyers stepped in and Berry was given co-writing credit with Brian).

The sound that toppled Spector wasn't pushy and street-smart like Phil's widely imitated urban jangle. It was more idyllic and companionable. Wilson's Beach Boys were a tabernacle of untutored, unabashedly nasal male voices joined in seamless Four Freshmen–inspired harmonies, these underscored by slip-and-slide bass lines; layered, muffled percussion; and a bit of Chuck Berry–flavored lead guitar offset by primitive, unorthodox rhythm chords—all of it rippling across wide-open oceans of monophonic space.

What was especially significant about this novel recording tack was that Brian actually was its creator and command pilot. It was probably the first time that a major rock artist had total control in the studio, free from the subjugation and wire-pulling hectoring of tyrants like Spector. Brian's first solo production was a revised version of "Surfer Girl," a 1963 hit released as a follow-up to "Surfin' U.S.A." It turned up again that September as the title song on the group's third album, an all-Brian production that marked a milestone in artistic sovereignty in the recording industry.

Thematically, the Beach Boys were just as innovative. The subject matter of their records sidestepped the shadow-tangled urban tableaux and mordant evocations of delinquency dominating so much rock and roll in the late 1950s, focusing instead on an endless summer Saturday: a glorious adolescent afternoon of deuce coupe shutdowns...quick, radio-blasting lifts to Del Mar, Trestles, and Manhattan Beach in a wheezing woodie station wagon...spilled Cokes at highway hamburger stands...drive-in movies, packed amusement parks, hop scotch ho-dads...and scores of virginal, tanned sun bunnies who dug surfers.

PRECEDING PAGES
*Page 90: Brian Wilson, 17—a yearbook photo (courtesy Michael Koehn).
Page 91: Wilson in the 1980s. A child is father to the band (Neil Preston/ Camera 5).*

THE BEACH BOYS WERE ON A TOUR OF THE SOUTHWEST—PROMOTING A recent hit single, "Dance, Dance, Dance"—when Brian had his first nervous collapse. It was December 23, 1964, three months and a day since the Warren Commission had issued its reports that Lee Harvey Oswald had acted alone in the killing of John Fitzgerald Kennedy, and the nation was in its own state of shock. Camelot was in ruins, and the only distraction from the shattered dream of a New Frontier was the rising tide of Beatlemania, kicked off in February 1964 with the landing of the British foursome at JFK Airport. Their moppish innocence and infectious good cheer had been something of a godsend for a country with a broken spirit. Overnight, the Beatles captured the country's hearts and radio waves. And crushed a tormented Brian.

The Beatles' success, Brian's breakdown, his earaches, his heartaches, all culminated in the demise of a pop fantasy and the birth of an appalling legend. His concert career terminated, Brian submerged himself in songwriting, arranging, and exotic studio experimentation—not to mention hallucinogens—while his band carried on without him. Years passed and rock and roll changed, growing harder, heavier, more cynical, and finally more grave. Lovely Brian Wilson–produced Beach Boys records continued to emanate from some orphic source, but these too had changed. Now they were more concerned with feelings than with experiences. The abandon of "Fun Fun Fun" and "I Get Around" was replaced by the isolation of "That's Not Me" and the rueful resignation of "I Just Wasn't Made for These Times."

Meanwhile, as Brian grew more remote, the bizarre rumors cropping up about the man multiplied. It was rumored that he had built a sandbox in the dining room of the Beverly Hills home he occupied in the mid-1960s, placing a grand piano in it so that he could continue to draw on the beach for inspiration without ever having to visit it again. His neighbors whispered that he was a hashish head, that he lived on candy bars and milk shakes, that he would record marvelous music and then destroy the tapes, that he had locked himself in his bedroom and stayed there for six straight months, that he was a perpetually panic-stricken paranoiac, that he was generally out of his mind. They were incredible stories. And all of them were true.

BRIAN WILSON WAS BORN IN CENTINELA HOSPITAL IN INGLEWOOD, California, in the summer of 1942, the first of three sons born to Murry Wilson and the former Audree Karthof. His father was an amateur songwriter who sold heavy machinery for a living. A strong-willed, insecure man, Murry Wilson had a tempestuous relationship with Brian. He was no Ozzie Nelson in the dad department; Brian was no Ricky. At one point, a quietly enraged Brian defecated on a plate and set it at his father's place at the dinner table. On another occasion, Murry reportedly punished Brian by taking out his glass eye and forcing the boy to look into the socket.

The Wilson boys and their cousin Mike Love organized several combos. As Kenny and the Cadets, Brian, Carl, and Audree recorded "Barbie" and "What Is a Young Girl Made Of?" for the local Randy label. The more the boys became interested in the music business, the harder Murry pushed to force their commitment to a full-blown music career. But while Brian was spending hours in his room perfecting his falsetto, and Carl was diligently practicing his guitar, the lazy, free-spirited Dennis (who remained a member of the various bands only because Audree insisted on it) was goofing off at the beach. He'd come back and tell Brian—who was terrified of the water—about the burgeoning surfing craze. Brian became enthralled with a world he was too fearful and withdrawn to participate in and pumped Dennis for details about the girls, the gremmies (young novices), the tubes. Retreating to his room, he'd fashion songs from the raw material. Murry was furious; Brian wouldn't leave the house, and he refused even to consider singing any of his father's material. When Audree and Murry left for a holiday in Mexico, their sons, Mike Love, and pal Al Jardine took the allowance and food money the Wilsons had left them and cut their demo of "Surfin' " at Keen Recording Studios in Beverly Hills.

BY THE END OF 1965, BRIAN'S VICARIOUS INFATUATION WITH THE seaside faded as he lost interest in virtually everything but bettering the Beatles. Anguished at how they continued to batter the Beach Boys in the record charts, and awed by the artistic cohesion of *Rubber Soul*, Brian brought his group's output to an abrupt halt. He wanted to make a concept album, one that, like *Rubber Soul*, would have a unity of mood, but one that would have a cumulative emotional impact as well. *Pet Sounds* was to be Brian Wilson's bid for acceptance as an "artiste." It was to be an analysis of

OVERLEAF
Brianless Beach Boys on tour (Fin Costello/ Retna Ltd.).

Brian redux: God only knows (Michael Putland/Retna Ltd.).

romance, centering on the theme of a young man growing into manhood, falling in love and out again, all the while probing himself for the reasons behind his restless yearnings.

Much of the pessimism and dejection that pervaded the album was tied to the problems Brian and his wife, Marilyn, were experiencing at the time. The record produced two hit singles, "Sloop John B" and "God Only Knows/ Wouldn't It Be Nice," but the album itself sold poorly. Brian was devastated but still determined. He rebounded in October 1966 with "Good Vibrations," an ingenious synthesis of the sounds and imagery of the current psychedelic wave, plus close harmonies sung to the hilt. While he included enough exotic instruments (sleigh bells, jew's-harp, wind chimes, harpsichord, flutes, organ, and theremin) to send Phil Spector packing, the songs retained the Beach Boys' ingratiating airiness. It was the complete statement Brian had been aiming for, and "Good Vibrations" became the group's best-selling single.

Having outdone himself on every level, earning the accolade of "studio genius," Brian Wilson next set about doing himself in. Much of the next year was set aside for the recording of another epic album, at first called *Dumb Angel*, then renamed *Smile*. Collaborating with impressionistic songwriter/composer Van Dyke Parks, Brian (who was now heavily into LSD) locked himself in the studio for days at a stretch, recording, erasing, creating, and then destroying days and weeks of work. In September 1967, a revamped album, *Smiley Smile*, was issued. Acid mania, creative depression, and sinister acquaintances scarred the next two years, during which the Beach Boys released *Wild Honey*, which had been recorded in the increasingly reclusive Brian's Bel

Air living room, and *20/20*, an album featuring a song—co-written by Charles Manson and Dennis Wilson—originally entitled "Cease to Exist," but released as "Never Learn Not to Love."

Late in 1969, the Beach Boys jumped to Reprise, which gave them a custom label, Brother Records. Working largely in Brian's house or out of their own studio in Santa Monica, the Beach Boys tried to downplay the fact that Brian was no longer a fully functioning group member, not even in the control booth, as they worked on the charming but poorly selling 1970 album, *Sunflower*. Van Dyke Parks and Brian produced some material for the follow-up, *Surf's Up*, but it also failed to find favor in the marketplace.

In 1972, the group lured the retired Brian, who had opened a North Hollywood health-food shop called the Radiant Radish, to the Netherlands. He refused to work on anything but a twelve-minute children's fantasy called "Mount Vernon and Fairway." When Warner Bros. heard the finished product, *Holland*, they rejected it. It was accepted only after Van Dyke Parks forced an admittedly deranged Brian to sit down at a piano and write a decent single for the spacy album. ("Hypnotize me into thinking that I'm not insane! Convince me I'm not insane!" Brian pleaded in the taped demo session. "Cut the shit, Brian!" Van Dyke answered.)

It was four years before Brian was pulled back into service again. Producer-singer Terry Melcher (Doris Day's son) had signed Brian to a production deal, but it proved a bust. ("He wouldn't touch anything in the control booth," said Melcher. "He acted like he was afraid to.") In 1976, Warner Bros. released *15 Big Ones*, an anniversary compilation of covers of rhythm and blues oldies like "Blueberry Hill" and new songs from Brian and company. Brian got production credit on the LP and was touted as having undergone dramatic drug rehabilitation through the psychiatric care of Dr. Eugene Landy. But it wasn't long before he was back in the shadows again.

Internal struggles plagued the Beach Boys throughout the late 1970s and early 1980s. They fought openly, sometimes even onstage. A mutual restraining order prohibited Mike and Dennis from physically provoking each other. Undistinguished albums came and went. The group had reunited once more when Dennis Wilson, a problem drinker who had voluntarily submitted to treatment at St. John's Hospital in Santa Monica, drowned in the Pacific three days after Christmas 1983. He had checked himself out of the hospital and gone swimming off a friend's yacht in Marina Del Rey.

Brian—who had recently been in the news when Carolyn Williams, his former aide-companion, charged that he had been snatched from his bed at Cedars-Sinai Hospital by his brothers and Dr. Landy and flown to Hawaii against his will—issued a public statement that he would write a song for Dennis. "He was always my source of inspiration," he said.

Giving himself over to another round of Dr. Landy's twenty-four-hour therapy in 1983, Brian was installed in a Malibu beachhouse with a live-in staff who were expected to keep him occupied with activities and drills for all but a few unstructured intervals. One day, after Brian couldn't find his car in a parking lot, one of his Landy-appointed nursemaids phoned the doctor to ask what their next move should be. "Make him look for it, just like anyone else!" Landy ordered.

With considerable prodding, Brian eventually found the car on his own. It was one small step in a new direction, but was it the grist for a great song?

JOHN LENNON

S A BOY, HE WAS FOND OF RISK. HIS CHILDHOOD HERO WAS Just William, the untamed scamp in a popular series of youth novels by Richmal Crompton. A favorite game involved hanging by a rope knotted to a lofty tree limb overlooking Menlove Avenue in the Liverpool suburb of Woolton, pushing off into the path of approaching double-decker buses, and swinging out of the way at the last minute. He also enjoyed "slapping leather" (as he called shoplifting) and taunting nuns. His Uncle George taught him one of his first songs, an alternate version of a popular favorite that began, "In the shade of the old apple tree / Two beautiful legs I can see...."

A choirboy at St. Peter's Church, he was eleven years old when he was permanently barred from Sunday services after repeatedly improvising obscene and impious lyrics to the hymns. He was caned for squirting his schoolmasters with a bicycle pump filled with ink. Fond of circle jerks in which he and his classmates called out the names of starlets as they "tossed off," he was infamous for once yelling out "Winston Churchill!"

His first exposure to American rock and roll was through "The Jack Jackson Show," a late-night program on Radio Luxembourg. The first song to make a marked impression on him was Bill Haley's "Rock Around the Clock," and Gene Vincent's "Be-Bop-a-Lula" cemented his fascination with the form; but it was the ascension of Elvis Presley that captivated him.

In his late teens, John Lennon began to make a name for himself as a musician, appearing with his combo in dives in the notoriously tawdry Reeperbahn section of Hamburg, Germany. Holding forth on the tiny stages of strip joints like the Indra Club, the Beatles played from 7 P.M. to 3 A.M. six or seven nights a week. Like the other band members, Lennon dressed in a white T-shirt, leather pants, cowboy boots, and a denim or leather jacket, and he had his greasy D.A. haircut transformed into a bowl-shaped, banged "French cut." Imitating the gimpy strut of rockabilly star Gene Vincent, whose withered left leg was the result of a motorcycle injury, Lennon would sometimes stalk the stage in his jockey shorts, a toilet seat around his neck, shouting, "*Sieg Heil!* Wake up all you bloody Nazis!" A jealous lover, he attacked a hulk who was flirting with girlfriend Cynthia Powell, cracking a bottle on the chap's skull. John himself, however, eschewed fidelity and was a frequent habitué of the Herbertstrasse red-light district.

By day, John and the boys were lonely bantlings, hungry for remnants of home. By night, they were drunk, loutish bullshit artists, riding high on speed and looking forward to some predawn whoring with a penicillin chaser. On the Sabbath, they rested—all but John. His lodgings abutted a Catholic church, and he liked to urinate on the clergy from on high, or to rattle parishioners by dangling a crude dummy of the Son of God out his window, a ballooned condom between its legs.

PRECEDING PAGE
*John in 1971: he
loved the Beatles' TV
cartoon series (staff
photo by Mathew
Lewis/The Washington
Post).*

RIGHT
*Lennon (left) asks
Ringo to focus in on
him (David Hurn/
Magnum Photos).*

ONE OF ROCK AND ROLL'S GREATEST ROUSTABOUTS, SOCIAL MAVER-
icks, and sharp-tongued philosophers, John Lennon was born on
October 9, 1940, at an Oxford Street maternity home in the midst of
a blitzkreig attack. His father, Freddy, was a ship's waiter aboard a
passenger liner; his mother, the former Julia Stanley, was a cinema usherette.
Freddy disappeared in 1940, and his son would see him only twice more in the
next two decades.

When Julia took up with Bobby Dykins, an alcoholic hotel waiter with his
own children, her sister Mimi volunteered to raise the boy. During his late
adolescence, John came to know the errant Julia as someone more akin to a
carefree older sister than a parent; her house, a short bus ride from Aunt Mimi's, was always a haven for truancy.

John cloaked his feelings in an unending sardonicism, reinforced with an
off-putting sartorial display that approximated the turnout of the foppish
"Teddy Boy" toughs of the era. Dressed in black drainpipe jeans, a colored
shirt, and a raincoat with padded shoulders, his light brown hair swept up into
a "Tony Curtis" roostertail pompadour accented by "lice ladder" sideburns,
he was a menacing presence in his quiet country village.

In 1956, Julia bought John his first guitar, a secondhand model from

Hessy's Music Store. John formed a group with best friend Pete Shotton and other local boys, which Pete christened the Quarry Men. Their first significant public appearance was at an outdoor summer fete in some fields beside St. Peter's Church on July 6, 1957. After the set, John met Paul McCartney, an accomplished guitarist (he could *tune* one!) who soon after joined the group. Then George Harrison began to tag along. Shotton, who was afflicted with stagefright, got the idea he was no longer appreciated when John broke his tin washboard over his head. Paul and John began to write songs together, sometimes performing as the Nurk Twins.

After breaking up for a time following the death of Julia Lennon in 1958 (she was killed instantly after being hit by a car), the group re-formed in 1959 as the Silver Beatles (in waggish emulation of Buddy Holly's Crickets), with John, Paul, and George on guitars; art student Stu Sutcliffe on bass; forklift driver Tommy Moore as a sometime drummer, to be replaced in time by Pete Best. In 1961, while in Germany, the (no longer "Silver") Beatles recorded "My Bonnie Lies over the Ocean." Sutcliffe was replaced on bass by Paul, and Best was dropped to make way for Richard Starkey, a.k.a. Ringo Starr. The transformation of the Beatles was complete.

In short order, the Beatles became the scruffy royalty of the "glad-all-over" Merseybeat sound, with its bright, chiming rhythms and heavy bass-drum sound. A national tour fomented Beatlemania, stoked by "She Loves You," the best-selling single of all time in the United Kingdom. In 1963, they gave a Royal Command Variety Performance for Princess Margaret and the Queen Mother. Lennon introduced the finale, "Twist and Shout," by nodding to the royal box and announcing, "Would the people in the cheaper seats clap your hands? And the rest of you—if you'd just rattle your jewelry...."

While John and company were celebrated enough to kid the Queen Mother, they carried no weight in America, where beach music was the order of the day. Manager Brian Epstein flew to America with an acetate copy of "I Want to Hold Your Hand" and met with the producers of the *Ed Sullivan Show.* Having been at Heathrow Airport the previous year as the Beatles returned from Sweden, Sullivan knew firsthand how rabid their British following was, and he gambled, booking them to headline for two consecutive Sundays, February 9 and 16, 1964. During the numerous press conferences held during their fifteen-day visit to the States, John jousted with reporters, who thought the Beatles an easy mark. Asked if the group could sing a song for the press, he said, "No, sorry. No, we need money first." How did they account for their fantastic success? "Good press agent." Why did millions of Beatles fans buy millions of Beatles records? "If we knew, we'd form another group and be managers."

In April 1964, "Can't Buy Me Love" was No. 1 on both sides of the Atlantic, with "Twist and Shout" and three other singles fleshing out the remainder of the American Top 5. That summer, the film *A Hard Day's Night* opened in America. The planet was charmed. Tens of thousands flocked to the venues on the Beatles' first and only world tour. Next came another movie, *Help!*, a soundtrack LP, and a mature new collection of work, *Rubber Soul.* On October 26, 1965, the foursome received Member of the Order of the British Empire medals from Queen Elizabeth II. By this time, Lennon and McCartney had ceased their active songwriting collaboration. Yet John insisted that all future Beatles songs by either would be credited to "Lennon-McCartney," a manifestation of the irrational private insecurities that pestered John all of his career.

OVERLEAF
The Beatles backstage in 1964: no collars, no cares (Philip Jones Griffiths/Magnum Photos).

New York City: Lennon loiters outside the Improv (David Gahr).

SUMMER, 1966. THE WORLD GETS A CONSUMMATE TASTE OF LENNON'S acerbic iconoclasm. An earlier interview he'd given the *Evening Standard* (after reading the book *The Passover Plot*) attracted recirculation and outrage: "Christianity will go. It will vanish and shrink. I needn't argue about that. I'm right and will be proved right. Jesus was all right, but his disciples were thick and ordinary. It's them twisting it that ruins it for me. We're more popular than Jesus Christ right now."

DRAINED AND DAUNTED BY THE RIGORS OF TRAVEL AND MINDLESS audience clangor, the Beatles relinquished touring after an August 29, 1966, concert at San Francisco's Candlestick Park and retreated to the studio, where they began work on *Revolver* (originally titled *Abracadabra*). This often chilling record reflected their growing, albeit random, interest in drugs and mysticism. "Dr. Robert," for example (released in the U.S. on *Yesterday and Today*), was coy praise by John for Charles Roberts, a New York physician greatly appreciated by the Beatles and Andy Warhol's crowd.

In June 1967, *Sgt. Pepper's Lonely Hearts Club Band* was released. A remarkably aggressive and prepossessing exploration of state-of-the-art four-track control-room technology and abstract conceptual density, it featured John's "Lucy in the Sky with Diamonds," a shimmering pastiche of childlike imagery and dreamy, celeste-laden chant vocals that many charged to be an evocation (if not endorsement) of LSD. John bristled, insisting that the title and lyrics were prompted by his son Julian's description of a painting he'd done at school. Lennon was bitterly amused that an earlier hit of his, "Day Tripper"—which *was* about LSD and included the line "She's a prick teaser"—seemed to bother no one. He took an increasingly rueful interest in slipping vulgarisms and maddening non sequiturs into his songs to mock and befuddle nitpickers and message mongers. After the death of Brian Epstein by sleeping-pill overdose in 1967, there was no one to screen out such pranks.

Magical Mystery Tour appeared in 1967, released as a double EP in England and an album in the States. The film that accompanied it was roundly panned—even the Queen made a negative public criticism of it. Still, critics had marveled at the surreal power of Lennon's "Strawberry Fields Forever" and "I Am the Walrus."

After the Beatles appeared worldwide via satellite to sing "All You Need Is Love" for the *Our World* international TV special, they retreated to Wales to spend what would be a half-year of absorption in the teachings of Maharishi Mahesh Yogi. The Beatles' part in a nine-week 1968 celebrity sabbatical with Mia Farrow, Donovan, and Mike Love at the Maharishi's ashram beside the Ganges ended abruptly when John got fed up with the guru's niggardly rationing of the secrets of the universe. Lennon also resented the advances the Maharishi allegedly made toward Mia Farrow and other female guests; and while in India, John wrote "Sexy Sadie" to ridicule his guru. When John informed him that the Beatles would soon depart, the Maharishi blanched and asked, "Why?" "You're the cosmic one," John answered. "You ought to know."

I N MAY 1968, SHORTLY AFTER A PARTICULARLY POTENT TAB OF ACID HAD momentarily convinced John Lennon he was Jesus Christ, he rang up one of his quirkiest groupies, Yoko Ono. Their affair translated into the *Unfinished Music No. 1: Two Virgins* album, released the same month as the Beatles' so-called *White Album*. John's six-year marriage to Cynthia dissolved shortly after.

From then on, the lines in Lennon's life were sharply drawn; everything was seen in either pro-Yoko or anti-Yoko terms, the Beatles increasingly relegated to the latter category. John and Yoko were married in the Crown Colony of Gibraltar on March 20, 1969, and they spent their honeymoon staging a week-long antiwar "Bed-In" at the Amsterdam Hilton. During the next two months, John changed his hated middle name from Winston to Ono, and the couple released "Give Peace a Chance."

Abbey Road, the Beatles' best-selling album, was released in 1969. John's songs for the record included "Because" and "I Want You (She's So Heavy)," both written about him and Yoko. Thirteen days prior to the LP's release, Lennon further asserted his independence from the group by flying Ono, guitarist Eric Clapton, bassist Klaus Voorman, drummer Alan White, and himself to a rock and roll revival show in Toronto; he billed the group as the Plastic Ono Band. A few weeks later, John told Paul he wanted a "divorce" from the Beatles; he was dissuaded from any action until legal disputes between the group's company and short-lived manager Allen Klein could be settled. In November 1969, Lennon returned his MBE, giving England's involvement in war-torn Biafra and its support of U.S. troops in Vietnam (plus, wryly, the poor sales of his "Cold Turkey" single) as reasons. He and Yoko mounted an abortive "WAR IS OVER! IF YOU WANT IT!" peace campaign and issued another single, "Instant Karma," produced by Phil Spector.

By the spring of 1970, the Beatles were in tatters. *Let It Be*, the last album, was resurrected from a stack of session tapes. Then, in April 1970, Paul issued a solo album and the surprise statement that the Beatles were over with—to John's ire and chagrin. Even as he strayed from it, John saw himself as the

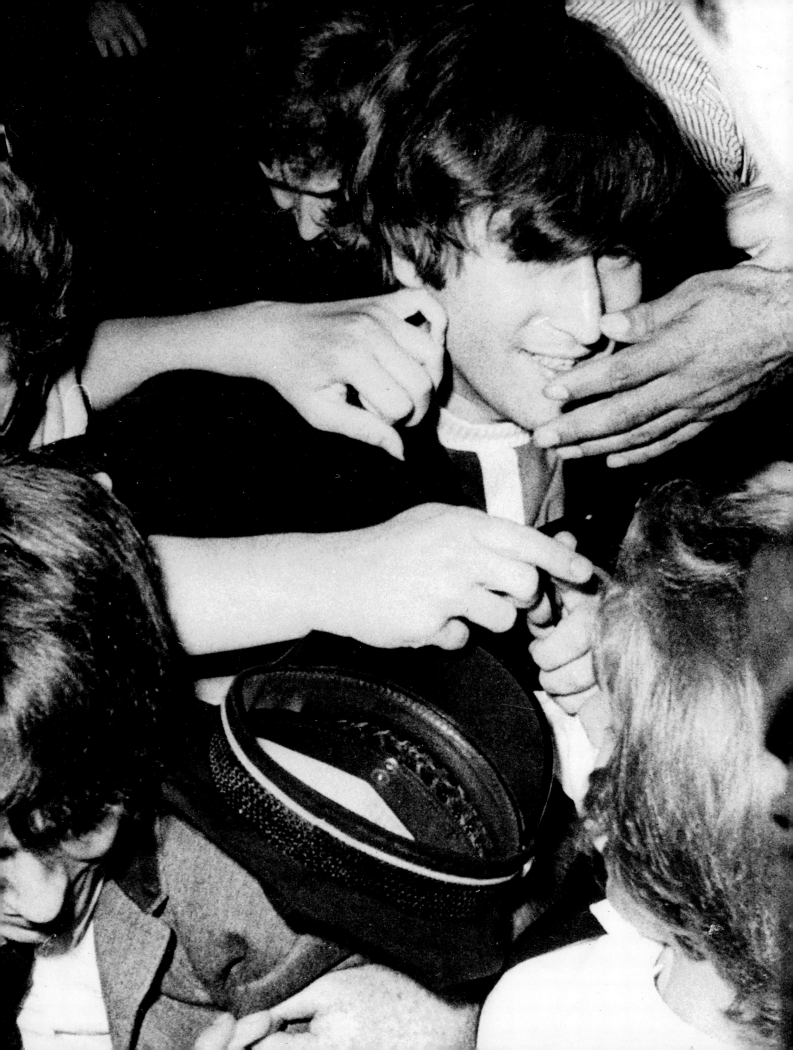

prime mover in the quartet. Moreover, Paul had been the one to talk John out of an earlier decision to announce the split. John felt Paul had robbed him of his much-needed chance to show the world he'd been the one who was confident enough to ring down the curtain on the Beatles *and* Lennon-McCartney.

IN THE DECADE THAT FOLLOWED, JOHN AND YOKO RELEASED VARIOUS SOLO and collaborative albums under the Plastic Ono Band umbrella. Their initial efforts were brutal refutations of his counterculture-costumed contemporaries' lofty ambitions and of their greed, contrasted with a brutal owning up to Lennon's own delusions and dybbuks. The songs were gripping in their vulnerability and eloquent in their spare settings. Later work, though, often comprised obnoxious scoldings and overproduced drivel.

In the mid-1970s, John and Yoko were badgered by the FBI and at odds with the Nixon White House, which wanted to deport Lennon, seeing him as an undesirable drug felon and leftish rabble-rouser. The couple separated for a year and a half, during which John dated aide May Pang (at Yoko's suggestion), drank heavily, and partied with Harry Nilsson, at one point causing a ruckus in a Los Angeles club while wearing a Kotex napkin on his head. He returned to his wife in March 1975 and began life as a "househusband" after Yoko gave birth to a son, Sean, on John's thirty-fifth birthday. John and Yoko released *Double Fantasy* in November 1980, and it yielded a No. 1 hit, "(Just Like) Starting Over." Then, on December 8, 1980, a pudgy twenty-five-year-old drifter pumped seven bullets into John Lennon as he strode through the arched entryway of the Dakota, his apartment residence on New York's Upper West Side. Earlier in the day the singer had given his assailant an autograph. When police arrived, they found the murderer standing on the sidewalk, calmly reading *The Catcher in the Rye.* Yoko was bent over John's blood-soaked body.

In January 1984, John Lennon's last songs, plus additional compositions by Yoko Ono, were released as *Milk and Honey—A Heart Play.* The album included the bouncy, outspoken "I'm Stepping Out" and a haunting ballad John wrote for Yoko, "Grow Old With Me."

After his death, there was a tendency to view Lennon as a saintly figure for an idealistic generation. More accurately, he was a ceaseless, ravenous experimenter whose natural disdain for any sort of constraints led him into every sort of clearing and cul-de-sac, and even into a willfully preemptive self-restriction. He was both in awe and in terror of the power he had over his own life, but he never lacked the courage to exercise it in new ways.

FACING PAGE
Starting over: John and Yoko (Bob Gruen/Star File).

PAUL McCARTNEY

H IS SEEMS AN EXISTENCE PLAYED OUT IN AN ENGLISH MUSIC hall, evoking that sentimental mid-nineteenth-century tradition—featuring pantomime, sketch comedy, and the song-and-dance man—that developed from entertainment in inns and taverns. In his music, misfortune is a pratfall, tragedy is dirgeful melodrama, happiness is a comic fluke, and fulfillment is an illustrated postcard captioned "Ardor." In his personal life, the same perspective holds true.

He is a man of minor mysteries, a casual creator of miniature shadows and quaint secrets, one who gently epitomizes another age, perhaps Victorian, in which styles and manners were needlessly flowery, excessively genteel. But Paul McCartney's role is more working-class in its textures, evoking a time when lowborn fellows of intelligence and ambition reached for such effects, yet leavened their deeply felt attempts with a playful self-deprecation.

S ELF-TAUGHT, PARTIALLY DEAF PIANIST JAMES MCCARTNEY LED A DANCE band in the 1920s, the Jim Mac Jazz Band, that provided amusement for Liverpool flappers and, on at least one occasion, musical accompaniment for the silent cinema at the local run of *The Queen of Sheba*. By day, Jim was a bachelor salesman for a cotton-brokerage firm, and the arrangement of his time and personal commitments was sufficiently cozy that he did not marry until he was due to turn forty. Mary Mohin, a visiting nurse in her early thirties, was the lucky girl. She was Irish Catholic, he was Irish Protestant, but there were no quarrels between them. They had two boys: James Paul, born June 18, 1942, and Michael, born two years later. Though money was tight in the postwar years, the McCartneys lived comfortably, even blissfully, in the Liverpool suburb of Allerton until Mary, a working mother, suddenly took sick and died of breast cancer.

Jim was crushed, the boys astonished that their world could be shattered on such short notice. "What are we going to do," lamented the forlorn, ever-practical Paul, "without her money?"

Paul was fourteen years old, an excellent student, a considerate son, worthy of the trust invested in him by his loving but sometimes careworn father. Galvanized by the rise of skiffle star Lonnie Donnegan, Paul requested a guitar, and his parent happily obliged. Jim McCartney recognized that a mutual interest in music was a way of keeping his boy close to the hearth. In the evenings after work, Jim would man the piano in the parlor and call out chords for his son to try. Paul's efforts were problematic until he realized that, although right-handed, he played better with his left. Skiffle quickly took a back seat to rock and roll. At first, Paul fell hard for the lunatic warbling of Little Richard, but ultimately he preferred the less raucous approach of the Everly Brothers, their interlocking harmonies and lilting chordings demonstrating the melodic beauty possible in a music best known for its bombast.

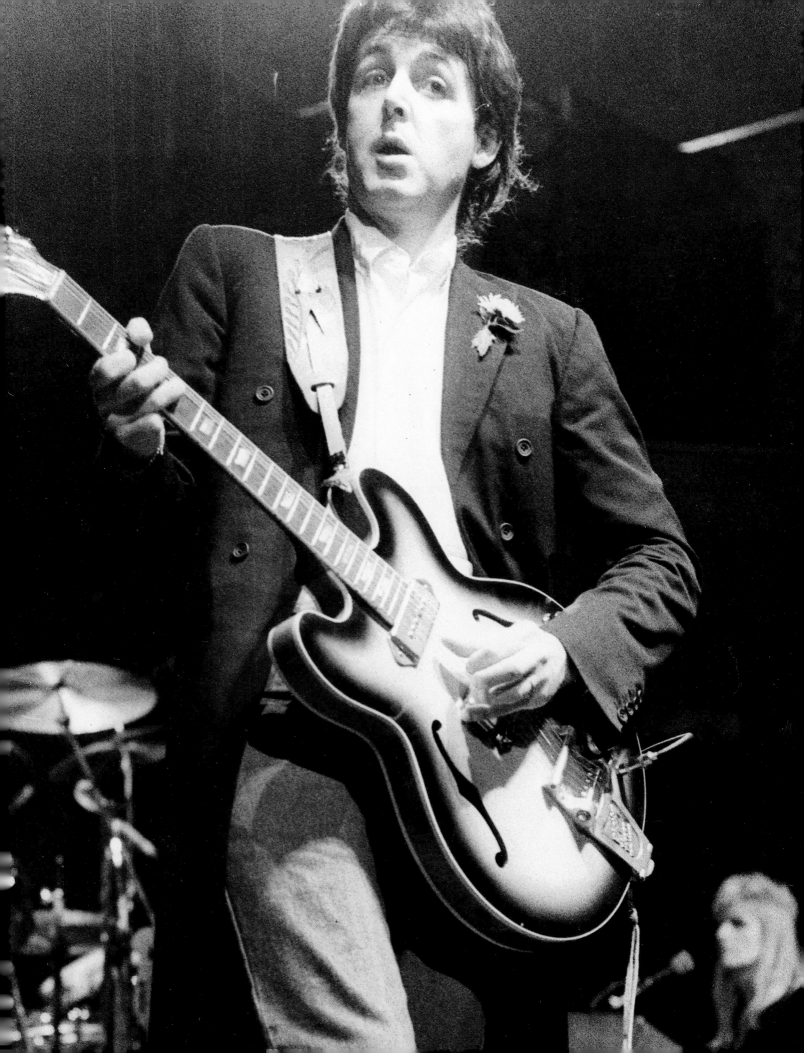

When Paul was invited to join the Quarry Men, neighbor John Lennon's skiffle group, he and John immediately turned what had been a chance encounter into a two-man guitar clinic, passing entire afternoons and evenings in Paul's living room mastering their instruments. Paul was the more accomplished of the two, and John peered through his accursed hornrims at every fingering in his new mate's repertoire. An outsider might have presumed that pushy, high-strung John was the prime mover in the group, but it was Paul who suggested they adopt formal uniforms, counseled (and was overruled) against giving its manager equal pay, and stressed the importance of long rehearsals and esprit de corps. Under their tutelage, the Quarry Men began to attract a broader range of bookings; audiences were either amused or agitated by John's biting bandstand banter, but they were consistent in requesting Paul's Little Richard imitation. Then one night, in the midst of a date at the Broadway Conservative Club, Paul unveiled "I Lost My Little Girl," a song he'd written himself. Intimidated, John intensified his own compositional explorations, and the two began to pace each other.

Jim McCartney got a kick out of his son's involvement in the Quarry Men, but his initial approval turned to consternation and then dismay when the boys began to hold court at the Cavern and then to plan a trip to Hamburg. Paul had just passed his final exams at Liverpool Institute, and Jim was keen to see him go on to teacher-training college. Paul and his brother had to gang up on their father. They minimized the summer stint in Germany as a lark before settling down to more weighty matters. Jim was naïve enough to believe them, practical enough to envy the itinerary, and harried enough to recognize he had no choice.

Considering the sheltered life he'd led in Allerton, Paul was totally unprepared for the tawdry glories of the Reeperbahn. The first lodgings the Beatles were given were next to the public toilets in a porno theater called the Bambi Kino. When he wound up being deported after supposedly trying to burn the place down (actually, he set fire to a prophylactic as a joke—the kind of stunt John Lennon had acquainted him with), neither he nor his father could decide if things had turned out for the best. One thing was certain: the experience left Paul with a permanent grin on his suddenly worldly looking babyface.

The breakthrough in the Lennon-McCartney songwriting alliance occurred in the autumn of 1963, when the two of them dreamed up a tune called "I Want to Hold Your Hand." As their output grew, it became obvious that McCartney and Lennon, while supportive of each other's writing, had divergent styles. Paul preferred story songs of a whimsical or heartfelt nature. Both concerns dovetailed in an offhanded melody called "Scrambled Eggs," which grew plaintive in tone when lyrics were added, becoming "Yesterday." "Penny Lane" was a childlike recollection of everyday commerce and the social niceties in the villages of Allerton and Woolton, focusing on activities at the traffic circle between the two. "She's Leaving Home," the doleful narrative from *Sgt. Pepper's Lonely Hearts Club Band*, stemmed from an account Paul read in the *Daily Mail*.

By the time of *The Beatles* (the so-called *White Album*) in 1968, Lennon was producing tracks like "Happiness Is a Warm Gun" while McCartney penned "Martha My Dear" about his dog of the same name. John favored raw, shrill, confessional music with an often belligerent feel to it, and he considered Paul's dulcet ballads "granny music." The dichotomy was never more obvious

Ed Sullivan introduces the Fab Four, 1964 (CBS Photo/Emil Romano and Lennie Lautenberger).

than in the infamous single from the *White Album*, Paul's wistful "Hey Jude" paired with John's "Revolution."

Contrasting family backgrounds had forever colored the sensibilities that grew from them, John working through the grudge he had against the Fates, Paul simply wanting to create the kind of music that his father could have played for his own sweetheart. That the Lennon-McCartney partnership would end was inevitable.

The parting with John emerged from the faltering fellowship of the Beatles as a whole, but, in the end, it was a personal falling out. *McCartney*, Paul's first solo LP, appeared in the stores on April 17, 1970, about a month before *Let It Be*, the last Beatles studio album, saw the light of day.

M CCARTNEY TOOK A LOT OF HEAT FROM CRITICS FOR THE distinctly homemade qualities of *McCartney*. Beatles' albums weren't noted for nubbly textures, and any product that failed to include (that is, excluded) the others was bound to draw fire. The critical derision was redoubled in 1971 when *Ram*, the LP credited to Paul and Linda McCartney (whom he'd wed in 1969), was issued: it was charged that Linda couldn't sing, that her presence as an artist made a mockery of Paul's previous standards, that Paul was casting sloppy seconds and table scraps into the marketplace. No one could fathom the man's reasoning. For all the barbs— the most cutting being a venomous song by Lennon, "How Do You Sleep?"— *Ram* had a No. 1 single in the U.S. with "Uncle Albert/Admiral Halsey." When the song publishing on the album was attributed to Mr. and Mrs. Paul McCartney, thus giving Linda 50 percent of the royalties, Lew Grade, overseer of the Beatles' publishing arm, Northern Songs, cried foul, disputing Linda's competence. A lawsuit resulted—which Paul and Linda won. As a conciliatory gesture, Lew Grade was asked to produce a TV special, *James Paul McCartney*, which saw worldwide distribution a year later and helped cement the new team of Paul and Linda in the minds of the public.

In an unusually bold move, McCartney next took steps to begin all over again, auditioning musicians in New York City and London for a band he would call Wings. *Wild Life*, their debut album, bombed, as did Paul's 1972

single, "Give Ireland Back to the Irish," which hit the stores shortly after the "Bloody Sunday" incident in Londonderry, Ireland, in which British paratroopers killed thirteen civilians during a demonstration. Furious that the BBC banned the record, McCartney retaliated with a single version of a children's nursery rhyme. Surprisingly, "Mary Had a Little Lamb" did well.

Throughout the mid-1970s, Wings prospered; personnel shifted periodically, and albums appeared with Beatles-like regularity. Complaints, often justified, of insipid songwriting continued to be leveled at McCartney, but his popular success easily eclipsed that of the other solo Beatles, and his sales sometimes achieved Beatles-sized dimensions. Two more Wings albums rounded out the decade. One, *Back to the Egg,* was an annoying series of song snippets that prompted the following overview in *Rolling Stone:* "This ex-Beatle has been lending his truly prodigious talents as a singer, songwriter, musician, and producer to some of the laziest records in the history of rock and roll."

One pursuit to which McCartney had applied himself with considerable vigor was indiscreet ganja-smoking, and his record of arrests is formidable. But the Eastman family (Paul's in-laws) and their law firm have served McCartney well, repeatedly helping him beat the marijuana raps. Also through their efforts, Paul gained control of the entire Buddy Holly catalogue, as well as the music to *A Chorus Line, Grease,* and *Annie,* making him the richest rocker (estimated to be worth $500 million) ever.

In the early 1980s, after the breakup of Wings, McCartney released three albums. The mature, sophisticated *Tug of War* earned the greatest praise accorded a McCartney project since *Band on the Run,* primarily for the record's thoughtful reflections on Paul's tempestuous relationship with the late John Lennon. McCartney seemed to be turning a new corner as a talent. Yet with the release of *Pipes of Peace* late in 1983, he was back creating syrupy melodies intertwined with mawkish lyrics, exasperating critics and confounding even his loyal fans. His heavy-handed film, *Give My Regards to Broad Street,* also fit the bathetic mold. These were projects that would never have passed muster in the Reeperbahn, but surely they made Jim McCartney proud.

MICK JAGGER

HE WAS CRYING, TEARS SPILLING IN THIN STREAKS DOWN HIS pimpled face. She was shocked that London's leading bad boy could be broken so bloody easily. "You ought to use the experience," she chided through the prison bars. "You should write a song about it or something."

It was June 29, 1967, and Michael Phillip Jagger was spending his third night in jail, having just been fined £100 and sentenced to three months confinement for illegal possession of several Benzedrine tablets of Italian manufacture. The bust had occurred several days earlier at Redlands, the country home of guitarist Keith Richards, where police had discovered eight men and one woman (she attired only in a fur rug) lounging about.

The lady swaddled in the rug was Marianne Faithfull, actual owner of the pep pills, girlfriend of Mr. Jagger, and visitor this very day at Brixton Jail. She assured her blubbering beau that he'd be out of stir within the next twenty-four hours; the overpaid lawyers were working tirelessly to countermand the trumped-up verdict. And sure enough, the High Court sprung both Jagger and Richards the next day. At month's end, an appeals court gave Jagger a conditional discharge and overturned Richards's conviction.

The established order that the Stones held in such smirking disdain had come through in a pinch. Mick was on the street again, hitting the pubs, his fleshy lips set in his best bratty sneer. But his main squeeze and other insiders would never forget how easy it had been to wipe that cocky wrinkle off his sallow face.

MICK JAGGER—BORN JULY 26, 1943, IN DARTFORD, ENGLAND—GREW up on the same block as Keith Richards. The son of a physical-education instructor, Mick was five years old when he met Richards (also born in 1943) at Wentworth Primary School. They lost track of each other when the beleaguered Richards family moved to a housing project at the other end of town. Then, in 1960, Mick and Keith met again by chance and realized that they both had an advanced interest in American rhythm and blues. They also discovered they had a mutual friend in Dick Taylor, a classmate of Keith's, who played guitar with Mick in a combo called Little Boy Blue and the Blue Boys. Keith joined the band and became tight with Jagger. At a gig at Alexis Korner's Blues Incorporated, they met Brian Jones, a blond-haired lady's man whose rousing slide-guitar solos quickened the crowd. Brian thought they should form their own group, and they invited Dick Taylor, pianist Ian Stewart, and traveling salesman–drummer Tony Chapman on board. Brian named the pack the Rolling Stones in homage to a Muddy Waters standard. A pat appellation; a sapient lot.

Brian, Mick, and Keith began sharing a flat in Edith Grove, Chelsea. They lived on boiled potatoes and pipe dreams, pestering entrepreneur Giorgio Gomelski for a Sunday-afternoon spot on the bill at the Crawdaddy Club, the

epicenter of the emerging blues craze. Advertising designer Charlie Watts replaced Chapman, and Bill Wyman took over the bass slot from Taylor. Gomelski finally acceded to their pleas. The Rolling Stones drew sixty-six people the first time out at the Crawdaddy and made £24.

Two weeks later, a nineteen-year-old hustler named Andrew Loog Oldham signed the Stones to a management contract. The Stones scored a deal with the Decca label, and straitlaced Ian Stewart was demoted to session-pianist status as Oldham moved to freeze the group's image as loutish snots, thus putting them at odds with the well-scrubbed Beatles. In the space of seven more days, the Stones cut "Come On," an obscure Chuck Berry song, and Willie Dixon's "I Want to Be Loved." Both sounded terrible, and Decca insisted they be redone. A reworked single of the two songs, with "Come On" as the A side, was released on June 7, 1963. Oldham secured airtime on the *Thank Your Lucky Stars* television show, and the Stones' first release rose to No. 22 on the British charts. The pushy young manager ignored the producer of *Lucky Stars* who urged him to dump the mangy lead singer with the "tire tread" lips, and instead put Jagger and his ruffians onstage at the National Jazz and Blues Festival.

The *Daily Mail* was succinct in interpreting the Stones' escalating appeal: "They look like boys whom any self-respecting mum would lock in the bathroom! But the Rolling Stones—five tough young London-based music makers with doorstep mouths, pallid cheeks, and unkempt hair—are not worried what mums think!"

By April 1964, the Rolling Stones had an album out in the U.S. and in the U.K., had sparked riots in Chicago, and had seen their chart-topping British single "Little Red Rooster" banned in the States as obscene. The pandemonium that attended their appearance on the *Ed Sullivan Show* moved the host to bark, "I promise you they'll never be back on our show."

Renegades of the well-groomed British Invasion, the Stones were denied the mainstream acceptance of the Beatles. They did, however, win over a loyal fringe that steadily expanded. "The Last Time" was their first big international success, kicking off the banner year of 1965. Jagger's spastic elan and puckered pout invested white rhythm and blues with a snippy vainglory typified by "(I Can't Get No) Satisfaction."

THE STONES WERE ASKED BACK TO THE SULLIVAN SHOW IN 1967. BUT, behind the scenes, the cocky group was in dire disarray. The drug raids that plagued Jagger, Richards, and Jones from 1967 on had been precipitated by dabblings in black magic, hard drugs, and innovative debauchery that had strained all bonds in the group's cosmology. Jagger had taken to mocking the adulation of the uncomprehending audience; rabblement became commonplace at concerts on the Continent, giving the Stones a reputation as a bad risk in a social climate already characterized by civil unrest and youthful calls for revolution.

As the Stones withdrew from live performances, Jagger—who had adopted a healthful regimen of exercise and nutrition that was downright bizarre for a rock star—became in all ways the leader of the group. Richards, meanwhile, established himself as the sublimely parlous soul of the outfit, the waggish wastrel and indefatigable party shark who single-handedly defined the lethal grandeur of rock excess. Jones, the Stones' finest musician, was usually too wasted or unbalanced to play. He withdrew into himself, undergoing a severe personality disintegration further aggravated by barbiturates, LSD, and drink.

Jagger assumed the cachet of a lanky Lucifer after the Stones tried in 1967 to better the Beatles' *Sgt. Pepper* LP with their dourly psychedelic *Their Satanic Majesties Request*. The record bombed with Christmas shoppers, but Jagger and Richards rebounded with the demonic "Jumping Jack Flash," an invocation of the patron fiend of hoochie-coochie men and soul-cursed sorcerers. Jagger starred in the film *Performance*, an "amorality play" intertwining bisexuality, drugs, and rock; Mick described it as "the perverted love affair between *Homo sapiens* and Lady Violence." On and off the set, he took to wearing pancake makeup, eye shadow, and lipstick.

Nineteen sixty-eight closed with the appearance of *Beggar's Banquet*, which featured the chilling "Sympathy for the Devil" and the incendiary "Street Fighting Man." "Anarchy is the only slight glimmer of hope," citizen Jagger told critics who quaked at the album's air of indiscriminate provocation. "Anybody should be able to go where he likes and do what he likes."

In June 1969, Brian Jones was drummed out of the Stones. It was after midnight on July 3 when friends found his body at the bottom of the swimming pool at Cotchford Farm, the Sussex estate where A.A. Milne had written *Winnie-the-Pooh*. The coroner ruled his death at twenty-six as "due to immersion in fresh water under the influence of drugs and alcohol."

On July 11, the day following Brian Jones's burial in his hometown of Cheltenham, the Stones released "Honky Tonk Women," followed in six months by *Let It Bleed* (a callous rejoinder to the Beatles' *Let It Be*). Jagger and Richards co-wrote the two tracks on the LP that received the most radio exposure: "Gimme Shelter," notable for its hellish chorus—"Rape! Murder! It's just a shot away!"—and "Midnight Rambler," a reptilian nocturne to Albert deSalvo, the Boston Strangler.

J AGGER WAS DETERMINED TO MOUNT A CONCERT THAT WOULD OUTDRAW the Woodstock Festival. He vowed that the event would be "the last and greatest concert of the sixties." Altamont Speedway in Livermore, California, was the last-minute choice for a venue.

As Jagger stepped out of the helicopter that had dropped him at the site, a man broke through the crowd and struck him in the face, screaming, "I hate you!" All around the grounds, the scene was ugly. A drunken contingent of Hells Angels had been hired to police the crowd and had spent the hours previous to the Stones' arrival beating members of the audience with pool cues and clubs, breaking jaws, shattering teeth, smashing heads. Then, during "Sympathy for the Devil," a black man in a green suit popped up from a sea of contorted faces and seemed to point a pistol at Jagger.

Bystanders watched as the Angels killed the gun-wielding figure, an eighteen-year-old named Meredith Hunter. Hunter had pulled the gun out to defend himself after he had been slashed in the back by a biker who'd singled him out because of Hunter's white, blonde girlfriend. Hunter was maniacally stabbed in the face and the back as he tried to run. Once down, he was kicked until his nose and jaw were shattered. A steel bucket was twisted into his eyes until his piercing cries of agony crested and ceased.

Mick Jagger left Altamont with a bulging suitcase of cash and flew straight to Switzerland. In his wake were a slew of lawsuits and condemnations, few more virulent than that from American promoter Bill Graham: "I ask you what right you had, Mr. Jagger . . . to leave the way you did, thanking everybody for a wonderful time, and the Angels for helping out? . . . What right does this god have to descend on this country this way? . . . Mick Jagger is not God Junior. . . . But you know what is the greatest tragedy? That [man] is a great entertainer."

IN MAY 1971, JAGGER WED BIANCA PEREZ MORENO DE MACIAS, THE FINE-boned daughter of Nicaraguan shopkeepers. The wedding took place in St. Tropez, and no one missed the obvious: she was a ringer for Mick. Friends snickered that the popinjay preener could now make love to himself. As a harbinger of the new jet-set lifestyle he and his bride lusted after, Mick was named one of the Hot Hundred Best Dressed Men by the natty *The Tailor and Cutter*. He later had an emerald implanted in his front tooth, replaced it with a ruby, then settled on a diamond.

The Stones secured their own label, Rolling Stones Records, which would be distributed by Atlantic. Andy Warhol designed an official logo—a carica-ture of Jagger's full lips and wagging tongue. *Sticky Fingers*, the debut release, and the scandalously sexist single "Brown Sugar" (in which a white slave mas-ter trades cunnilingus for fellatio with a black dancer while comparing her to unrefined heroin) made them a darkly chic international sensation. *Exile on Main Street* completed the masterful trilogy of macabre urban reconnoiters that had begun with *Beggar's Banquet* and continued with *Sticky Fingers*. Music that lionized the underbelly of human existence, it was not the sort of aural ambiance one would wish in an empty room after sundown, but it was true to the pernicious spirit of the tar-hearted delta blues denizens of yore.

Mick Taylor left the Stones in December 1974, and runty, bird-haired Ron Wood, lead guitarist for the Faces, signed up in April 1975. Stones al-bums continued to tumble out of a quarry where the sun rarely shined, some of them awful (*Goat's Head Soup, Black and Blue, Love You Live, Sucking in the Seventies, Still Life*), some mediocre (*It's Only Rock and Roll, Tattoo You, Un-dercover*), and one of them excellent (*Some Girls*) for all the right—that is, effectively irksome—reasons.

Jagger shed Bianca in a hotly contested 1979 divorce, sharing custody of their daughter, Jade. In 1983, he turned forty as an effete multimillionaire whose official residence became the Caribbean Island of Mustique, and a fam-ily man who'd fathered three girls (the second by actress Marsha Hunt, the third by model Jerry Hall). He was the most famous rocker on earth, a survivor of the star wars, but most young comers considered him to be either a fading hero or an irrelevant old fart.

Two days after Christmas 1983, Mick showed up on the backstage celebri-ty list for an electric blues concert. Tired of watching from the wings, Jagger slipped out into the hall to catch the spirited show from the orchestra section. After dancing amongst the audience for some ten minutes, he attempted to return backstage. Beefy security guards barred the way. He tried to barge past them. They threw him back. Told him to beat it.

Abruptly, it dawned on him that absolutely no one recognized who he was. He cursed. Squinted at his tormentors. Reasoned with them. Cursed. Paced. It was not until he flashed his American Express card that anyone be-lieved him.

This was indeed Mick Jagger.

FACING PAGE
Jumping Jack Flash, complete with knee-pads (John Bellissimo/ Retna Ltd.).

OVERLEAF
In 1981, the Stones' might as a live act was undiminished, and Jagger had become a guitarist (Martin Benjamin).

KEITH RICHARDS

BLACK IS HIS FAVORITE COLOR.

His mother claimed he had perfect pitch since age two.

As a boy, his idol was Roy Rogers.

When he was ten, his aunt sent him a map of California, a treasure he guarded for years afterward.

At thirteen, Keith joined the Boy Scouts but quit after the initiation ceremony.

The first record he purchased was a Woolworth single on the Embassy label. On it, a singer imitated Ricky Nelson.

His mother bought him his first guitar for £7.

He won his first fight by swinging a bicycle chain at his opponent.

He was a regular at the one snooker hall in his hometown.

He was expelled on his last day of school for leaving half an hour early.

He considers his most admirable virtue to be compassion.

While in art school, he liked to pop Benzedrine and Midol tablets. Sometimes, he shared his pills with a cockatoo in the zoo.

He was strongly against releasing "(I Can't Get No) Satisfaction," feeling the song he'd largely written was "album filler" . . . "terrible" . . . "It could just as well have been called 'Aunt Millie's Caught Her Tit in the Mangle.'"

After being fined for driving without a license, he arranged for an aide to impersonate him for his driving test. The aide passed, forged Keith's signature on the necessary documents, and the Ministry of Transport granted a license.

"What I'm doing is a sexual thing," he told a journalist in 1966. "I dance, and all dancing is a replacement for sex. What really upsets people is that I'm a man and not a woman."

During his trial in June 1967, following the police raid on Redlands, his country home, Richards told the judge, "We are not old men. We are not worried about petty morals."

Girlfriend Anita Pallenberg talked him into purchasing a Nazi staff car in the late 1960s. He had the huge Mercedes refitted at a cost of $5,000. The day it was delivered, he wrecked it. The car went back to the auto shop. A year later, it was roadworthy once more. The day it was delivered, he wrecked it again.

The character from fiction he would most like to have been is Smiley from John LeCarré's *Tinker, Tailor, Soldier, Spy*.

In 1970, he moved with his family to Nellcote, a Roman-style villa above Villefranche-sur-Mer on the Côte d'Azur, as a tax dodge, and he had heroin shipped to him on a regular basis, concealed inside his son's toys.

While in France, he graduated from snorting smack to shooting smack.

In April 1972, Anita Pallenberg gave birth to Dandelion, her second child with Keith. As with Marlon in August 1969, Dandelion was delivered while Anita was addicted to heroin.

On December 14, 1972, police descended on Nellcote, discovering quantities of heroin, cocaine, and hashish.

When Anita was arrested in Jamaica in December 1972 for possession of

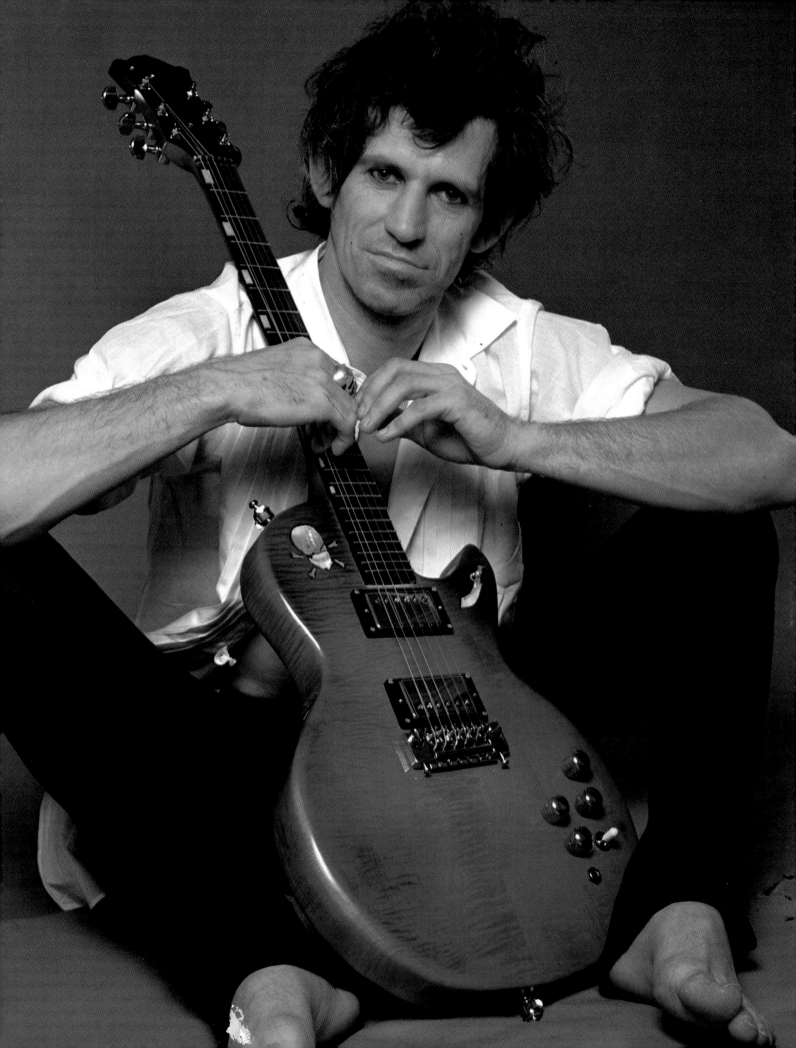

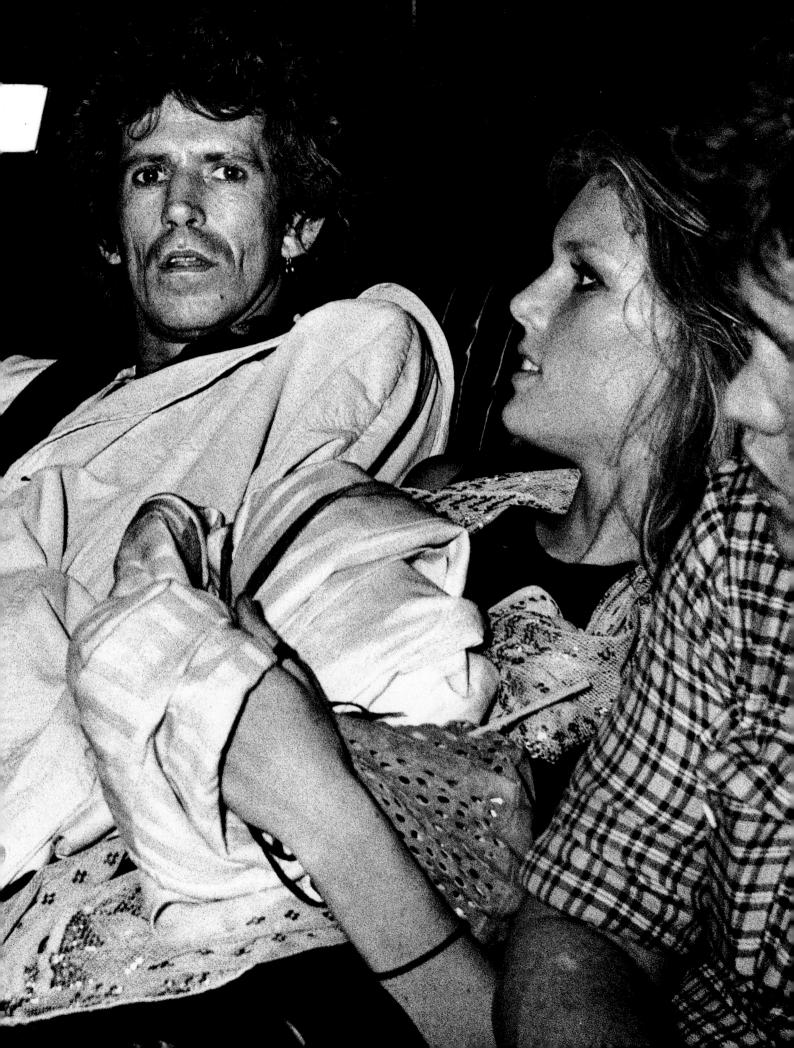

marijuana—and repeatedly beaten and raped in her jail cell—Keith privately offered $12,000 to anyone willing to kill the man who had set up the bust. He had no takers.

His favorite bourbon is Rebel Yell.

His idols are the Great Train Robbers.

His definition of the height of misery is being caught with a cold and no handkerchief.

He and Anita Pallenberg acquired a reputation around London for corrupting the servants supplied by a Chelsea employment agency with heroin, thereafter taking the money they needed for requisite fixes out of their wages. Eventually, the agency refused to send any more prospects to the couple.

Following the shooting of George Wallace at a political rally in May 1972, Keith began to carry a .38 police revolver for his personal protection.

On July 4, 1972, Keith introduced Rolling Stone Records chief Marshall Chess to heroin in Washington, D.C.

He once told a London reporter that he believed Redlands was a site for UFO landings.

On June 26, 1973, London bobbies uncovered guns, Chinese heroin, and Mandrax tablets during a raid on Keith's home on fashionable Cheyne Walk.

A desperate Marshall Chess reportedly phoned Keith from a Knightsbridge hotel late one evening in the early 1970s, informing him that he believed he was dying from an overdose of the $1,000 worth of bad heroin they'd split earlier that evening. Keith is said to have hung up on him—repeatedly—later telling an aide to buy back whatever smack Chess had left over.

Needing to clean up for the Rolling Stones' 1973 European tour in support of *Goat's Head Soup*, Keith and Marshall traveled to Switzerland to get a forty-eight-hour blood transfusion—a supposed cure for heroin addiction. A Florida doctor named Denber officiated. The cure appeared to work. Shortly afterward, both men took up the drug again.

On March 26, 1976, Anita Pallenberg gave birth to a second son, Tara Richard, in a Swiss clinic. Ten weeks later, the infant died. No public explanation was ever given for his death.

On May 19, 1976, Keith fell asleep at the wheel of his Bentley and ran it off an English highway into a field. No one in the car was hurt, but an investigating officer found an unidentified substance in the car. After arriving two hours late for the trial, Keith told the judge he was waiting for his trousers to come out of the dryer. "I find it extraordinary," replied His Honor, "that a man of your stature has only one pair of pants."

While Richards was being sentenced in Canada for heroin possession and trafficking, Sid Vicious slit his wrists. "He's trying to steal my headlines!" said Richards.

After he and Anita Pallenberg allegedly kicked heroin through neuroelectric acupuncture treatment in New York, a Canadian judge gave Richards a suspended sentence for the heroin rap and ordered him to perform a benefit concert for the blind.

"The last thing I could bear," he says, "is to feel guilty about smack."

He would like to die "humbly."

In December 1983, he married Patti Hansen outside Cabo San Lucas, Mexico. She was nine years old when "Satisfaction" was an international hit.

On his guitar picks are stamped the words: "I'm innocent."

ARETHA FRANKLIN

WHAT BEGAN IN THE SUNNY GLOW OF A DAYTIME phone call almost ended in a backwater brawl in the fathomless predawn. Atlantic Records vice-president Jerry Wexler had received a hot tip: Aretha Franklin had just gotten out of her contract with Columbia Records. Wexler rang Aretha immediately. He chatted sweetly with the shy singer and her husband, Ted White, and within days they had a deal.

For Wexler it was a godsend. He'd been emerald with envy ever since Columbia's John Hammond had picked up on the eighteen-year-old spiritual singer. Aretha had been the centerpiece of the pew-pounding services at her father's New Bethel Baptist Church, and Hammond hired her shortly after she'd wriggled loose from her father's wayfaring evangelist caravan. "She was the best natural singer I'd heard since Billie Holiday," said Hammond. Columbia tried to steer her away from the narrow gospel category in which James Cleveland and Aretha's aunt Clara Ward had excelled and toward the fully orchestrated show tunes and bleached jazz-pop that were leading the Hit Parade. She started out in 1960 with "Today I Sing the Blues," got detoured to "If Ever I Should Leave You" from *Camelot,* and, after ten albums, had seen only one feeble pop hit, "Rock-a-Bye Your Baby with a Dixie Melody." Nothing could have been less "natural."

Wexler booked a week at Rick Hall's Fame Studios in Muscle Shoals—plenty of time to cut an entire LP—and requested a certain integrated roster of musicians that would include a leading black horn section. It didn't go down that way, and when Aretha and her testy spouse found themselves in the deep South, with a sea of white faces peering over their music stands, it was bad ethnic arithmetic. Aretha remained game, quietly going to the piano to explain the parts she'd worked out, but Ted White clenched his teeth. Sure enough, one of the trumpet players started trading thinly veiled racial repartee with White as they got drunk from the same bottle. Curt winks gave way to cold stares and cutting retorts. The sun sank like a sick joke, taking all civility with it, leaving too much liquor behind and the wrong men intent on consuming it. As the witching hour approached, Wexler took to his bed in the motel where everyone was staying and prayed for the storm to pass.

He awoke to the sounds of heavy footsteps in the night. Doors slammed. He thought he heard shots going off. The phone rang. It was Aretha, calling from a diner. A boiling brouhaha of no small scope had developed between Ted and the trumpet player and had spilled over in all directions. She and Ted had an ugly fight, and she'd run away.

At 7 A.M., Wexler found himself in Aretha's room, Ted White laying him out, cursing a blue streak, and calling down dreadful oaths. "Man," he fumed, as Aretha wept, "why did you bring her down here with these rednecks!" Husband and wife split on the next flight North, vowing never to return.

Wexler was left with only one completed track, "I Never Loved a Man,"

and "Do Right Woman—Do Right Man," a work-in-progress. He knocked off some master tapes, mailing them out to prominent rhythm and blues DJs for feedback. He got a tremendously positive reaction. Problem was, Wexler couldn't put the single out because he had no completed B side, and he was unable to locate Aretha. Catching up with her a couple of weeks later, Wexler suggested that they try to make amends in neutral territory—New York City. She gave her cautious assent. The basic band from Muscle Shoals was brought up, plus the Memphis horns buttressed by saxophone great King Curtis, a favorite of Aretha's.

"I Never Loved a Man (the Way I Love You)" became a Top 10 hit in 1967, and it was the prelude to Aretha Franklin's five-year reign as the preeminent black artist in the world: Lady Soul, the Spirit in the Dark.

She also gained repute as a remote, woe-laden woman of precarious fortune but irreducible dignity. For all her hard luck and travail, she would never circulate complaints, never broadcast bitter asides, never so much as acknowledge a single reversal. But the pain was in her singing, a pliant, plangent wail that childhood houseguest Sam Cooke had believed would never be palatable outside of a witness-bearing holiness shout in church. As Wexler put it, she became "the mysterious lady of sorrow."

SHE CAME OUT OF DETROIT'S EAST SIDE, HUMBLE HOME TURF TO THE Supremes and Smokey Robinson, but her house was a large one on a tree-lined street. Her father, Reverend Clarence L. Franklin, was one of the best-known preachers in the country, making thousands of dollars per homily on his barnstorming runs, and boasting a brisk-selling catalogue of over seventy albums of sermons on the Chess label.

Aretha was born on March 25, 1942, in Memphis, Tennessee, one of five children by the former Barbara Siggers. Her father brought the family North when Aretha was two, first to Buffalo and then to Detroit, where he became pastor of the New Bethel Baptist congregation. Aretha was six when her mother abandoned the family. In 1952, word came that she had died. The children often found themselves in the care of hired help when her father traveled with his troupe. At twelve, Aretha soloed in church to a joyous reaction and cut some sides with JVP Records; then Clarence Franklin took her to see his people at Chess. Two singles resulted.

Inspired by Sam Cooke's bold break with the church in the mid-1950s, eschewing Sundays at New Bethel for Saturday nights at the Flame Show Bar, Aretha moved to New York City and auditioned for theatrical agent Jo King. A Columbia contract was offered and snatched up, but Aretha wasn't ready. Outside of a church, without the uplifting press of pious spectators, she lost her bearings. Under Wexler, however, the environment was funky, relaxed, even cloistered. There was no excess, and plenty of rehearsal time in which to gestate and experiment. Aretha relaxed and began writing more songs; her innate approach—with its piercing heights and supple melisma—flowered and steadied. "I Never Loved a Man" sold a million copies; four more gold singles were cut that year, including the peerless "Respect"—a wonder, written by Otis Redding, that was captured live in the studio. Aretha's first albums on Atlantic, *I Never Loved a Man the Way I Love You* and *Aretha Arrives* were cohesive works, free of filler, and their honesty and directness made them standards by which blacks measured themselves.

The Southern Christian Leadership Conference gave her a special citation for her contributions to black culture, and she was a bona fide heroine, devoid of the gloss and cynical self-aggrandizement of a Diana Ross or the rhinestone-studded vapidity of a Nancy Wilson.

Riding the acclaim of her superb *Lady Soul* LP and "Chain of Fools" single, Aretha opened the 1968 Democratic Convention with a truly soul-stirring version of "The Star-Spangled Banner" that said more about rightful citizenship in the land of the free than any speech delivered at that accursed convocation. She placed four more singles in the Top 10 before Christmas: "Since You've Been Gone," "Think," "The House That Jack Built"/"I Say a Little Prayer," and "See Saw."

Her homelife was less transcendent. She gave birth to three children during her teen years, products of an unhappy union. Fans were outraged when Ted White roughed her up in public in 1967. Their divorce some two years later was as unpleasant as their time together, lightened only by the birth of a son in 1970.

By the end of 1971, Aretha had had more million-sellers than any female singer, thanks to "Don't Play That Song," "Bridge Over Troubled Water," "Spanish Harlem," and "Rock Steady." But her mood swings increased in the 1970s. Then, during a session down in Miami, she contracted pancreatitis. It was Wexler who looked after the singer, wheeling her to the X-ray room, monitoring her care. Oddly, her entourage had deserted her. "There was nobody but me," said Wexler. "I couldn't understand it."

In 1970, she brought out *Spirit in the Dark*. It boasted "Don't Play That Song," a brilliant performance that connected with the peaks of *Lady Soul*. *Live at the Fillmore West* in 1971 brought her together with Ray Charles and King Curtis and primed the pump for *Young, Gifted and Black*, the 1972 LP that would be her last soul-baring effort, a wrenching look back on her tormented marriage. She found solace and renewal in gospel on *Amazing Grace*. But further epiphanies failed to occur. Aretha's stage shows and television appearances defied interpretation in their gross ignorance of her intrinsic charm. She would hurry through scores of costume changes in an unintentional send-up of *Gentlemen Prefer Blondes* or waddle onstage attired as a black Emmett Kelly.

In 1978, Aretha married actor Glynn Turman; the Rev. C. L. Franklin performed the ceremony as the Four Tops sang Stevie Wonder's "Isn't She Lovely." In 1979, her father was shot by burglars and left in a coma. She left Atlantic amid financial difficulties augmented by her father's medical bills and signed with Arista, and once again was given simpler settings in which to work out her vocal insecurities, let her heart be heard, and permit some magic to take hold. Rising singer-producer Luther Vandross gave her a hit with the title track of *Jump to It* in 1982 and won her new fans with *Get It Right* in 1983, both exceptional records. She made her stage debut in 1984 with *Sing, Mahalia, Sing*, a musical based on the life of gospel legend Mahalia Jackson.

As the future brightened, Aretha kept her own counsel. A rare soliloquy from the start of her boom years with Atlantic serves as the best summation of her trials and of her spirit in the dark: "Trying to grow up is hurting, you know. You make mistakes. You try to learn from them, and when you don't it hurts even more."

B O B   D Y L A N

DURING AN INVERVIEW IN THE FALL OF 1983, SINGER/SONG-writer Paul Simon was asked: *Who besides John Lennon do you believe has been a positive inspirational figure in rock?*

"Dylan. He made us feel at a certain time that it was good to be smart, to be observant, that it was good to have a social conscience. These are all things that are out of fashion now. Real art remains when the fashion changes, but art can run conjunctively with fashion. Both can occasionally be quite intelligent at the same time."

Blessed with the hindsights of adulthood, what's the smartest thing you ever heard anybody in rock and roll say?

(Long pause, small smile) "Be-bop-a-lula, she's my baby."

PAUL SIMON, THEN FORTY-THREE, COULDN'T HELP BUT CHUCKLE AFTER confessing that the opening line of rockabilly star Gene Vincent's palpitating 1956 pop yodel about puppy love was the most luminous he could recall. But he wouldn't retract the statement.

Paul Simon's career took shape in Bob Dylan's shadow, and he held the man in the same awe as the rest of his contemporaries. He envied Dylan's intuitive ear, was charged by his trenchant wit and his understanding, admired his temerity, was humbled by his talent, arrested by his mystique. During a songwriting workshop at New York University in 1971, Simon told his class about the first time he met Dylan. He trailed Bob around his messy, paper-strewn house; he picked up every loose scrap of paper behind his host's back and stuffed them into his pockets, dying to discover "how Dylan did it."

DYLAN'S SKETCHY BACKGROUND WAS DELICIOUSLY INTRIGUING AMERI-cana. He was born Robert Allen Zimmerman in Duluth, Minnesota, on May 24, 1941, son of a hardware-store owner, formed a high-school group called the Golden Chords, took Dylan Thomas's first name as his last when he began playing at cafés while at the University of Minnesota. He came to New York City in 1961, sought out a dying Woody Guthrie in an East Orange, New Jersey, hospital, and begged him for his blessing. John Hammond, A&R sleuth at Columbia Records, discovered Dylan at Gerdes's Folk City.

Ahh, but that was 1962, when his debut *Bob Dylan* LP on Columbia set smug Greenwich Village talking about a gangly broccoli-haired stick of a kid who could lend fresh import to traditional ballads, a street poet who could get people thinking about something other than current pop pap like Ray Stevens's "Ahab the Arab" with such originals as "Song to Woody" and "Talking New York." By 1963, he'd become *The Freewheelin' Bob Dylan*, pictured on the album cover heading down West 4 Street with a honey blonde on his arm, not dressed against the cold, making you feel just how cold it was going to get with such songs as "A Hard Rain's a-Gonna Fall," "Blowin' in the Wind,"

and "Masters of War." In 1964, *The Times They Are a-Changin'* made him a protest singer without peer—lauded and loathed—but he showed the world that he was one leftist troubadour who could come down off the barricades and write exceptional love ballads when he closed out the year with *Another Side of Bob Dylan*. Come 1965, his *Bringing It All Back Home* continued in the folk-rock direction he'd started when he'd given his "Mr. Tambourine Man" to the Byrds. Dylan endured boos at the Newport Folk Festival for the electric guitar around his neck, then got a No. 2 record with the savage "Like a Rolling Stone." Nineteen sixty-six saw the beginning of Dylan's incarnation as the star-crossed satirist-savant, his public pleading with him for clues to the cerebral songs on *Highway 61 Revisited* and *Blonde on Blonde*, Dylan racking up another No. 2 hit with the unruly wobble-rhythms of "Rainy Day Women #12 & 35," Dylan getting a broken neck and amnesia after a motorcycle crash in Woodstock, New York. . . .

THEN CAME 1968 AND DYLAN'S COMEBACK WITH THE MORDANT *JOHN Wesley Harding,* his marriage to twenty-five-year-old model Sarah (Shirley Noznisky) Lowndes, his interest in Zionism and his Jewishness. His further movement toward country music came in 1969, with *Nashville Skyline* and "Lay Lady Lay." There was a tepid return to Greenwich Village in the early 1970s with *Self-Portrait* and *New Morning;* a tentative redux of social consciousness with the Concert for Bangla Desh, and his "George Jackson" single. And then the cagey dismantlement of the myth, testing, tearing, pushing it to the limits with the soundtrack and cameo role (his character's name was "Alias") in Sam Peckinpah's *Pat Garrett and Billy the Kid;* the *Planet Waves* LP; the 1974 tour documented in *Before the Flood;* the unexpectedly poignant, contemplative, and prismatic *Blood on the Tracks* (1974) and *Desire*

(1975); *The Basement Tapes* (1975), cut with the Band during Dylan's recuperation from the cycle spill; the ragtag Rolling Thunder Revue caravan that enlisted Allen Ginsberg, Ronee Blakley, Joni Mitchell, Roger McGuinn, Arlo Guthrie, Mick Ronson; his divorce from his wife in 1977; the release in 1978 of his disastrous four-hour parable of rock ennui, *Renaldo and Clara.*

By 1979, after two uneven live albums *(Hard Rain, Live at Budokan)* and a moribund studio LP *(Street Legal)*, Dylan showed himself to be an arrogant, uncharitable, born-again Christian, but his music had regained snap and bite, especially on his *Slow Train Coming* and *Saved* albums. He was certain of its strangeness, excited by its obscurity. *Infidels*, released in 1983, was intended to be a setting aside of his ever-shifting religious obsessions, and it suffered from a transparent self-consciousness. The broad irony, evident in such famous remarks as, "Oh, I think of myself more as a song-and-dance man, y'know," was long gone.

B OB DYLAN'S SONGS, SO FIERCE IN THEIR ENDURING VITALITY, ARE OF THE "time-and-place" stripe. They are welded to signposts, highway ramps, overpasses; places his contemporaries have done time in, raced through, moved away from. They run wide and deep, but they somehow do not exist on their own terms. "Be-Bop-a-Lulu" does. It is an emotion preserved in song, unconditional, wholly without boundaries. It is too guileless to be quaint. Too forthright to be trivialized. Impervious to age. As universal as a planted kiss.

Paul Simon is rich now, famous, his distinguished place in the rock annals is secure. He can sit quietly in his offices in New York's Brill Building, the one-time headquarters of Tin Pan Alley and teen pop, and recall songs that bring back the challenges of his youth, the various phases of his career, the aura of coffee houses, SNCC, the Mobilization, Kent State, the fall of Saigon, the Hearst kidnapping, the gradual embracing of adulthood, the accomplishments of his rock and roll colleagues. Dylan songs remind him of these things, and vice-versa. They have rich meaning; they challenged conventional wisdom and helped get things done. They depict a time when a young man in a hurry could locate himself in and measure himself against his heroes, change his name and identity to gain proximity to their legends—maybe even eclipse them—and then win applause for the nerve these deeds require. Such songs are too shrewd to be pure, too clever to be instinctive, too studied for practical reasons to be the smartest of the smart.

Once Bob Dylan had been like no one else. Now he was like all of us. A still-restless dabbler, the tale of his reinvention too often retold, an ordinary man whose eyes stared inward, branded with his generation's now-familiar expression of perplexity. He was a common victim of the American Curse: too many choices.

STEVIE WONDER

I T HAD BEEN DESCRIBED AS A "DAY IN THE KEY OF LIFE" ON THE EN-graved invitations. Some 200 journalists, celebrities, and music-business executives were cordially requested to spend twelve hours with Stevie Wonder, Motown's resident soul visionary, for the unveiling of his magnum opus, *Songs in the Key of Life*. It was autumn 1976.

Guests were welcomed at a groaning-board breakfast buffet at a midtown Manhattan hotel, escorted to a conga line of chartered buses, and carried to the airport. A private jet redeposited them on an airfield in the woods of Massachusetts. The tarmac landing strip was a trifle too short for the large plane, and only the judiciously violent braking of the pilot kept the craft from veering too close to the heart-halting drop at the end of the strip. Those unfazed passengers who'd held onto their eggs benedict and sauteed zucchini swiftly deplaned and were met by more buses that hauled all comers to the end of the line: Long View Farms.

A billowy white banquet tent had been pitched between the house and the barn; and while the guests milled about sloping acres of woods, lawns, and meadows, a chef and his staff readied lunch. On the second floor of the farm-house, a slim, broad-shouldered black man was being dressed by two middle-aged valets.

The man was twenty-six years old, blind from birth. He hummed a melody, sporadic and low. His cream-colored western shirt was being buttoned by one valet and a matching Stetson hat set upon his head by the other. He said little, playing with the drawstring on his hat, tightening it under his chin so that it pulled the brim near to his eyebrows.

"You don't be wanting the hat to be on your head all that hard, it's too far down," said one attendant. Steview Wonder sat expressionless, saying noth-ing, scratching his moustache, humming, rubbing his goatee, ceasing to hum. His feet were guided into a cream-colored pair of boots, and he was asked to stand. Around his waist was put a leather holster belt. Its pistol sheaths had been replaced with two cardboard mock-ups of his album jacket; flat wooden handles, painted to resemble the butts of cocked sixguns, protruded from them. Sunglasses were put in place, and Stevie pressed these against his brow. Downstairs, an awkward announcement was made by a well-dressed black woman, then repeated verbatim by an equally elegant black man; they were going to play the first side of Wonder's new record.

The studio monitors began to hiss as guests crammed themselves into the dark, circular room, and multi-tracked "oohs" burst forth, followed by Won-der's sung introduction to "Love's in Need of Love Today."

The song was a mournful plea for brotherhood, Wonder's almost viscose tenor sinking from a wistful falsetto to an emphatic growl, a harmonized gospel descant drifting in and out, while drums, bass, tinkling rhythm guitar, and synthesized blurps nudged the doleful lyric onward. The next song, "Have a Talk with God," was equally somber and keyed to the ominous striking of a bell. "Village Ghetto Land" was a pastoral on poverty and neglect, complete

with a synthesizer parroting both a preachy pipe organ and strings that whined a dirgeful minuet. "Contusion" was a herky-jerky jazz-rock fusion instrumental. The side ended with "Sir Duke," a peppy tribute to Duke Ellington that punctured the dolorous mood with a kooky horn fanfare.

As the cerebral sermonizing faded from the monitors, the tall, trusting Wonder was led downstairs by the elbow to meet the assembled. His unwieldy holsters repeatedly got caught in the bars of the railings; the crown of his hat dented slightly as he strained to keep his head down during the cramped descent. At the sight of this unconsciously ostentatious space cowboy, the crowd fell silent, perplexed. Wonder looked miscast, fleeced of his innate dignity, his incongruous costume communicating an unintentional whimsy, much like that of a guileless trick-or-treat toddler who is paraded before the oldsters before his Halloween rounds. A break for lunch was called, and Wonder was taken outside and eased into a crooked swing hung from a great tree to pose for photos. A copy of the album jacket was held up ceremoniously, and many guests were taken aback at its ugliness, raggy concentric rings of burnt orange enclosing a blurred sketch of Stevie that was at best a clumsy likeness.

"Is that the finished cover?" one writer asked with trepidation. "This is it!" replied a Motown rep in an expansive tone. Asked to comment on the graphics, Wonder said he guessed they symbolized "universal love." Fifteen minutes later, Wonder was taken back upstairs. He made no further appearances.

For the remainder of the afternoon, installments of *Songs in the Key of Life* were unveiled at half-hour intervals. For almost two hours of music, it was low on padding and well-produced. Relieved that the fete had offered more than

sumptuous hype, the guests settled into a sunny alfresco afternoon of eating, drinking, and casual conversation. But there was something distinctly off-center about the affair, an absence of naturalness and grace, supplanted by a feeling of having been offered a haphazard peek at an unfortunate, even unnecessary puzzle. Eyes kept straying to the second-floor window. What was it like to be Stevie Wonder? To be the centerpiece of splendid parties in which he did not participate, a musical wunderkind who lived in his head, dependent on the ministrations of others, a victim of their visual, sartorial, and who knows what other tastes? On the plane back to New York, one writer for a newsweekly turned to another reporter and insisted that, as far as it was known, Wonder was extremely well-cared for by his devoted family, freed from petty concerns to focus totally on his music, but made all important decisions himself. The results of the arrangement spoke for themselves.

"All I know," murmured one black journalist, "is that if somebody ever tried to get Ray Charles into some weird getup and put him on display like a doll, Ray would have personally kicked their ass."

HE WAS BORN BLIND ON MAY 13, 1950, IN SAGINAW, MICHIGAN, STEVE-land Morris according to his birth certificate. Adept at playing piano, drums, and harmonica by his eleventh year, he was signed to the Hits-ville U.S.A. label (later renamed Motown) through the good graces of singer Ronnie White of the Miracles. White had auditioned the boy, introduced him to staff songwriter Brian Holland, and got owner Berry Gordy, Jr., to take on the twelve-year-old prodigy. Little Stevie Wonder, Gordy called him. In concert, Wonder was presented as a pint-sized musical jack-of-all-trades, jumping from drums to organ to piano and then pulling out his silver mouth organ to bring his mighty feat to a furious close. He was seen by many as an inspirational novelty attraction who'd conquered a handicap with astounding style, but white acceptance was always much on Motown's mind, so, in 1964, Wonder was a featured performer in two surf movies, *Muscle Beach Party* and *Bikini Party*.

In 1966, he deepened his crossover appeal with an affecting cover of Bob Dylan's "Blowin' in the Wind." By 1968, he was having hits with such superior rhythm-and-blues ballads as "I Was Made to Love Her" and "For Once in My Life." By the time he'd turned nineteen, his balladry, though sugar-coated, had the trappings of sophistication, as in the well-received "My Cherie Amour" and "Yester-Me, Yester-You, Yesterday."

As the history of Motown shows, Wonder's renegotiated 1976 Motown pact, a reported $13 million deal whose terms filled 120 pages, was an epoch-disintegrating document. Formed in the late 1950s after retired Detroit boxer Berry Gordy lost his record store to bankruptcy, Motown Records was an autocratic organization. Every facet of its artists' careers and finances—of their entire lives—was controlled by "the Corporation" with Gordy acting as Big Daddy. Each act was selected by Gordy and groomed under his patronage, sent to charm schools, given voice and diction lessons, grilled in choreography. Then they were placed in the hands of a battery of staff writers and producers like the trio of Lamont Dozier and Brian and Eddie Holland, who specialized in gospel/blues-rooted grit primed to fit a lustrous pop grid. When royalties rolled in, the cash was consigned to banks and paid out to the performers in weekly allowances.

Wonder was the pioneer in eroding this chafing hierarchy, but, as was characteristic of others who were similarly assertive, he reflexively spun an opaque and secretive new human cocoon around himself, one that was the scaled-down equal of the immediate Motown "family" from which he'd distanced himself. Moreover, he set the oft-repeated precedent of peopling his new world with personnel from the parent organization. Besides introducing the fortressed factory tradition into the black arm of the modern record industry, Gordy had implanted in his people a paranoid "Motown mentality," a "them-or-us" bunker sensibility that spread to other black-owned or black-dominated record labels. Stevie ignored the fear-mongering but adhered to the familial code of camouflage and covert action.

The albums that Wonder did for Motown in the 1970s were no baker's dozen of hit-bound confections. Wonder produced highly integrated statements, the socially conscious (if mystically detached) songs overlapping to impart a complex overall impression. *Where I'm Coming From* (1971) was a rickety bridge into this new terrain, but *Music of My Mind* (1972) got the sensibility across confidently. *Talking Book* was issued several months later and, aided by an opening berth on the Rolling Stones' continental caravan in 1972, it became Wonder's mainstream calling card and spawned two chart-toppers, "Superstition" and "You Are the Sunshine of My Life." *Innervisions* (1973) and *Fulfillingness' First Finale* (1974) continued in a similar vein.

On August 6, 1973, while riding along a North Carolina highway, a log from a flatbed truck slid through a windshield and pinned Wonder by the head, robbing him of his sense of smell and nearly ending his life. That he rebounded from such additional cognitive loss with a statement as lush as *Songs in the Key of Life* is perhaps indicative of his peculiar strengths.

He next set aside three cloistered years for *Journey Through the Secret Life of Plants*, a gossamer grab bag of euphony meant to be the soundtrack of an unreleased nature film. But just what sort? Walt Disney's *The Living Landfill? National Geographic Visits the South Bronx?* And to what end? The two-record set (a pale-green package that when opened gave out a Shalimar-inspired scent) was a puerile tangent long in the making. Only a recluse with bankable mystique could have finessed such a skewered chorale of botanical babytalk. No one bought it, but no one was too piqued by the florid sidetrip. Nineteen eighty's *Hotter than July* was a bucket brigade of scrupulous Motown tunecraft that put a glossy finish on newly arrived pop forms—for instance, his ratification of reggae (inspired by Bob Marley) in "Master Blaster (Jammin')"—and erased all memory of Stevie's bald indiscretion. He then pressed on contritely in sanguine hits like "That Girl," "Do I Do," and "Ebony and Ivory," the last a duet with Paul McCartney.

By mid-decade, the limits of Wonder's intuitive prowess were manifest: his signature songs are a voracious accumulation of contemporary instrumental leitmotifs, wedded to addled but affecting lyrics that are transporting when experienced, embarrassing when written out. Aptly—too aptly—there is scant emotion in his work save wonderment, few instincts beyond a sublime disavowal, no outlook firmer than anticipation—the blind bedazzling the blind. For the record, no singer has ever offered such uniform, unearthly escape to integrity.

JIM MORRISON

INGRID THOMPSON'S HUSBAND WAS IN PORTUGAL ON ACCOUNT OF business. Jim Morrison's wife was in France on account of her husband— he was unendurable. On November 19, 1970, Jim took a room at the Chateau Marmont Hotel, located just off the Sunset Strip in Los Angeles, and he and Ingrid began spending nights there.

November nights passed in the Chateau Marmont with Ingrid were largely devoid of moderation. One moonless evening, he brought home champagne and a film canister filled with cocaine; Jim and Ingrid devoured both in the space of three hours. Ingrid, tipsy, hoping the evening had not yet peaked for herself and the bloated, bearded singer of the Doors, began to ruminate about her layabout friends in Scandinavia. These friends, she said, occasionally drank blood. Jim perked up. He pressed Ingrid into finding a razor blade. She stabbed herself in the fleshy mound between her thumb and forefinger. He caught the blood in a champagne glass. They sipped at their plasma cocktail, had intercourse, and smeared the gore on their bodies.

The next morning, they awoke far too sober to smirk at the sight: the sheets blotchy and musty-sour, the rust of death upon their pale skin.

IN OCTOBER 1970, THE BODY OF SINGER JANIS JOPLIN HAD BEEN FOUND IN A room at the Landmark Hotel in Hollywood, the red pinpoints on her arm fresh evidence of an accidental heroin overdose. Two months earlier, Jimi Hendrix had been asphyxiated by his own barbiturate-soaked spew. Morose and inebriated, Morrison had recently informed friends, "You're drinking with number three."

Jim Morrison was, a few days after a memorable Miami concert in March 1969, arrested and charged with committing a felony (lewd and lascivious behavior) and three misdemeanors (indecent exposure, open profanity, and drunkenness) while on stage. The court claimed that he "did lewdly and lasciviously expose his penis, place his hands upon the penis and shake it, and further the said defendant did simulate the acts of masturbation upon himself and oral copulation upon another." If there had been an encore or a curtain call, the bill of particulars failed to note them. It also lacked such footnotes as the twenty-odd paternity suits that were pending against Morrison.

In September 1970, a Miami jury acquitted Morrison of lewd behavior— the felony charge—and public drunkenness. However, they did convict him of profanity and public exposure. On October 30, Judge Murray Goodman sentenced Morrison to a total of eight months at hard labor, to be followed by twenty-eight months of probation, plus a $500 fine.

The case was in appeal when he met Ingrid. The case was pending when he joined wife Pamela Curson Morrison in Paris in 1971. The case was still undecided when he was found dead in a bathtub on July 3, 1971, from a heart seizure, at the age of twenty-seven. He was buried in secret by Pamela and some associates at Père Lachaise, the oldest cemetery in Paris, site of interment for Oscar Wilde, Frederic Chopin, and Edith Piaf. Pamela herself perished in Hollywood in April 1974 due to a heroin overdose.

THE DOORS WERE FORMED IN 1965 BY KEYBOARDIST RAY MANZAREK AND Jim Morrison, both of whom had attended the UCLA Graduate School of Film. They got the idea of starting a band while on the beach in Venice, California; Jim would write the songs, Ray would set them to music. Manzarek's brothers pitched in on guitars until drummer John Densmore and guitarist Robby Krieger, Formerly with the Psychedelic Rangers, joined the group. Morrison christened them the Doors, courtesy Aldous Huxley's William Blake–derived book on mescaline, *The Doors of Perception*. Their intentions were deeply profound, but their music was fairly pedestrian, and the bulk of Morrison's opaquely platitudinous lyrics was chuckleheaded word spinning.

During Jim's life, the Doors made eight LPs for Elektra Records, a company that had capitalized on the folk-pop boom of the early 1960s. The best albums were the first, *The Doors*— which was released in 1967 and which contained the No. 1 hit "Light My Fire"—*Strange Days*—which yielded "People Are Strange," a Top 20 success—and the last, *L.A. Woman*—which contained the Top 20 songs "Love Her Madly" and "Riders on the Storm."

JAMES DOUGLAS MORRISON, SON OF CLARA CLARKE MORRISON AND HER husband, Steve, a career naval pilot, was born on December 8, 1943, in Melbourne, Florida. The family moved often. After graduating from George Washington High School in Alexandria, Virginia, and spending a year at St. Petersburg College in Florida, Jim slipped off into his own discrete trajectory. By 1965, he was a listless maunderer who had read enough reasonably cerebral literature to describe his depressions, written enough half-hearted suicide notes to call himself a poet, and grown tired enough of his poems to want a rock band to put them to rest. Saturnalia, incestuous rape, and other debauched sensualisms were the working themes, but they were the narcissistic fantasies of an imaginary sybarite. Morrison himself was not overly particular about his pleasures, his pastimes, his surroundings.

Why the bathtub? Because it was there.

PRECEDING PAGE
Jim Morrison, the Lizard King in his lair (Klaus Schnitzer).

FACING PAGE
A dime-store Rimbaud striking a pose (Kino Eye Inc./Todd Gray).

PETE TOWNSHEND

SOMETHING IN HIM LONGED FOR THE NEW ROMANTICS, FOR THEIR fashion sense, their renegade style, their club lust, their dance fever, their natty nonvalues, their *outré* experiments in scene making, their shedding of conscience—and then of consciousness. He'd been around the bend at least twice before, leading a group called the High Numbers in the Shepherd's Bush section of London during the heyday of the mods; dressing up in mohair, madras, stovepipe slacks, two-tone chisel-toed shoes; popping amphetamines; and becoming, in famed mod manager Peter Meaden's words, "neat, sharp and cool; an all-white Negro of the night."

In 1965, the Who (once the High Numbers) released "My Generation," whose stuttering narrator was the apotheosis of the natty mod brat, braying, "Hope I die before I get old." The singer was Roger Daltrey, he with the blond bouffant and circus-stripe trousers, but the writer was Pete Townshend.

The Who went on to reap the sunny, acid-stoked spoils of being hard rockers in the halcyon days of the late 1960s and early 1970s, when it was de rigueur to thrust guitars into amplifiers, reduce drum kits to pearly splinters, back limousines into swimming pools, heave color TVs out of hotel windows, and then invite underage groupies up to the executive suite to watch you scrawl bad poetry on the walls.

At thirty-six, Townshend was getting a bit too stiff in the knees and long in the tooth to be dallying with Steve Strange and other New Romantic movers at the Club for Heroes. But then the central message of "My Generation" had been a deeply held philosophy of his, a plea for justice, actually, and in the two decades since, he'd never admitted to himself that he hadn't given up on the "live fast, die young, leave a good-looking, mohair-swaddled corpse" ethic. It was as dear to him as rock and roll itself.

BORN PETER DENNIS BLANDFORD TOWNSHEND ON MAY 19, 1945, TO CLIFF Townshend and his wife, the former Betty Dennis, he grew up, along with younger brothers Paul and Simon, in a Shepherd's Bush household where frying pans were always airborne and crockery forever being smashed. His parents had never been able to get along, and their rows were outlandishly destructive. Peter's grotesque homelife was in synch with his own self-image. A long-faced boy with a trowel-sized nose and small, deep-set eyes, he thought he looked like a carnival freak. At the age of twelve, his grandmother gave him an inexpensive Spanish guitar. The guitar gave way to a banjo, and Peter was quickly drawn into the traditional jazz fad of the late 1950s. He joined a Dixieland band with trumpeter/schoolmate John Entwistle. Entwistle quit in 1960, taking up the bass guitar he'd been toying with since his early teens, and joined the Detours, a group led by guitarist-singer Roger Daltrey, also a Shepherd's Bush mate. When they lost their rhythm guitarist, Townshend was invited to fill the gap. They changed their name to the Who after seeing a band called the Detours on TV.

Publicist Peter Meaden and doorknob manufacturer Helmut Gorden began to manage the group, Meaden cajoling them (with much initial resistance from Townshend and Entwistle) into adopting the mod look and thus acquiring a guaranteed following. Meaden renamed them the High Numbers, drummer Doug Sandom was excused, and seventeen-year-old Keith Moon, an apprentice electrician formerly with a surf band called the Beach Combers, auditioned. More or less. What Moon did was talk himself onto the bandstand during a gig at the Royal Oldfield Hotel, bragging he could do better than the guy onstage. He sat down, demolished the drum set, and got the job.

A mods-angled single written by Meaden, "I'm the Face," was released by Fontana Records in 1964 with a sizable publicity campaign, but it was a miserable failure; hip mod listeners were aware that the melody was a direct rip-off of Slim Harpo's "Got Love If You Want It." The band took up with new managers, filmmakers Chris Stamp and Kit Lambert, and became the Who again. When Townshend inadvertently snapped the neck of his guitar one night while wielding it in a low-ceilinged club, he lost his temper and smashed it. Moon, always happy to play Betty Townshend to Peter's Cliff, leveled another drum set. Lambert noted the frenzied response from the audience and made the destruction sequence the standard sign-off at all Who concerts.

The Who were signed to Decca and cut a Townshend song, "I Can't Explain," in 1965, the group taking off after Peter pulverized his guitar with sledgehammer grace. Their cocky, cacophonous sound, peppered with Moon's reverberant drumming, Townshend's loud, slashing chord-based lead guitar (a technique originally devised to conceal his technical limitations), and Daltrey's scrappy vocals—Entwistle stood stone-still—made them a top act in the U.K. "Happy Jack," from their 1966 *A Quick One* LP, broke into the Top 30; but it wasn't until an appearance at the Monterey Pop Festival in 1967 and a spot on the Smothers Brothers' television program that they had any lasting impact in America.

The Who Sell Out, a concept album built around an antic radio broadcast, did well in the U.S. in 1967, and the single "I Can See for Miles" went Top 10. *Magic Bus*, a sampling of singles and obscure sides, was released in 1968 to a tepid reception, but 1969 brought *Tommy*, the ninety-minute rock opera about a dictatorial deaf, dumb, and blind "pinball wizard" that became one of the most acclaimed records since the Beatles' *Sgt. Pepper's Lonely Hearts Club Band*. Various stage productions of the album were mounted, and director Ken Russell directed an atrocious film version in 1975. Daltrey, Moon, Tina Turner, Elton John, and Eric Clapton all took part.

Live at Leeds, one of the finest arena-sized live albums ever recorded, appeared in 1970. *Who's Next*, a sagacious synthesizer-woven studio experiment, ruled FM for the entirety of 1971. Prodigious tracks such as "Won't Get Fooled Again" and "Baba O'Reilly" received enormous airplay and helped to make the record a multimillion-seller. Townshend had become a disciple of Indian spiritual master Meher Baba, temporarily renouncing drugs and alcohol and dedicating a solo LP, *Who Came First*, to his guru in 1972.

Nineteen seventy-three's *Quadrophenia*, Townshend's second rock opera, explored the bleak underside of the adolescent mod ethos, its creator looking back in anger and bewilderment. After its release, the Who began to lose the thread of its battered mission. Members turned out spotty solo albums; group projects in the late 1970s and early 1980s on the MCA and Warner Bros. labels (*The Who by Numbers, Who Are You, Face Dances, It's Hard*) largely lacked fire, and the band's leader and chief songwriter was in shaky shape. Only *Rough Mix*, a 1977 collaboration with Ronnie Lane, and *Empty Glass*, a searing 1980 solo album that scrutinized Townshend's tendency toward personal excess as well as the collapsed punk movement and its perspectives, satisfied.

Fans first got wind of the fact that Townshend was bent on getting terminally blotto when, in the spring of 1981, the guitarist fell asleep onstage while performing solo during the first night of the Secret Policeman's Ball, a series of concerts to benefit Amnesty International. After roaring through "Pinball Wizard" and "Drowned," spraying the crowd with a magnificent barrage of fat riffs as he attacked his axe with his trademark windmill motion, he went to his dressing room to await the finale. A bottle of brandy was sent up to keep him company. By the time the call came to return, he was a bit bleary, sallied onstage, and nodded out with his Gibson acoustic cradled in his arms. It was a very short snooze, but people had come to expect a bit more than a public nap from rock's most athletically agitated guitarist.

What the faithful weren't aware of was that Townshend was well into what had been a more than year-long binge, having all but abandoned his family (wife Karen, daughters Emma, thirteen, and Minta, eleven) for the bottle, the nightlife, cocaine, and freebase laced with heroin.

Townshend had reason to want to draw the curtain on himself. Over $1 million in debt with no clear-cut route out, he'd found it almost impossible to write and compose. His band was falling apart and was soon to do a farewell tour. In terms of aging gracefully, the Who family had not been faring very well as of late. In August 1978, old standard bearer Pete Meaden committed suicide by drug overdose. On September 7, 1978 (Buddy Holly's birthday), Keith Moon expired from an overdose of Heminevrin. In April 1981, Kit Lambert died from a fall down the stairs at his mother's house.

In the clutches of a canyon-sized depression but desperate to pull out of it, Townshend took himself to an alcoholism clinic for help. Ativan was prescribed. Ativan is a tranquilizer. Combined with alcohol and coke, its punch is devastating, and Townshend, an alcoholic, became hooked on it. Those knowledgeable about such things maintain that Ativan is more ensnaring than smack. Shortly afterward, he was rushed to the hospital after overdosing on freebase and heroin with Ativan thrown in for good measure.

Early in 1982, Townshend flew to San Diego, California, to get the same electro-acupuncture treatment that had delivered Eric Clapton from heroin addiction. As he cleaned up, he resolved to save his marriage, decided to fold the Who (with Kenney Jones replacing Moon) after one fine-edged last hurrah, and discovered, to his astonishment, that he no longer wanted to die.

The day he was released from the San Diego clinic, he went for a walk on the beach and found a little bottle of white powder washed up on the shore. He uncapped it, licked a fingertip, poked it inside, and took a taste. It was cocaine of the highest quality—a lot of it—likely tossed overboard during some shore-patrol drug bust. He hesitated, his hand shaking, and then smashed it on the rocks at the water's edge. If the Devil can, he will fool with the best-laid plans of mice . . . and rock musicians.

FACING PAGE
Pete Townshend, aging Modernist (Davies and Starr).

OVERLEAF
From a blister to a scream, Townshend's superior stagecraft (both, Robert Ellis/ Sygma).

JIMI HENDRIX

IN 1968, JIMI HENDRIX SAID, "IT'S FUNNY THE WAY MOST PEOPLE LOVE THE dead. . . . Once you are dead you are made for life." It was not an opinion borne of low wit so much as a knowing judgment concerning a certain chilly kind of journey, a spirited jog along the River Styx. Some say it started for Hendrix in his fourth year, when his father renamed him, legally transforming Johnny Allen Hendrix into James Marshall Hendrix. There's an old superstition among certain Native American tribes that it's unwise to name a child twice because it splits his eternal spirit in two, half of it ascending into Heaven and half of it going straight to Hell. Jimi Hendrix's great-grandmother was a full-blooded Cherokee.

Lucille, Al Hendrix's tubercular, hard-partying jitterbugger of a war bride had given birth to Johnny at 10:15 A.M. on November 27, 1942, in damp, gloomy Seattle General Hospital. Another son, Leon, arrived in 1948, but by then the family unit was a bust; and the overdue divorce came down in 1950. Since the Marshall part of Jimmy's new appellation had been bestowed in honor of Al's brother (who'd been a professional dancer), Al Hendrix tried to develop the showboating capabilities of his favorite son, teaching him a bit of buck-and-wing, demonstrating how to play the spoons or to quick-strum a ukulele, and tucking a five spot into Jimmy's shirt pocket so he could buy his little buddy's old hollow-body guitar. Jimmy began skipping school to cruise the blues joints in the misty and mean Seattle ghetto, getting high on codeine cough syrup and Benzedrine, stealing sharkskin threads through the gratings of shop windows. He was jailed after getting nabbed joyriding in two stolen cars inside of a week. A lenient judge suggested he cool his heels in the armed forces, and Jimmy was assigned to the 101st Airborne outfit in Fort Campbell, Kentucky.

In January 1962, he wrote his dad, requesting that he ship down Jimmy's Stratocaster guitar, which the left-handed grunt had a habit of playing upside down. When the Strat arrived, Jimmy painted "Betty Jean" on the side in memory of an old inamorata and spent his evenings alone with it in the barracks. Sometimes he'd thrum it hard and pump the vibrato bar until the taut strings produced an oscillating whine resembling the drone of an air transport at 10,000 feet—or he would cuff the humming strings with the heel of his palm and hit a sequence of tarantular chords, the skinny, pointy fingers of his right hand crowding the strings to one side of the neck, invoking a rude, whistling bark.

Word spread around the base that Hendrix slept with his axe and conversed with it after mess hall as if it were a comely young doxy. He was shunned by most of the men, but a boisterous black bassist named Billy Cox sought him out. Once they were discharged, Jimmy and Billy headed for Nashville to get tight with other black musicians playing non–country & western dives like the Club Del Morocco. Jimmy then moved on to Vancouver, Canada, to join a lounge group. Little Richard blew through town in 1963, in need of support men who were willing to endure his egotistical psycho-prattle, and

he pulled Hendrix onto the road with him for long, long nights of "Keep A Knockin' " with "Tutti-Frutti" encores.

Hendrix made his first known appearance on record for the Los Angeles Revis label. The song, "My Diary," was a minor local hit. More recording ensued, all of it unimpressive, but onstage he was stepping out more and more from the rigid soul review ensemble rubric of the day, spewing out controlled bursts of daft virtuosity and histrionic sound. He picked up T-Bone Walker's old trick of soloing with the guitar held behind his head, and it seemed to other performers like vaudevillian gimmickry—until Hendrix brought forth sardonic hosannas and atavistic chaos from the instrument.

In 1965, Hendrix settled in New York City. Gangly, imposing, bushy-haired, he was tiring of the spit-and-polish regimentation of the soul groups and gravitating toward the bohemian life of Greenwich Village. It was in the Café Wha? that twenty-eight-year-old Brian "Chas" Chandler, bassist for the leading British group the Animals, discovered Hendrix. Chandler was knocked out by Hendrix's wild, atmospheric approach to rock guitar, knew it was time to pounce, and induced Jimmy to come back with him to England.

Hendrix obliged and fell headlong into the Swinging London upheaval and its psychedelic undercurrents. French rock star Johnny Halliday was astonished by Hendrix's solos and entreated him to appear on a bill in Paris two weeks later. With that deadline before them, Chandler and Hendrix created an instant group comprised of novice bassist Noel Redding and former British TV child star John "Mitch" Mitchell on drums. The Jimi Hendrix Experience was born.

When *Are You Experienced?*—the inaugural album—appeared in 1967, it was a London sensation, heralding, in both its streamlined fuzz-tone guitar monologues and the hip-gypsy garb of its members, the advent of psychedelic rock. And the exhortations of the chortling lead singer were a Rabelaisian invitation to a coitus-and-controlled-substances bender of the first rank. At Paul McCartney's urging, the Jimi Hendrix Experience got themselves added to the bill at the Monterey Pop Festival in the summer of 1967. Hendrix whipped the outdoor concert audience into a mighty lather with a barrage of electronic guitar distortion that soared, missilelike in its sonic arc, over their dazed heads. At the finale of the set, he doused his Stratocaster with lighter fluid and set it aflame, bowing out to an ecstatic roar as the unearthly drone of the burning instrument streamed out of the speaker towers.

In 1968, the Experience released the highly experimental *Axis: Bold as Love* LP, and critics marveled at the waterfall feedback and dazzling fluidity of this guitar avatar, not to mention the impenetrable quasi-Hindu acid hodgepodge that made up the lyrics. Later that year, *Electric Ladyland*, a blues-rooted two-record electronic soundscape appeared. The record became a bestseller in the U.S. and the U.K. and a staple on FM radio, but it was increasingly obvious that Jimi was growing faster than his audience—and that his Dionysian concerns were keeping pace with his musical ones. Throughout the album there is a feeling of floating, spiraling sexual contentment that is then despoiled by crude violence or rent apart by anonymous agents of rage. All of *Electric Ladyland*'s songs alternately deify and defame womankind, the bitch goddess pulled through the wringer over four sides of supernatural seduction, menace, and mayhem. Hendrix's guitar solos on the record are in a dozen different styles, and his singing is equally kaleidoscopic. He can sound like a rol-

PRECEDING PAGES
Page 156: Jimi Hendrix, voodoo avatar (Joel Axelrod/ Retna Ltd.).
Pages 158–159: Jimi was a jaunty gypsy and a sardonic sensualist (left, Joseph Stevens/Photo Trends; right, Mike Charity/ Photo Trends).

licking blues shouter, his crackling good humor hugely engaging, and then his spirit turns saturnine, bitter, and ultimately maniacal.

Rolling Stone pegged him: "Hendrix is the Robert Johnson of the sixties." *Electric Ladyland* became the album of choice among pot-smoking American troops fighting in the rice paddies and rain forests of Vietnam—just in time for the band to break up. Redding and Mitchell were put off by Hendrix's expanding ego and his habit of leaving the stage in the middle of sets if the audience didn't seem sufficiently adoring. His excessive drinking and his round-the-clock drug taking were making him difficult to communicate with. The only people to get his full attention were the phalanxes of groupies who attended him. The groupie underground pronounced Jimi "Best Score" because he never denied any of their swollen ranks. Things got ugly, however, when it was rumored Hendrix had thrown one girl down a flight of stairs. During the same period, he wrecked two new Corvette Sting Rays on two successive nights. His drug intake was also on the rise. In the early days he kept it down to several acid trips a week, lots of good reefer, beer, and liquor to keep the edge off, and party favors like a plastic baby bottle filled with Methedrine-spiked water. Now he was interested in anything and everything, around the clock, and the rest of the Experience could not keep up. On July 1, 1969, the group was spontaneously dissolved in Denver.

HENDRIX PLAYED THE WOODSTOCK FESTIVAL WITH A LOOSE AGGREGAtion called the Electric Sky Church. Afterward, he bowed to pressure from Black Power groups and formed an all-black outfit called the Band of Gypsies. Their debut concert at New York's Fillmore East was taped and turned into a live album, but the band existed for only one more show. Hendrix, who was reeling from a tab of bad acid in Madison Square Garden, took his guitar off in the middle of a song and told the 19,000 people gathered in the arena, "I'm sorry, we just can't get it together."

In 1970, Hendrix cut an uneven album entitled *The Cry of Love.* During the fall, he was immersed in composing the music for an occult film heavily influenced by the Tarot, which was to be called *Rainbow Bridge.* With a straight face he had begun informing close friends that he was from "an asteroid belt off the coast of Mars."

Jimi Hendrix died at 11:25 A.M. on September 18, 1970, at St. Mary's Abbot Hospital in London. He had been sleeping at a friend's flat; vomit had been discovered coming from his mouth and nose, and Jimi could not be awakened. In an ambulance en route to the hospital, he was placed in a sitting position; this contributed to his suffocating on his own vomit. An autopsy showed that Hendrix had consumed nine tablets of a prescription drug called Vesparax, normally taken in one-half-tablet doses. Also in his system at the time of death were tranquilizers, amphetamines, depressants, and alcohol. The coroner ruled the cause of death to have been "inhalation of vomit due to barbiturate intoxication." There was an "open verdict" on the question of suicide.

S L Y   S T O N E

THE FIRST RULE OF ROCK AND ROLL IS TO SHOW UP. THERE IS NO second rule; the rest is entirely up to you, including *when* and *how* you choose to show up. Sly Stone is the man who somehow stretched the lone precept of this profession far beyond its almost limitlessly elastic limits, until, incredible as it may seem, he ultimately broke it.

Back in his hometown of Dallas, Texas, he had been a punctual churchgoer and a child prodigy who launched a recording career with a sacred single, "On the Battlefield for My Lord," released at age five. Born Sylvester Stewart on March 15, 1944, Stewart sang the song with a family group, the Stewart Four, as well as playing drums and guitar on with several doo-wop groups. At sixteen, he cut "Long Time Away," a solo record that did well in the region. At Vallejo Junior College, he majored in music for three semesters, with an emphasis on theory and composition, and sang in the college choir. He used his education to put various bar bands together for weekend dates at go-go joints in North Beach and rock and roll dances at American Legion halls. He met Tom "Big Daddy" Donahue, the renowned Bay Area disc jockey, at just such a Legion hall, and Donahue told him he'd left radio to concentrate on a record company he'd formed with another ex-DJ, Bob Mitchell. Stewart joined Autumn Records, a zealous enterprise that aimed to harness the uncategorized local rock upheaval, and sharpened his arranging skills. He made two undistinguished records of his own, "I Just Learned to Swim" and "Buttermilk, Parts 1 & 2," before turning his attention to a band called the Beau Brummels. He also put Grace Slick's first group, the Great Society, through over 200 takes of "Free Advice," a song that landed on the flip side of the original release of "Somebody to Love."

In about 1966, he departed Autumn Records, using his royalties to buy his folks a home in Daly City, and took a job as a jock with KSOL in San Francisco. Smarts acquired in a three-month course at the Chris Borden School of Modern Broadcasting helped keep the airwaves wriggling with the sounds of "Super Soul." Employing request lines and such stunts as flushing-toilet sound effects after Ex-Lax commercials and live piano renditions of "Happy Birthday" for listeners, he built a solid following. Later, at KDIA in Oakland, he became a star attraction from 6 to 9 P.M. But his main interest remained in his band, the Stoners. When it dissolved in 1966, he and trumpeter Cynthia Robinson formed the Family Stone band, a clutch of "soul hippies" that included sister Rose on piano and brother Freddie on guitar.

Everybody in Haight-Ashbury was preaching togetherness in 1967, and Sly wanted to merge white rock and black soul into a musical archetype of everybody's stoned-out musings. After a trip to Vegas with the Family Stone, he left the safety of the radio booth for the great indoors of the Bay Area's rock palaces.

Sly and the Family Stone's first single, "I Ain't Got Nobody"/"I Can't Turn You Loose," led to a signing with Epic Records; but their first LP, *A*

Whole New Thing lacked the fizzy familial feel of their live shows. *Dance to the Music* was a raging rebound. *Life* gave the group a No. 1 single, "Everyday People," whose call for racial harmony floated on rippling waves of march-tempo glee. The primeval funk of James Brown had been broadened, blended, turned more pliant on this brilliant track and then embroidered with all the soot and smiles of a superior street fair. *Stand!*, released in the summer of 1969, was the album-length masterwork that "Everyday People" had presaged; in one fell stroke it gave black music a new inner complexion while revolutionizing every other rock rhythm section extant.

The hits kept coming—"Hot Fun in the Summertime," "Thank You Falettinme Be Mice Elf Agin," "Everybody Is a Star"—but where was Sly? Concert promoters across the nation were promised he'd arrive any minute...or thereabouts. He canceled twenty-six of the eighty dates he'd committed to in 1970 and roughly half of the next year's shows. When he did put in an appearance, he was often as much as five hours overdue.

A *Greatest Hits* package was hurried out, selling 3 million copies, but an all-new LP was two years late when his manager sued Sly for $250,000 in loans and back commissions. The idea of having a lien put on every shaky show moved Sly to refuse to tour. The suit was dropped in exchange for promises of productivity and reorganization. Yet even when Sly began living in a van parked out in front of the recording studio, he proved tardy—if not missing in action. Epic put him on suspension and froze his royalties. He was evicted from his $250,000 house because he couldn't make the mortgage payments. He took refuge in a Beverly Hills apartment house, where he blared sound equipment from sunset to sunrise; his landlord filed a $3 million lawsuit, charging him with conspiracy to drive off the other tenants.

Complaining of Sly's cocaine use and dual personality, his manager read Sly the riot act. Sly answered with *There's a Riot Going On*, a broody, militant, savage indictment of all the decayed determinism of the 1960s—Sly's, the country's, the world's *Riot* codified his fury at *having* to produce, his rage at needing to retreat and then hide, his self-loathing about the drugs he could not let go of when the street fair dispersed, his bitter disappointment that his wildly sequined sense of style had not transmogrified into an acceptable excuse for content.

Out of morbid fascination, his audience bought enough copies of this symphony of detritus that it made No. 1. It was a fortuitous accident that could not be sustained, and members of the Family Stone were reshuffled or replaced in the confusion and mayhem that followed.

In the meantime, police across the country had grown hostile toward Sly and his seeming endorsement of the Black Panthers; the Panthers seemed to grow equally angry with the singer's fickle fence-straddling. The cops took the initiative. Sly had no less than five confrontations with the law in the latter part of 1972. July found him in custody after the Family Stone's mobile home was stopped on Santa Monica Boulevard in Los Angeles. Two vials of narcotics and two pounds of marijuana were found in the vehicle, but charges were later dismissed; a judge decided there was insufficient evidence to prosecute. Then, while sitting in a car in a friend's driveway, he was busted for disturbing the peace. As he was leaving a sickle cell anemia telethon in Los Angeles, he was stopped and searched. Before a concert at Madison Square Garden, Sly was arrested on West 45 Street for supposedly threatening an old lady with a

Colt .44 cap pistol he was wearing in a holster. In December, police invaded his Bel Air home, saying they'd had an anonymous report of a robbery and dead bodies on the premises. Finding nothing, they handcuffed Sly for having no identification and led him away.

Early in 1973, he canceled an East Coast concert swing, without explanation, after two shows. Later in the winter, Sly was arrested in another raid on his L.A. home and charged with possession of cocaine, cannabis, and dangerous drugs, and possession of the last for sale. He got a year's probation.

Come spring 1973, the word was that Sly was moving to New York and getting married to his nineteen-year-old Asian girlfriend, Kathy Silva, who was expecting their child in August. He also announced that a new LP was in the works and told the *New York Times* why he had missed so many concerts and how he planned to save his band: "Sometimes you don't feel your soul at 7:30. But we've been recording, rescheduling, regrouping and recoping on everything we like to do, what we have to do, and things we wish we could do."

Fresh was released before the year was out, with "If You Want Me to Stay" becoming a hit as much for its sad-sack irony as for its own modest merits. In June 1974, Sly and Kathy Silva were wed in a televised ceremony prior to a sold-out concert at Madison Square Garden. By October, Silva had sued for divorce, asking custody of their one-year-old son, Sylvester Bubb Ali Stewart, Jr., plus alimony and child support.

There were more missed concerts, among the most decried no-shows being a benefit for muscular dystrophy in Washington, D.C., in December 1974, which nearly sparked a full-scale melee—until the crowd was let in free. A spokesman from Sly's record company said the star bowed out, insulted, when he'd discovered that he'd been paid for what was supposed to be a free appearance. Sly would have nothing to do with the money or the event. "I think it was a failure of communication," said the Epic source.

Sly made three albums in the next eight years, all of which had sheepish titles (*Heard You Missed Me*, *Back on the Right Track*, *Ain't But the One Way*). None attracted much attention. He also worked with Funkadelic on a 1981 album called *Electric Spanking of War Babies* and continued to book, cancel, and sometimes actually give concerts of suitably erratic quality.

In August 1981, Sly was arrested on charges of cocaine possession. July 1982 brought new misadventures: he was nabbed after a brawl at a hotel in the Westwood suburb of Los Angeles. Sly identified himself as his brother Fred, but a fingerprint analysis established his true identity; police said they had found a freebasing kit in his room and a small handgun and cocaine in his briefcase, and they charged him accordingly.

Nineteen eighty-three. Another bumper year for busts. In February, Sly and four other men were detained in Paxton, Illinois, because the registration for their van had expired. During a search of the vehicle, authorities found a sawed-off shotgun and a quantity of "white powder." In June, Sly was found passed out in a motel room in Fort Myers, Florida, with a woman companion; he was arraigned on charges of possession of cocaine and drug paraphernalia. In August, he was charged with grand theft in Fort Lauderdale. He was collared at a gay night club where he was appearing, police offering a detailed explanation of the deeds that preceded the arrest. While at the King Neptune Hotel, where he and his manager were staying, Sly had allegedly admired a $5,000 gold ring belonging to Maryanne Magness, part owner of the hotel. He

Chapel of Love: Sly weds Kathy (Ron Galella).

tried it on and then, as Magness became "distracted" by her duties, "forgot" about it, moving on to play a Pac Man video game. Leaving town for a quick trip back to his home in San Francisco, he noticed he was still wearing what police described as the "huge" ring and gave it to Novi, his one-year-old daughter by new wife, Olinka. When he returned to Florida, Sly found himself confronted by an irate Magness, who demanded he cough up her absent jewelry. She told police the ring was particularly valuable because she had received it from her father just before his murder three years ago.

At his September arraignment in Broward County Jail on the theft charge, Judge Howard Ford was in the midst of releasing Sly on $10,000 bail when he paused to yell, "Are we keeping you awake?" at the slumped, dozing star. It later came to light that Robert Eaton, the arresting officer, couldn't resist the temptation to get an autograph from the accused while he had him in custody, so he impulsively made the singer sign the back of his Miranda Rights Waiver Form. "It was the only thing I had," said Eaton.

In May 1984, Stone made a statement from the Lee Mental Clinic in Fort Myers, Florida, where he was undergoing a six-month program to kick free-base: "Drugs can take you up, but they can also take you out.... I want to do music and have that express itself." Again.

JIMMY PAGE

FROM THE VIEWPOINT OF A PRACTITIONER OF MAGICK, THERE IS no happenstance in this world or any other. The planet does not revolve, the rain does not cease, the woman does not conceive, the illness does not set in, the sparrow does not drop from the sky—unless some animate force wills it to occur. The maker of magick does not believe in the existence of accidents.

Aleister Crowley was a magickian, purportedly one of the most formidable who ever lived. He was also a painter, poet, world traveler, mountain climber, bisexual satyriac, and heroin addict. He was a member since 1898 of a secret fraternal organization called the Order of the Golden Dawn. Founded by several Rosicrucians for the purposes of practicing magick, its objective was that mankind "may ultimately regain union with the Divine Man latent in himself." Crowley's aim was to gain the know-how to invoke his Holy Guardian Angel; his philosophy was distilled in his customary greeting: "Do what thou wilt shall be the whole of the law."

William Burroughs, for one, feels Crowley was on to something, and that rock and roll is a modern force with a kindred perspective. "Rock," he wrote in 1975, "can be seen as one attempt to break out of this dead and soulless universe and reassert the universe of magic[k]."

Crowley's home was at Boleskine, near Loch Ness in Scotland. The building was erected on the site of a church that had burned to the ground with all of its unfortunate congregation trapped inside. Prior to Crowley's taking occupancy, a beheading and a host of suicides had taken place within its walls. After Crowley's passing, several tenants went straight from the house to insane asylums.

Thus acquiring something of a sinister reputation, the address became difficult to rent or sell, but, in the mid-1970s, a realtor negotiated its purchase for Jimmy Page, avid devotee of mysticism and magick, lead guitarist of the Yardbirds and of Led Zeppelin, the latter one of the most popular rock bands in the world. Asked why he picked the remote place as a hideaway, Page said, "I'm attracted by the unknown."

JIMMY PAGE WAS BORN ON JANUARY 9, 1944, IN HESTON, MIDDLESEX, England, and spent his early years in Felton, a community in the shadow of Heathrow Airport. An only child, he enjoyed the isolation his status afforded him, and the gift of a secondhand acoustic guitar when he was twelve further enhanced his sense of apartness. After hearing Elvis Presley's "Baby, Let's Play House," he made up his mind to be a professional musician.

Yardbirds' bass player Paul Samwell-Smith left the group in 1966, and Page took his place. When physically ravaged lead guitarist Jeff Beck dropped out of the band five months later, after suffering a nervous breakdown (according to Beck: "Inflamed brain, inflamed tonsils, and an inflamed cock and everything else..."), Page took over the reins, asking studio bassist John Paul Jones and drummer John Bonham, with whom he'd worked on Donovan's

Hurdy Gurdy Man LP, to join him. Robert Plant, vocalist with a group called the Band of Joy, completed the revamped act, and they fulfilled the previous lineup's lingering commitments in Scandinavia as the New Yardbirds. Various other names for the band were proposed, but Led Zeppelin was agreed to after Keith Moon of the Who predicted the band would go over like a "lead balloon."

Led Zeppelin, released in 1968, was unlike any other album of its era. Its hollow, thudding percussion, stupored melodies, and strangled, clarion vocals suggested a somnambulistic Goliath in the throes of an opium trance. The playing was blues-based but coated with fuzzy overtones and splenetic distortion. This was "heavy metal," fully realized in all its precise, ponderous, pealing pomp. The lazy afternoon of psychedelic idylls and flower power was over, and *Led Zeppelin* heralded the approach of the great storm. Zeppelin was destined to be an FM radio taste, their albums selling millions, their tours gigantic affairs, their image one of gloom and mystery. *Led Zeppelin II* did yield a Top 10 hit in 1969 with "Whole Lotta Love," but the group disdained singles.

The spell they cast was a potent one. Few groups could control a vast crowd with the broody confidence of Led Zeppelin, the gawky, bedraggled Page lording over the worshipful with a flourish of the violin bow he used for various ear-hemorrhaging solos. Stooped over his Les Paul electric guitar or a gleaming acoustic, dispensing songs rife with Celtic mythology and Druidic symbolism, he resembled a man-sized praying mantis in a gothic sci-fi novel.

Even as Page led Led Zeppelin to the pinnacle of rock preeminence, its members were decimated by bizarre misadventures and tragedies, hotel trashings and groupie fests giving way to full-scale riots and other, weirder twists of fate. Robert Plant and his wife and two children narrowly escaped death in the summer of 1975, when their car rolled off a narrow highway on the Greek island of Rhodes. Plant later said that all he could hear in his head during the incident was the obsessive chant ("Oh my Jesus! Oh my *Jee-sus!*") he sings in "In My Time of Dying" (from the *Physical Graffiti* LP). The band's activities were curtailed by the crash and a series of other coincidental setbacks that some believers attributed to Page's occult involvements. In 1976, the semidocumentary *The Song Remains the Same* and a soundtrack album were released, the film filled with the iconology of the black arts. In 1977, Plant's young son Karac died of a rare virus infection, sending the singer into a tailspin of grief that lasted two years. The group's last studio album, *In Through the Out Door,* appeared in 1979. In 1980, drummer John Bonham died at Page's Windsor home, asphyxiated on his own vomit, after falling asleep in a state of acute intoxication. In December, a press release was circulated, indicating that the group would not continue; *Coda* sealed the crypt in 1982.

Page continues to enthrall as a studio guest star and solo artist. But he remains a gloomy, arcane figure, seldom granting interviews, his personal and artistic goals unclear. He may have offered a clue in a Crowleyesque statement he made in 1975: "Just say that I'm still searching for an angel with a broken wing. It's not very easy to find them these days."

PRECEDING PAGE
Jimmy Page, guitarist as necromancer (John Bellissimo/Retna Ltd.).

FACING PAGE
A grin that gives nothing away. Page in the early 1970s (Michael Putland/Retna Ltd.).

ERIC CLAPTON

I N HIS HANDS WAS THE TURNKEY TO HEAVEN AND HELL, THE INSTRU-
ment of damnation and exultation; his touch gave it life, triggered its
power, and—as he wielded it—it turned his fingers a translucent white
or a charred black. When he played a barbarous blues lick, it transformed the people clustered before him into demons bathed in red.
When he played a brace of sweet chords, the onlookers became angels,
basking in an incorporeal glow. It was San Francisco. It was 1971. Eric
Clapton was out of his skull on LSD, but the apparitions he was provoking with his guitar had a gravity to them that superseded the deceptions of any
drug.

"I am and always will be a blues guitarist," said Eric Clapton at the start of
his career, and he has repeated the oath with regularity ever since. He prefers
playing to angels, he says, but admits that devils claim the bulk of his
concentration.

A N ONLY CHILD, ERIC CLAPTON WAS BORN ON MARCH 30, 1945, AND
raised by grandparents in Ripley, Surrey, England, after his mother
abandoned him and moved to Canada. Scrawny, belligerent, with
small, sad eyes and a downturned mouth, he had few friends beyond
a group of schoolmates in Ripley who were labeled "the loonies" for their well-
deserved outcast status. He became curious about American blues after reading that "rock and roll has its roots in the blues" on the sleeves of import
albums by artists like Chuck Berry and Buddy Holly. At seventeen, he took up
the guitar, wanting to find an outlet more visceral than the stained-glass design
he was studying at Kingston Art School. Like most British working-class kids,
he loathed the rigidity of the country's social order and was titillated by the
freewheeling essence of American culture, preserved and expanded by genera-
tions of hot-footed rounders and musical vagabonds who maximized the pleasures of a land without a heritage of proprieties. Like himself, a bluesman had
no lasting ties, no forebears to shame, no background worthy of acknowledge-
ment, no obstacles to wantonness.

He adopted the blues creed almost immediately, finding a polestar in the
orthodoxy of Big Bill Broonzy, Sonny Boy Williamson, and Buddy Guy. But,
like a dedicated seeker, he settled at last on Mephistopheles's bandmaster,
Robert Johnson. Clapton spent his novitiate period as a street musician around
Kingston and Richmond, then, for the better part of 1963, worked with a
rhythm and blues group called the Roosters. Meeting most of the best young
blues-focused musicians of the day in the usual London haunts, he preached
his doctrine of grueling purity with all who would listen and, with any luck,
elect to jam on the issue with him. Hard up for funds, he briefly compromised
his mission in a seven-date flirtation with a commercial cover band, Casey
Jones and the Engineers. But late in 1963, he settled into the Most Blueswail-
ing Yardbirds, a five-man band that played electrified Chicago blues. Chum-
my with the Rolling Stones, the Yardbirds gained a standing invitation to

Wystąpią:

ERIC
CLAPTON

I JEGO NOWY ZESPÓŁ

Dnia 15-16 października, godz. 19.30
Sala Kongresowa PKiN

Przedsprzedaż biletów tylko w kasach SPATIFU Al. Jerozolimskie 25

Teatr Stara Prochownia

Warszawa, ul. Boleść 2

Kierownik artystyczny
WOJCIECH SIEMION

REPERTUAR

1979 r.

Andrzej Witkowski
Witold Gruca
W scenach zbiorowych
godz. 19.00.
ERZY LAPIŃSKI
BAJ
OTFRIED

headline the Crawdaddy Club in their absence. It was a compliment attributable to the bewitching wiles of their immoderate and at times lacerating vamps on the blues, aggravated by the stinging outbursts of Eric "Slowhand" Clapton, their lead guitarist. Amplified to the threshold of pain and pegged to storm-trooper percussion, the Yardbirds' sound was the precursor of a new form of rock, later labeled "heavy metal." *Five Live Yardbirds*, their first album, was released in England in 1964. *For Your Love*, their American debut, came out a year later and won numerous fans with its scruffy verve, the archetypal single "For Your Love" doing well on the charts.

Sonny Boy Williamson and the Yardbirds and *Having a Raveup with the Yardbirds* both appeared in 1966, but Clapton was present on only four tracks on the second record, having quit the group in 1965 (right after the "For Your Love" session) rather than comply with the pop direction they were veering toward. He held body and (blues) soul together as a day laborer on construction sites for several weeks before finding a kindred spirit in Manchester guitarist John Mayall. He took the top guitar post in Mayall's Bluesbreakers and recorded with the group, as well as doing studio sessions with bassist Jack Bruce, keyboardist-singer Stevie Winwood, and guitarist Jimmy Page. He became preoccupied with speed and articulation in an extended-solo style that attracted idolizing fans for whom the electric guitar was a symbol of masculine heroism and potency. "Eric Clapton is God" was scrawled in the tunnels of the London Underground and became a graffiti staple of the late 1960s.

Gloomy, troubled, and greatly dissatisfied with his playing, Clapton dropped out of the club and recording scene for a year, reportedly locking himself away with his guitar and receiving no callers—communing, like his musical forebears, with the infernal muse, coming to grips with the sepulchral depths of his blues calling. His next band was Cream, a saga-sized 1966 merger of ashcan power drumming and bare-knuckles British blues, also featuring

Blues Power (Michael Putland/Retna Ltd.).

Jack Bruce and wiry Ginger Baker, a flailer of no small repute. Whenever the three combined to construct their self-described "neocontrapuntal" numbers, the total effect was that of a Concorde backfiring in a wind tunnel. Clapton himself had tapped into some obscure source of voltage and assumed a uniquely elegant appetency for fluid, unerring phrasing. For two years, Cream was at the pinnacle of the rock pile, Clapton the premier guitarist, his back to the crowd and his face in shadow as he played an extended version of Robert Johnson's "Crossroads" that was supernatural in its virtuosity. Cream's onslaught created audience reactions that nearly drowned out the pandemonium onstage, and the four albums they cut during their short existence sold hugely. In 1968, *Wheels of Fire* became the first album to be certified as a platinum (million-units-sold) record.

Clapton, who insisted that the band "was originally meant to be a blues trio," began to grouse publicly that it had become "a jazz-rock group" and therefore distasteful to him, although he was pleased that "Crossroads" had been one of the group's hits. The farewell concert came on November 26, 1968, at the Royal Albert Hall and *Goodbye* capped the breakup in 1969.

Confused about his future, Clapton was induced in a moment of weakness into becoming part of Blind Faith, a "supergroup" that counted Ginger Baker, Stevie Winwood, and bassist Rik Grech as its other stars. The decision pulled him further from the blues than before and made him susceptible to other, less wicked influences. While backstage during the group's first and only U.S. tour, he chanced to meet two devout Christians who entered his dressing room and said, "Can we pray with you?" He nodded, knelt, and supplicated himself, amazed to find that he suddenly felt better than he had in years.

Strolling around the room, overwhelmed by a feeling of elation and well-being, he told his pious acquaintances that he wanted to show them a poster of Jimi Hendrix he treasured. Unfurling it, he found another poster rolled up inside it, a poster that he'd never seen before. It was a portrait of Christ. He reacted to the image like St. Paul on the road to Damascus and embraced the faith on the spot. Earlier, he had written "Presence of the Lord" for the *Blind Faith* album in order to celebrate his relocation from London to Surrey, a move that enabled him to escape the clutches of Officer Pilcher, a cop who'd made a career of busting rockers; this action was now seen by him as having been a portent of his conversion.

After the Blind Faith tour—more a high-decibel circus of excess than a string of concerts—Clapton knocked around with Bonnie and Delaney Bramlett, whose country-fried blues and blue-eyed gospel-rock had made them an esteemed opening act on the supergroup's bill. He recorded with the Mississippi guitarist and his singing wife, and they with him. Delaney produced the *Eric Clapton* solo LP in 1970; the album hit with J.J. Cale's "After Midnight."

Clapton's career was acquiring a semblance of stability, but his personal life was a ticking bomb due to a love triangle in which he'd become enmeshed. The other guy was best friend George Harrison, and the woman was Harrison's wife, Patti Boyd. Rattled by the strain of the situation, Clapton upped his already flourishing intake of cocaine. His drug dealer would only score quantities of Colombian marching powder for him if he agreed to buy smack as well, and Clapton kept stashing the unwanted heroin in a drawer at his home in Sussex. When Patti threw him over and went back to Harrison, the anguish of unrequited love drove him to despondency and then to the drawer. Clapton became a junkie.

Sinking into a measureless netherworld, he gave himself over to his misery and the monkey that rode his back, writing languid tunes steeped in the clouded tunnel vision of heroin hunger, living death, and the disintegration of the heart. These found their way onto *Layla and Other Love Songs*, a sardonically titled album made in 1970 with a collection of intemperate associates from the Delaney and Bonnie days, the most flagrant being fellow junkie guitar wizard Duane Allman. Eric named the band Derek and the Dominoes. With the exception of Neil Young's 1975 *Tonight's the Night* (an LP about the drug deaths of two friends), no record has ever come closer to making distilled emotional horror physically tangible. In the 1730s, London gin shops used to advertise "drunk for a penny, dead drunk for tuppence, and straw for nothing." *Layla* offered cold alienation on side one, acceptance of humiliation by side two, forlorn freefall by side three, and a screaming fast fade with "Layla," a seven-minute, ten-second onrush of harrowing guitar virtuosity that conveyed the perverting power of ruined love and defined despair itself. It was aimed at the soul of Eric Clapton, with direct quotes from Robert Johnson's "Love in Vain," by way of Patti Boyd Harrison, and it found its mark with devastating accuracy.

CLAPTON EXPECTED TO DIE BEFORE HE REACHED THIRTY. HE WASN'T alone in this presumption. He told friends that ever since he'd begun singing, he wanted to have a voice as tortured as the chords he wrenched from his guitar, a voice like Ray Charles's at the height of his addiction. In order to truly sing the blues, your soul must be as empty as your stomach, and only smack can take you all the way to a perfect vacuum, to a place where you learn how it feels to feel nothing at all and come to love the sensation. The last scrap of caring he still possessed was incinerated when

Clapton learned on September 18, 1970, of the death of his own guitar god, Jimi Hendrix.

"I went out in the garden and cried all day because he'd left me behind," said Clapton in 1974. "Not because he'd gone, but because he hadn't taken me with him. It just made me so fucking angry. I wasn't sad, I was just pissed off."

For nearly three years—the better part of 1971, 1972, and 1973—Clapton did not play in public. He'd left the Dominoes after some touring, showed up for the Concert for Bangla Desh in August 1971, and that was it. In Surrey, heroin was his housekeeper, his lover, his refuge. Then Pete Townshend of the Who, genuinely believing the end might be near for Clapton, coaxed Eric out of his lethal lair to prepare for a comeback concert at the Rainbow Theater in London in September 1973. His performance was unsteady, jagged, but he found the courage to turn it into a live record just to convince himself he could still function at an accountable level. He kicked heroin through electro-acupuncture treatment, convalesced on a farm in Wales, and then flew to Miami in 1974 to record *461 Ocean Boulevard*, an insouciant, humbly spiritual album that had a No. 1 hit with his cover of Bob Marley's "I Shot the Sheriff."

"I've got this death wish; I don't like life," the twenty-nine-year-old guitarist confessed after *461* was released. He said he knew he could never get out of the hardcore blues alive, so they were now relegated to the drawer in which the smack had once been stowed. He preserved the blues textures in his music, but merely as catchy coloration, and looked to other rustic, but more upbeat, idioms to carry his now-becalmed singing, which was sometimes shaded by female vocals. His guitar solos, when they appeared at all, were compact and muted. *Slowhand* and *Backless* gained Clapton a new, younger audience that admired his laidback romanticism. The rosy "Lay Down Sally" floated to No. 3 in 1978, and "Promises" went Top 10 the following year, when a slim, fit, but still sad-eyed Clapton won back the love of his life, marrying Patti Harrison. He put out four soothing albums in the early 1980s and did well in 1981 with the lively "I Can't Stand It."

In 1983, he released *Money and Cigarettes* and, when stricken buddy Ronnie Lane (formerly with the Faces) approached Clapton to raise money for the cause, appeared on a benefit tour for Action Research into Multiple Sclerosis (ARMS) that started in London and traveled to America.

Clapton, dressed in a sleek silver-blue suit, led the band in an offhanded set that included "Layla" and blues like Freddie King's "Have You Ever Loved a Woman?" As a rule it started out subdued and built steadily to a stately climax. On occasion, though, the guitarist's studied reserve would rupture, and he would spin away from the audience, bowing his head, shutting his eyes, unleashing a fusillade of punishing runs, jarring fans too young to be aware that this benign balladeer had once beseiged the blues like a man possessed . . . and showing that the fiendish spirit behind his past offensives had not yet been exorcised.

ROD STEWART

A GRAVELLY VOICE CROONED, "I TOOK HER TO AN ALL-NIGHT laundry; we watched her bra go'round in the machine." It could be a lyric from a whimsical Sam Cooke song, perhaps a couplet left off "Another Saturday Night." But no, the line belongs to asthmatic British rock-and-rhythm rasper Rod Stewart. It is his explanation of how he met and wooed Britt Ekland.

A gifted raconteur and songsmith, Stewart is adept at such picturesque on- and off-the-record summations of his recreational involvements. It's a bit tricky discerning whether he's jerking one's chain; but that's part of the fun, as well as the problem. Rod *should* be best known for his deeply felt admiration of Sam Cooke, whose gospel passion, soul virility, and pop humor he was able to mirror and even recast. But his reputation, like that of Cooke, has come to rest on his cockamamie run-ins with the opposite sex.

The best known is his years-long dalliance with Britt Ekland, whom he encountered on and off during the early 1970s before getting cozy with her after she came backstage when Stewart and the Faces were playing the Los Angeles Forum in March 1974. Stewart must have liked what he saw in the washer (or was it the dryer?): Britt promptly moved both herself and her laundry into Rod's estate. After a few years of listening to Stewart's vague stories about marriage and keeping some semblance of fidelity while watching him bird-dog anything in skirts (excluding the traditional ancestral male costume of his beloved Scotland), Britt slapped Rod with a $15 million palimony suit. The protracted litigation was a Hollywood horror show, the screen version of which might have been entitled *It Came from Beneath My Kilt*. In the end, he settled out of court and returned to his promiscuous habits, a lifestyle immortalized in a limited edition foldout poster included with a 1971 Faces LP called *A Nod's as Good as a Wink to a Blind Horse*. The gamy giveaway was a compilation of snapshots showing band members flagrante delicto. The record company regained its senses and deleted the freebee from the second round of packages pouring out of the pressing plant, but the legend of Rod Stewart and the Faces' march-or-die party ethos had been born.

It was with dropped jaws, then, that fans of the singer received the news that "Rod the Mod," as the dandified crooner had been known since his early days in London rhythm and blues clubs, had wed starlet Alana Hamilton in April 1979. While the bloom was still on the rose, Alana assured the British tabloids that "there could never be any question of me suing Rod for money because our marriage is forever. We both know that."

Stewart seemed to take such dictums with a grain of salt—"Da Ya Think I'm Sexy" (the biggest single of his on-and-off solo career) was released that same year. He and Alana had two children, but Rod kept his eye on the passing parade. Rod and Alana tussled, separated, and reconciled with great frequency—something he and Britt had also specialized in. Finally, in 1983, Alana sued for divorce. Stewart's manager, Arnold Stiefel, issued a uniquely exasper-

ated public statement: "God knows this is so confusing—like something out of *As the World Turns*."

Only Stewart seemed to know what he was doing. He released a new LP that year, *Body Wishes*.

ALTHOUGH HE WAS BORN IN LONDON—ON JANUARY 10, 1945—STEWART defers to his Scottish lineage. He left home at seventeen and spent months busking with companion Wizz Jones, singing American folk music in Belgium, Italy, and France with a light-hearted fervor. He started to blend the blues and a Gene Vincent–Eddie Cochran rockabilly itch into his folk bag, and, in 1963, he landed a spot as a singing harmonica player with Jimmy Powell and the Five Dimensions. They backed up Chuck Berry, who announced they were his best pickup troop in recent memory, and they got the house-band position when the Stones left town with Bo Diddley. After recording some singles with the Five Dimensions, Rod left to do session work, playing harmonica on Millie Small's "My Boy Lollipop" and cutting gooey versions of pop hits for drugstore album collections.

Gaining an awareness of his vocal strengths, Stewart put out a solo single, "Good Morning Little Schoolgirl," on Decca, the Stones' label. Next came two more solo singles for Columbia, "Day Will Come" and "Shake." Then came a brief stay in 1966 with Baldry's Steampacket. After a clash of egos with Baldry, he hooked up with future Fleetwood Mac members Peter Green and Mick Fleetwood; they called themselves Shotgun Express. In 1967, "flash" guitar snob Jeff Beck hired Stewart to front the Jeff Beck Group and two LPs, *Truth* in 1968 and *Beck-ola* in 1969, brought Rod's tortured soul timbre to the attention of a large rock audience. Mercury Records offered him a solo contract, and some superb albums resulted—*The Rod Stewart Album* and *Gasoline Alley*.

After Beck broke up his band, Stewart signed on with the Small Faces, which thereupon shortened their name and cut a number of LPs as the Faces, beginning with *First Step*. In June 1971, Stewart released his own *Every Picture Tells a Story* and became an immediate star, the album being the first record to chart at No. 1 in the U.S. and Britain simultaneously; the single "Maggie May" followed suit.

He put out an insipid album, *Smiler*, in 1974 to get out of fulfilling his obligations to Mercury, and then joined Warner Bros., where his output was by turns deeply felt and doltish. No one could hit all the jagged corners of a song of shattering love ("The First Cut Is the Deepest"), or renew a pledge of faith in the rigors of true romance ("Tonight's the Night"), or lend coloration to a sentimental, backporch valentine ("You're in My Heart [The Final Acclaim]") like Stewart. But when an arrogant sappiness set in, the best he could manage was such comic-book ribaldry as "Hot Legs."

Stewart seemed destined to become rock's human whoopie cushion, his clangorous music a purple party trick. *Camouflage*, a 1984 pass at reclaiming his storied past, petered out before the first side was over. None of his youngest fans could have guessed that he was once the humble, committed preserver of the blues line, so shy before his initial Jeff Beck Group audience at New York's Fillmore East in 1968 that he sang the kick-off song from the wings.

PRECEDING PAGES
Da Ya Think Rod's (Still) Sexy? (both, Bonnie Schiffman).

OVERLEAF
Stewart is a playful but sometimes transparent performer (Simonpietri/Sygma).

ROCK STARS

183

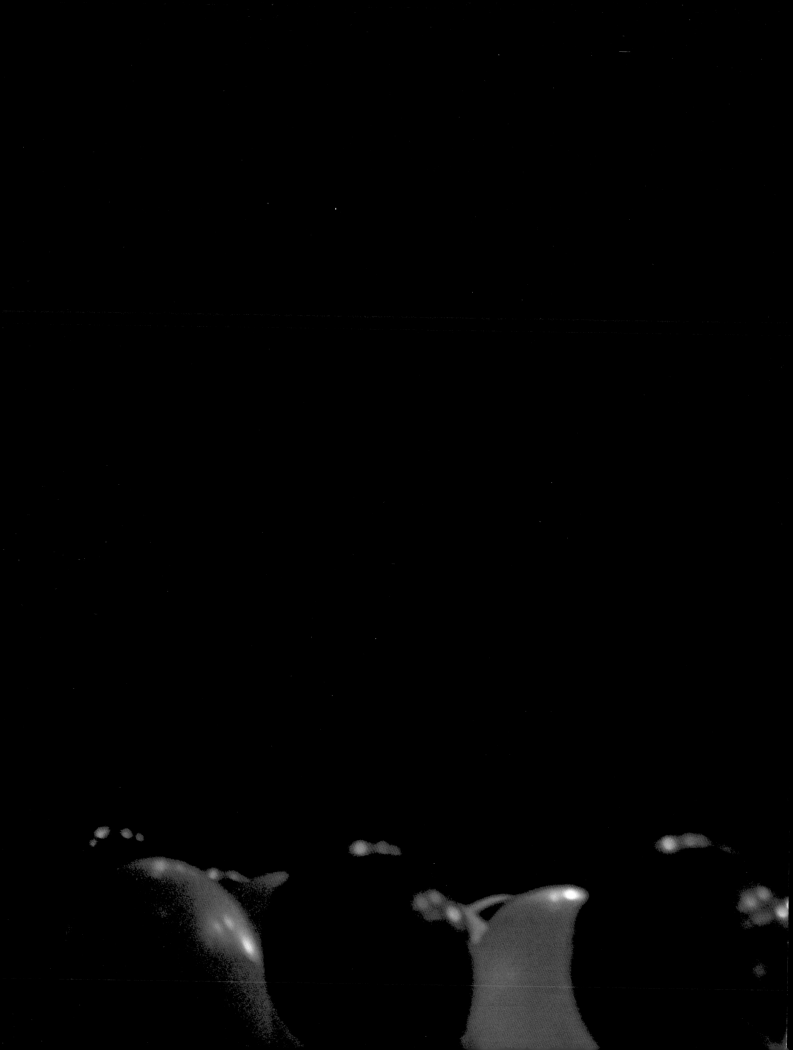

JONI MITCHELL

T HE FRENCH POET ALPHONSE DE LAMARTINE HAS WRITTEN, "God has placed the genius of women in their hearts because the works of this genius are always works of love." Yet love, like hate, is a natural exaggerator, seeking outlets but never limits, the unrelenting fire of life that either purifies or consumes.

Like the erotica of Anaïs Nin, the songs of Joni Mitchell have been a move, in a world generally dominated by men, to express the experiences of physical and spiritual love solely from a purposeful woman's vantage point. Through an often-angry admission of her emotional weakness for and dependence on the opposite sex, of her foolhardy miscomprehensions and unrewarded acts of faith, and of her ability, however imperfect, to make the process of self-love and the search for romantic fulfillment compatible, she has forged a fresh image of the autonomous female artist. It is not a political representation, tied to trends or to movements like Women's Liberation, but a forceful announcement of her own singularity. She began by embodying the archetypal fair-haired hippie-chick singer, ornamenting the male folk-rock enclave, taking lovers (Graham Nash, James Taylor) from among her associates, yet making it plain that they were her peers, that she claimed co-ownership of the experiences, and that she reserved the right to think out loud about them. Mitchell, like the rest of the obstinate rock and roll community, was on the way to satisfying herself, and she made no bones about it.

David Crosby—who is credited with discovering her in a club in Coconut Grove, Florida, and who produced her first album, *Song to a Seagull*—is said to have commented once that his protégée was "about as humble as Mussolini." Perhaps, but certainly no more arrogant than David Crosby. She has insisted on having her own mind, and she has flourished in a contest where she found she was "outside the uniform of rock and roll, and it annoyed people."

A NATIVE OF ALBERTA, CANADA, SHE WAS BORN ROBERTA JOAN ANDERson on November 7, 1943. At the age of nine, she contracted polio in an epidemic that swept Canada, and it was thought that she might not walk again. She remembers spending Christmas in a hospital, shouting Christmas carols at the top of her lungs in the polio ward as a gesture of defiance. Regaining her strength, she plunged into social dancing, organizing weekly Wednesday-night get-togethers. Joni was a precocious child, interested in painting and music. She began her art studies in Saskatoon and bought her first record in 1953, a Rachmaninoff theme used in the score of the Ethel Barrymore–James Mason movie *The Story of Three Loves*.

Mitchell took up the guitar and ukulele in order to play Kingston Trio songs at parties (the hootenanny-singalong craze was then extremely popular). She attended the Alberta College of Art in Calgary, planning to concentrate on commercial graphics, but got sidetracked by folk music and became a regular

at the Depression Coffeehouse. After moving to Toronto to have greater access to clubs, she met and married Chuck Mitchell; and they formed a loose duet. In 1966, they relocated to Detroit, where the relationship fell apart as her solo career took off. She headed for New York, where she became known as a songwriter, singer Tom Rush adding her material and that of newcomers Jackson Browne and James Taylor to his sets. In 1967, she signed a contract with Reprise and went into the studio with David Crosby, whom she credits with helping her fight to see that her writing wasn't diluted to fit the current folk-rock trend. A year later, her material had gained wide exposure; Tom Rush recorded her "Circle Game" as the title track of his 1968 LP, and Judy Collins hit the Top 10 with "Both Sides Now." Mitchell's own *Clouds* album, which featured her version of "Both Sides Now," benefited from the attention, and "Chelsea Morning" became ubiquitous on FM radio. Nineteen seventy's *Ladies of the Canyon* sold 500,000 copies, and "Big Yellow Taxi" landed on the charts.

Her next two records, *Blue* and *For the Roses*, were the sharply confessional works of a woman resentful of her inability to stand loneliness and eager to place the blame on others—even as she denies that she is doing so. But Mitchell's delightful vocal animation was a leavening factor, her trills, ululations, and sandpapery skips along the scale revealing a personality increasingly willing to laugh at its willfulness. Her guitar playing was also distinctive, the humming heft of her open-tuning chords and hard-strumming style anchoring the whole with impressive authority.

Court and Spark, released in 1974, showed that her overall musicality had matured to a point where she could look beyond herself for input and thereby achieve new dimension. A virtual collaboration with hornplayer-arranger Tom Scott and his E.A. Express, the LP was an immaculate jazz-rock exploration; the wide-open, freeway-entwined vistas of Los Angeles seemed to become aural landscapes in which the singer loses, rediscovers, and surrenders herself. *Court and Spark* was considered a brilliant new direction for both Mitchell and rock, and artists as diverse as David Bowie and Jimmy Page expressed envious admiration of the album.

From there, however, Mitchell became more obscure as she drifted further and further into a jazzlike fringe of her own invention. *The Hissing of Summer Lawns* in 1975 was as overwrought as the title implies, as was *Don Juan's Reckless Daughter*. *Mingus*, a 1979 tribute to the terminally ill jazz bassist, was brave but brittle. Two live albums released in 1974 and 1980 were only occasionally winning; while her 1982 release, *Wild Things Run Fast*, found Mitchell returning, almost apologetically, to the conventions of *Court and Spark*.

It had only been on *Hejira* in 1976, that she had crossed over into an entirely new realm of creativity, producing a ghostly, ethereal record of stalking, abandon, and flight, in which the dark side of love is directly confronted, the soul subsumed, an otherworldly eroticism achieved. It was the kind of craftsmanship Henry Miller was pushing Anaïs Nin toward when he kept advising her to concentrate on the carnal and "leave out the poetry."

PRECEDING PAGE
Joni Mitchell, Spy in the House of Love (Moshe Brakha).

FACING PAGE
A solitary searcher, Joni lives on "nerves and feelings."

DIANA ROSS

A SEQUINED DIANA ROSS STARTED TO RHAPSODIZE IN FRONT of 2,500 guests at Pasadena's Civic Auditorium in the spring of 1983. "Someday, we'll be together." The high-spirited crowd became positively transported when, from the wings, former Supremes Mary Wilson and Cindy Bird-song emerged to join in. The song was the trio's last No. 1 hit as a group, before Diana Ross departed in 1969 to go it alone. At the time of the breakup, the act was known as Diana Ross and the Supremes, and Diana's departure had been imminent for three strained years. She was replaced by Jean Terrell, sister of heavyweight boxer Ernie; Wilson and Birdsong were gone by the early 1970s, and their replacements disbanded the act before the end of the decade. Florence Ballard, founder of the group and the woman Cindy replaced in 1967 after Motown president Berry Gordy dismissed her, died of cardiac arrest in 1976, a problem drinker living on welfare.

While the audience was electrified by the reunion—which had been arranged as part of the live taping for Motown's twenty-fifth anniversary gala—the women themselves seemed awfully tense. That feeling might have remained a nettlesome notion, simply an unfounded suspicion, had "Reach Out and Touch (Somebody's Hand)" not been added to the program. That song was a Top 20 hit for Ross in 1970, her first accomplishment on her own. She seemed not to want to relive the memory in the company of the Supremes, however, because partway through the song, Ross gave Mary Wilson a sponta-neously spiteful on-camera shove of such force that it caused Wilson to drop her microphone.

Only the hasty diplomatic arrival of Smokey Robinson, offering himself as a gracious, smiling buffer between the two bickering women, saved the even-ing from further tarnish. It also provided a touch of nostalgia. In 1964, when the Supremes, the Temptations, and other Motown acts first introduced them-selves to America through the Motor Town Revue company bus tour, it was Robinson who continually served as a one-man rescue team when acts faltered. And it was Robinson, the senior member, who always closed the show. The Supremes were stuck in the vulnerable position of opening the evening's enter-tainment, but Diana shrewdly saw the latent advantages in the situation and exploited them to the fullest. "She stole everybody's act," Motown president Berry Gordy once recalled, referring particularly to choreography. "When [the others] came on, they looked ridiculous. They had to change their acts every day. They all hated her.

"There are winners and there are losers, and there are heavyweights, middleweights, and lightweights," Berry added. "Diana Ross has always been a heavyweight. She has been called the plastic queen of soul. That's a fallacy."

Gordy made certain that the shoving incident was excised from the tele-vised version of the special. Diana Ross is far too testy and tough to be mistak-en for something so unsuitable for conducting heat and electricity as plastic.

DIANA ROSS WAS BORN ON MARCH 26,1944, IN DETROIT, MICHIGAN, ONE of Fred and Ernestine Ross's six children (three boys, three girls). A stable lower-middle-class family, they lived in the Brewster-Douglass housing project in the "Black Bottom" section of the city. Her father was a foreman at the American Brass plant, her mother a maid for a wealthy white family. Diana recalls that, as a child, "all I wanted to do was sing and wear pretty clothes." While studying design at Cass Technical High School, she took a job as a night busgirl in one of the four restaurants housed within J.L. Hudson, one of the city's oldest and most exclusive department stores; as the first black ever hired by the store for a position outside the kitchen, she became a talked-about curiosity. Her salary was spent on weekend modeling and cosmetology classes.

At fourteen, shortly after an unsuccessful audition for a school musical, she was invited to join a singing group by neighbors Florence Ballard and Mary Wilson. Another girl, Betty Travis, was added. Manager Paul Williams approached the girls' parents for permission to use them in tandem with the Primes, a male vocal group; and he got an OK. The girls called themselves the Primettes. Travis dropped out shortly after they were signed to the local Lu-Pine Records label, and Barbara Martin came in to help them cut two singles, "Tears of Sorrow" and "Pretty Baby." The records helped them get bookings, and they worked with the Primes, but the act was shaky. Martin left to get married and Ballard was pulled out periodically by her mother whenever her grades dipped. Even when her parents agreed to her singing, Florence was a listless, unreliable participant, given to unexplained truancy and disappearances; occasionally, Ross and Wilson had to appear as a duet.

William "Smokey" Robinson of the Miracles, an informal talent scout for Hitsville, U.S.A. Records, later to be called Motown, had been involved in bringing the Primes into the company in 1960. That same year, he arranged for the Primettes to audition for Gordy. The boss was unimpressed, but he said he'd consider a deal after they'd finished school. In the meantime, the girls hustled for recording experience, singing backup on Motown sessions and hanging around the bungalow headquarters on West Grand Boulevard in hopes of pickup work. A few opportunities arose, backing Marvin Gaye, cutting demonstration sides with Martha and the Vandellas, as well as lending handclap effects to rhythm tracks, each at the rate of $2.50 a session.

After Ross's graduation in 1962 (she was voted Best-Dressed Girl), the Primettes were taken on by Motown, and they issued the tepid "I Want a Guy." Then the Primes became the Temptations, and Ballard suggested the Primettes also change, supplying the new name—the Supremes. After a so-so commercial response to their "Let Me Go the Right Way" single, Gordy put the girls together with the Holland-Dozier-Holland songwriting-and-production crew. Eddie Holland shaped their vocals; Lamont Dozier developed their melodies and background vocals; Brian Holland mastered a signature sound in the studio. The molding didn't stop there. Auxiliary tutelage was provided by the Artists Development Department of Motown, a team consisting of musical directors, a choreographer, vocal coaches, wardrobe consultants, and advisors on stage patter and social etiquette.

While Mary Wilson had always been the lead singer of the group, Gordy considered her vocal coloration uncommercial; of the three, Florence had the strongest pipes, but Diana's high voice was the most expressive. Her tart, wily

PRECEDING PAGE
Diana Ross, easily exposed (Douglas Kirkland/Sygma).

FACING PAGE
The Supremes and their high-flying clotheshorse (Frank Driggs Collection).

OVERLEAF
Ross, in concert in Central Park, 1983 (Gary Gershoff/Retna Ltd.).

phrasing, although in need of much guidance and goading, cut through the characteristic gospel density of Motown's backing and the pop crispness of its production values. As Diana's role as lead singer grew firm, she gained general dominion over the group. She became engrossed in their image, choosing and even sewing their costumes, devising their hairdos, pushing for the supper-club poise and sophistication she aspired to in her own outside charm-school classes. To her mind, appearances were the coin of ambition, a rococo wardrobe a wise means to a worthy end: come what may, you are not a star until you *look* the part. The results started to show in 1963, when the Supremes scored with "When the Lovelight Starts Shining Through His Eyes." The careful refining process clicked in 1964. "Where Did Our Love Go" topped the pop charts, initiating a stellar pattern—eight more consecutive No. 1 singles between 1964 and 1967. No female group, white or black, had ever done so well or been in such demand for concert bookings. But the lead singer was dissatisfied on both personal and professional fronts; she found the Diana Ross version of Dale Carnegie training still wanting and, in 1966, spent the group's only vacation in three years taking a charm-school refresher course.

Late in 1967, a change in the group's billing—to Diana Ross and the Supremes—showed up unannounced on "Reflections," which peaked at No. 2, and rumors and real disgruntlement within the trio began to grow. When Ballard missed dates pleading "illness" (drinking problems, melancholia, and bad blood between her and Ross were the true causes), Gordy put her on suspension. The proud, impulsive Ballard retaliated by firing off a letter to Ross and Wilson, saying that she was quitting. Cindy Birdsong was brought in, but Diana started to squeeze solo appearances into the crowded Supremes schedule, disturbing associates with the stress her acquisitive will was putting on the group and on her own well-being. In June 1969, she cracked. She found her poodle, Tiffany, and Yorkshire terrier, L'il Bit, dead in her dressing room at a New Jersey nightclub; they had eaten rat poison intended to rid the premises of field mice. Diana fled the scene and canceled a week of Supremes' bookings.

ROSS'S ANNOUNCEMENT OF A SOLO DESTINY CAME IN DECEMBER 1969. FOR the next two years, she began her own dates with the greeting, "Good evening, and welcome to the Let's-See-if-Diana-Ross-Can-Make-It-On-Her-Own Show," and her efforts were bolstered by a high-powered Motown campaign aimed at turning her into a glamorous "personality." Nick Ashford and Valerie Simpson supplied material with a tightly tailored combination of elegance and dramatic content; the studiedly torchy new arrangement of their "Ain't No Mountain High Enough" is a prime example of the expansive story-song setting they were after.

Ross expanded her activities in the early 1970s to include television and films, particularly *Lady Sings the Blues*, the Motown-backed musical biography of Billie Holiday in which she starred. (Ever vigilant in her unremitting quest for *le dernier cri* and its desired effect, she threw a much-publicized tantrum on the set in protest of the "tacky" costumes selected for the role.) She also eloped with Robert Silberman, an actor's agent who worked under the name Robert Ellis. *Lady* gained Diana an Academy Award nomination as Best Actress and fortified her international image as a glittering clotheshorse. Her second movie was *Mahogany*, the story of a black fashion model's rise and disillusionment; it was plainly a reflection of Diana's own hopes for herself as fashion plate—the character's gauzy regalia was of Diana's own design. While Diana's single of *Mahogany*'s theme song reached No. 1, the film was rejected as a pretentious mess by critics and fans alike. Then, in June 1976, her five-year marriage to Silberman went into divorce court.

"My wife *belongs* to that company," Silberman once said of Motown. He also expressed a weariness with its overweening corporate head, who even accompanied the couple and their children on their family vacations. "She's totally dominated by a man who never read a book in his life. I just can't stand it anymore to hear them calling Stevie Wonder a genius. What happened to Freud?"

Diana signed a new seven-year contract with Motown, and the company think tank called for a more youthful, sultry persona. She became interested in a film interpretation of Broadway's *The Wiz*, then being discussed at Motown. Sitting up one night with a videotape of the original movie, she phoned Berry Gordy at 4:30 A.M. and insisted on being given the part of Dorothy. "Have you been drinking?" he asked. Ross refused to budge, and she got her wish. Moviegoers were unwilling to accept her as an ingenue in the overblown production, and the movie flopped, but critics took note of her role in the emerging solo career of Michael Jackson, who played the Scarecrow in the film. In their scenes together, especially the dance sequence for their "Ease on Down the Road" duet, his unvarnished adoration of her was blatant.

"He kind of idolized me," she later said, "and he wanted to sing like me . . . everything; people couldn't tell which was me and which was Michael."

After two disappointing albums, she recouped in 1979 with *The Boss*, an audaciously self-assertive album that was produced by Ashford and Simpson. Her next LP, *Diana*, had hits with "Upside Down" and "I'm Coming Out" in 1980. She shared the spotlight with Lionel Richie for one of 1981's biggest singles, the theme from the film *Endless Love*, and then revealed her decision to leave Motown. The news took observers by surprise; Berry Gordy was thought to have an unbreakable hold on Diana's services—and on her heart. He offered her a multimillion-dollar sum reported to be the most offered any individual by a record label, but she turned it down, severing her twenty-year tie. She signed a $20 million arrangement with RCA, purchased a co-op in the Sherry Netherland Hotel and a Connecticut estate, released a new album, *Silk Electric*, and had a sizable hit with "Muscles." It was a brazen song about a woman's craving for well-developed men, written and produced by Michael Jackson.

In 1983, Ross celebrated her new independence by giving a free concert in New York's Central Park to raise money to build a children's playground named for her. The initial concert and its raindate the following night were chaotic, plagued by a torrential downpour on the first pass and marauding street gangs on the second. It was learned months later that the shows had wound up costing $2.5 million. The city lost $479,000. Not one cent was left over to build the playground, despite the fact that the city had footed all bills for police, sanitation, and other services. When the city asked the Ross organization for a full accounting, they learned of lavish spending for trappings: embroidered gown, $11,035; makeup, $625; limousines, $12,000 (Diana already owned a Rolls Royce). "Shaken and unhappy" with the disclosures, she presented the city with a personal check for $250,000 to get the playground construction underway. The overall fundraising project was judged a debacle. But then, all Diana had wanted to do, of course, was wear pretty clothes and sing.

DAVID BOWIE

DAVID BOWIE HAD JUST GLIMPSED SOMETHING GHASTLY. HE jumped up and hurried to the picture window. It was the summer of 1975, and he was a houseguest at the Hollywood home of lawyer Michael Lippman, his sometime manager. He'd been lolling about his small, book-lined, candle-lit room, taking his ease. Now he was shaken. He had just seen a body drop from the sky. He pulled the shade down, revealing a star drawn on the inside with a ballpoint pen; "Aum" was scrawled beneath it. He hastily lit a black candle. And then blew it out.

A few days later, Bowie fled Lippman's house, the second in a series of impromptu hostels he'd taken refuge in. He was enjoying a level of mainstream success unprecedented in his career. "Fame"—a single from his *Young Americans* LP that he'd written with John Lennon and Carlos Alomar in forty-five studio minutes—had given him his first No. 1 record in the U.S.; he'd starred in *The Man Who Fell to Earth*; he was a darling of American mass culture, his years-earlier admissions of bisexuality having lost their scandalous tint as he chatted on national variety shows with Cher and Dinah Shore and captivated his peers on the Grammy Awards television special. But privately, he was a complete mess; in his own estimation, a "hurt, broken mentality; a fractured person." And he was due to get worse.

He moved into Bel Air and rented a mansion with Egyptian decor; the interior design coincided handily with his developing interest in mysticism, the Cabala, and exotic clinical and organic drugs. He would stay awake for seven and eight days at a trot, eating little, painting massive, alien abstractions, and erecting fifteen-foot "superman" sculptures of polyethylene. After dark, he descended on Hollywood's Cherokee Studio to work through the night on songs with titles like "Golden Years" and "Wild Is the Wind." At sunrise, it was back to Bel Air for druggy, chain-smoking harangues with groupie-sycophants about how he could have made a good Hitler, ruminating on the uses of fascism in rock and roll, and regaling listeners with a dream of confrontation he'd been having—either awake or asleep, he wasn't sure—that went like this: he is hosting a rock summit concert with dozens of the biggest living names, and the monstrous event is being beamed around the planet by satellite; as the show gets under way he appears from the wings with a wheelbarrow of submachine guns, taunting the performers into laying down their guitars and taking up some *real* firepower.

In November 1975, Bowie actually did arrange a satellite hook-up to unveil plans for a six-month world tour. *Station to Station* was intended to bring civilization to its tender knees with its despotic brawn. Babbling on-camera from his Bel Air citadel, Bowie the red-haired ranter was well into discursive proof of his new-found fanaticism when the technicians' headphones began to buzz with word that the government of Spain was demanding emergency use of the satellite. Generalissimo Franco had died.

It was all too perfect. Franco! He's dead? So what! I'm alive and may be the next Franco! A rock and roll despot!

Bowie refused to relinquish the satellite.

Things continued in this manner for another month, the man careening from pompous nihilism to fear of his own shadow. For more than a decade, Bowie had played the pop chameleon, changing his sound with each conceptual album, assuming and discarding personas as he saw fit: the swishy blunt-cut Beau Brummel on the cover of 1970's *The Man Who Sold the World*; the Veronica Lake lookalike of 1971's *Hunky Dory*; pop messiah-stud Ziggy Stardust in 1972 for *The Rise and Fall of Ziggy Stardust and the Spiders from Mars*. In recent weeks, those characters had begun to prey on him. He was *seeing* them emerge from his wardrobe, jeering, telling him he no longer called the dance. *They* were going to take *him* over.

Two days before Christmas, one of his closest friends stood him before a mirror and informed him that he had grown impossible to deal with, be around, bear any longer. Look in the mirror, he was commanded, and take a good look at all the people you no longer are! You're drowning in a nihilistic fantasy world, but you're too far gone to be worth saving.

Thrown for a loop, Bowie packed up and flew to Jamaica to dispel his galloping schizophrenia, banish his alter egos to Never Again Land. But the cure didn't take. The Magus of Glam-Rock no longer had the psychic strength to pull the plug on his ghoul mill; they could now conjure themselves up and inhabit him at will.

When the *Station to Station* tour began in the spring of 1976, it was led by a new ogre, a blond Aryan dilettante who looked like David Bowie but answered to the sobriquet of the Thin White Duke. Dressed in black but for a white shirt, he stalked a Brechtian set that held nothing but high-tech hardware and sable-colored surfaces, an overhead network of blinding klieg lights lending the ambiance of a Bund rally in an abandoned bunker.

"I'll lead this bloody country," he seethed offstage. "The masses are silly." Onstage, he sang of "throwing darts in lovers' eyes," above one of the loudest, most monolithic electric bombardments imaginable. Eyewitnesses were afraid to leave their seats.

"It doesn't look good for America," Bowie concluded. "They let people like me trammel all over their country."

PRECEDING PAGES
Page 199: David Bowie, master chameleon (Gary Gershoff/ Retna Ltd.).
Pages 200–201: the Thin White Duke faces off against Ziggy Stardust (both, Michael Putland/ Retna Ltd.).

FACING PAGE
Bowie, the 1983 model (David Bailey).

DAVID ROBERT JONES CAME INTO THE WORLD AT 9 A.M. ON JANUARY 8, 1947, at 40 Stansfield Road, in Brixton, London, the sole child resulting from the marriage of Soho club-owner-turned-publicist Haywood Stenton Jones, whose previous wife had divorced him on the grounds of adultery, and Margaret Mary Burns, a cinema usherette. David had two siblings, Annette and Terence, and a family tree fraught with hereditary insanity. Terry—his father's child from his first marriage and David's elder by eight years—was prone to long, fitful bouts of unexplained weeping. Terry was in his early twenties when he returned from service in the Royal Air Force, greatly disturbed. David could only watch as his stepbrother gradually shut out the world, eventually ceasing to talk. Then Terry vanished for a few years; he was later discovered in a mental ward, where he has been institutionalized ever since. Other close relations have been prone to sudden, mysterious disappearances; aunts and cousins have been hospitalized after being found wandering

in the streets. His sister, Annette, is said to have gone to Egypt with a millionaire businessman and has never been heard from again.

At the age of sixteen, David himself became withdrawn, spending all his free time reading books recommended to him earlier by Terry. But after exposure to Kafka's "Metamorphosis," he became uncomfortable with his own thoughts and was harried by vivid nightmares of human insects, seeing himself becoming an unrecognizable monster. Breaking away from these insistent images, and haunted by the specter of his own impending lunacy, he endeavored to create an alternative world in his own mind, populated with more inviting figures and—most important—fresh characterizations of himself.

While attending Bromley Technical School, David made the acquaintance of Peter Frampton (future lead singer in the Herd) and one George Underwood, who became his closest crony. Their bond held even when Underwood formed a rival band (George and the Dragons) to David's (the Kon-Rads), and, in an unrelated incident, punched David in the eyes and put him in the hospital. (When David returned to school three months later, his left eye was stricken with aniscora, paralysis of the pupil.)

After graduation from Bromley Tech, Bowie took a job as a "junior visualizer" with a commercial art company and then spent six months working for a London ad agency. In 1963, he formed the King Bees with Underwood. In June 1964, seventeen-year-old Davy Jones and the King Bees released their first single, "Liza Jane," on the Vocalion Pop label. That fall, he appeared on a BBC radio program with members of several local bar bands to lobby for "the prevention of cruelty to long-haired men." He recorded singles with two other bands, the Mannish Boys (who had Jimmy Page on the session) and Davy Jones and the Lower Third.

In January 1966, he changed his name to David Bowie, and his new group—David Bowie and the Buzz—became regulars on the pirate Radio London station and appeared on bills with Long John Baldry, Elton John, and the High Numbers (later the Who). He cut three solo singles for Pye Records in 1966 before signing to Decca Records' new Deram label. He went on to a stewardship with Lindsay Kemp's Underground Mime Troupe, "living," Bowie remembers, "the most degenerate life with this rancid Cocteau-ish theater group and writing odd songs about child abusers and dykes" that found their way onto *The World of David Bowie* LP in 1967. When he'd had his fill of Kemp and company, he joined a Buddhist group headed by Chimi Youngdong Rimpoche, a monk who'd recently escaped from Communist China. Bowie came close to moving to the group's monastery in Scotland and taking his vows. But he changed his mind at the last minute and returned to pop music as a Dylanesque folksinger. He appeared in avant-garde films and made a commercial for Lyons Maid "Pop Ice Cream." In 1969, he formed the Beckenham Arts Lab, a creative arts cooperative. "Space Oddity," a single he wrote at the time of the moon landing, hit big in 1969; he was backed in an album, *Man of Words, Man of Music*, and a tour. Not knowing what audiences were like in rock and roll revues at the time, he found himself doing a Dylan/Anthony Newley–influenced set before droves of belligerent skinheads.

Then, seeing the kind of androgynous shock rock the kids were eating up, he formed a fey, mincing outfit called Hype. His head swimming with opiated hashish, Bowie sat about writing brutal songs about his own bizarre upbringing. *The Man Who Sold the World* was the result; it featured "All the Madmen," a track about brother Terry. In March 1970, Bowie was wed to Mary Angela "Angie" Barnett, the couple agreeing to an open marriage that would accommodate unrestrained infidelities and Bowie's bisexuality. In 1971, Bowie released *Hunky Dory*, a homage to the New York City art-rock scene led by the Velvet Underground.

By 1972, he'd told the British press that he was gay (the brocaded gowns he'd been photographed in over the last twelve months had been a tip-off) and created an ill-starred pop-savior persona—Ziggy Stardust. Like all the false faces in his wake, Ziggy was intended to be a painted nothing, an android from another planet who recognized rock solely as an energy exchange in the rubble of a doomed metropolis. His hair was sickly orange, his skin so translucently pale one could see the blood coursing underneath, his empty grin a prickle of milky spikes flashed with vampiric grace. As Bowie moved from genre to genre in search of superficial renewal, he derided substance, made a mockery of jadedness, and recast rock as a livid laughingstock of itself.

I T HAD ALWAYS BEEN AN ENTERTAININGLY STRENUOUS CHORE TO SEPARATE the man from the game plan. If only by virtue of its staying power, the *concept* of David Bowie had achieved an integrity all its own. David Bowie had brought artifice within spitting distance of art.

Before art could spit back, Bowie collapsed, the cumulative faces in the mirror laughing much harder than they had ever been authorized to. His psyche was in shambles.

After the *Station to Station* tour, colleague Brian Eno took the panicking poseur to Berlin, where Bowie lived in a small apartment over an auto-parts shop and collaborated with Eno on two technocratic, flush-the-pipes electronic albums (*Low* and *"Heroes"*). It took two years before he stopped suffering drug flashbacks and such manic imaginings as furniture shifting in the room. He moved on to Switzerland in 1979, thereafter finalizing his divorce from Angie and assuming custody of son Zowie, eleven, now known as Joseph. The intended trilogy with Eno was completed with *Lodger*, a tribute to human restlessness in all its forms. In 1980, he reviewed his traumas with *Scary Monsters (and Super Creeps)*, this time seeming to rule the shadow creatures instead of the other way around.

He left music to act on Broadway in *The Elephant Man* and on television in Brecht's *Baal*. He also starred in a couple of films: *Merry Christmas, Mr. Lawrence*, a study of captives and captors in a Japanese P.O.W. camp in Java in 1942, in which Bowie played an officer who refuses to break under torture; and *The Hunger*, Bowie opposite Catherine Deneuve as a two-hundred-year-old lover of a ravishing vampiress.

In 1983, he returned to rock and released *Let's Dance*, a cool, sleek R&B record that hearkened back to the horn-laden jump blues of Louis Jordan as well as to the modern ballroom funk of Chic, Prince, King Creole, and the Eurythmics. On the gigantic *Serious Moonlight* tour, Bowie played himself, a man of wealth, taste, and cunning. He looked entirely resurrected, but he refused to renounce his odious ravings of the past, saying, "I meant everything I said back then." To whit: "I believe that rock and roll is dangerous. We weenie boys with our makeup and funny clothes and whatnot, I feel that we're only heralding something even darker than ourselves."

OVERLEAF
What you see is what you get: the 1983 Serious Moonlight tour (G. Schachmes/ Sygma).

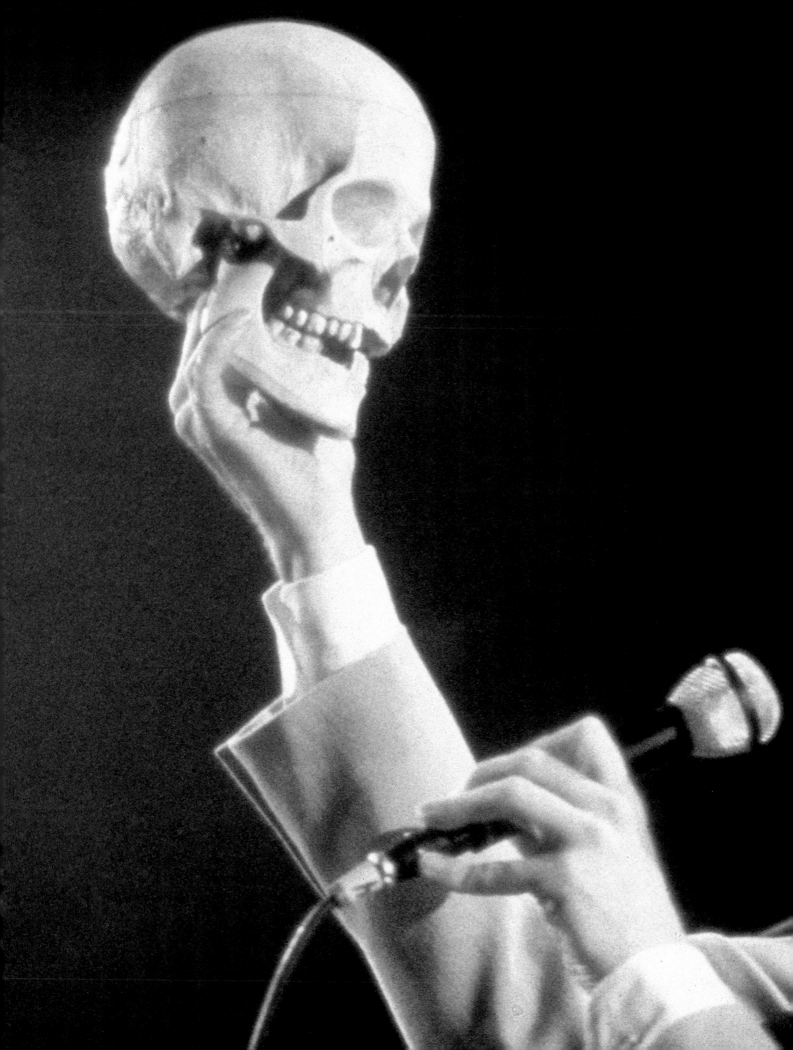

JAMES TAYLOR

JAMES TAYLOR WASN'T AWARE OF IT AT THE TIME, BUT THE COVER OF his 1979 *Flag* album was the nautical symbol for "man overboard." And in the months that followed its release, Taylor sank into as difficult a period as he'd known in his tormented crossing. Among his troubles, he counted a crisis in confidence in his career, duels with the bottle, strained relations with wife Carly Simon, and serious doubts about how to rear his son and daughter. In 1981, he released *Dad Loves His Work*, a record about the "curse" of his intemperance, wanderlust, and inability to be a reliable paternal presence. His own father, Dr. Isaac Taylor, was a compulsive expeditionist when James was a boy, forever dashing off from his work (he retired as dean of the University of North Carolina medical school in 1971) to go on extended research jaunts.

"James's own father's absence was very painful to him," his wife said in 1981, "and he felt slightly responsible. He had the very mistaken idea that because he loved and admired his mother and got to know her better than he did his dad, his father was jealous of their relationship and left all the time for that reason. James had built up an Oedipal dilemma in his mind.

"James's work is extremely good for him," Carly added. "It holds him together. And he's usually most healthy physically and mentally when he's on tour. But while he feels justified by his *Dad Loves His Work* philosophy, it's still difficult for his children. James is really a country boy, likes being on the loose and disorganized, and it's one of our incompatibilities. When he comes back from the road, there's always a feeling of anticlimax, of relief followed by 'Jesus! *Now* what?'"

After ten albums, dozens of tours, a movie career (*Two-Lane Blacktop*, *No Nukes*), and some composing for stage and screen (Studs Turkel and Stephen Schwartz's play *Working*, the films *Times Square* and *Brubaker*; his songs were not used in the latter two), Taylor's position as one of the foremost singer-songwriters of his generation is secure. In 1968, with the release of his first LP, *James Taylor*, on the Beatles' Apple label, he achieved instant prominence and received considerable praise for the confessional boldness of his dark folk narratives—inky, agony-strewn songs that would have made for unbearable listening had they not been structured around the bright resonance of his nasal North Carolina twang and the clipped, suspended chordings of his ringing acoustic guitar. He crooned about confinement in a mental institution, about nervous breakdowns and dungeon-deep depressions, and somehow he left such disquieting realities a little gentler on our minds.

He was handsome in a spindly, lantern-jawed way—his friends in boarding school had called him "Moose"—and everybody wanted to embrace and unravel his many riddles. By the time he scored a hit in 1970 with "Fire and Rain," a song partly about a friend who had committed suicide, he looked to be a talent capable of great things but possibly destined for self-destruction before he had applied himself to his gifts. James, like brother Livingston and sister Kate, had spent time in McLean Psychiatric Hospital in Belmont, Mas-

sachusetts, as well as another Massachusetts mental institution, Austin Riggs, in Stockbridge.

Without warning, this fragile young man with the gothic Southern lineage was a mainstream superstar. He was on the cover of *Time*. He had been hooked on heroin since the age of seventeen. He seemed doomed.

H E WAS BORN ON MARCH 12, 1948. QUIET AND RECLUSIVE, JAMES ENJOYED his boyhood years in the picturesque college town of Chapel Hill, North Carolina; he felt "centered" by the family home. When he wanted to be alone, he would walk out the front door of the imposing manse and down the great knoll on which it was built, disappearing into twenty-five acres of woods.

The South was a special place to him. James loved the lazy pace of its people, their tendency to back off when they weren't wanted and to draw near when they were. North Carolina was an elemental environment where the lushness of the landscape, the intensity of the sun, the fury of the thunderstorms, and the chittering sounds of the insects at night all culminated in a powerful, benign *presence*.

In the perpetual absence of his father, James clung to the rest of his family the way he hugged his big cello during the Taylor's "kitchen concerts"—informal recitals at which brother Alex played violin, Kate and Livingston manned the piano, and mother Trudy sang. During the summer, the clan migrated to Martha's Vineyard, and James was particularly fond of the fact that it was an island.

When he needed to open up to people, he had friend Stan Sheldon to turn to. But generally he avoided that kind of intimacy—until it was nearly too late.

James's unfettered existence disintegrated when his parents decided that it was time for him to choose a direction in life; so at the age of fourteen, he was sent off to Milton Academy, a Massachusetts boarding school, where he was expected to cultivate a new independence, succeed academically, and get his ass into a good college. For anybody else, it might have been the best move in the world, but for young James, it was "wrong, wrong." The school was "high-powered"; it functioned by means of "fear-tactic stuff"; and there were "no girls in sight." James was jolted. He began to realize that he was not wrapped tight enough for this kind of jostling, and he left school and returned to Chapel Hill, only to be confronted with another unsettling reality.

"I'd lost touch with everyone in Carolina. I thought, 'What the hell, finish boarding school and aim for college, because the past has nothing more to offer.'"

Milton Academy took him back—his grades had been good—but he felt as if he were ambling across a chasm. It didn't help matters that he was assigned a small room by himself in the headmaster's house. He'd always preferred to be alone before; why was it so fucking frightening now? He tumbled into an intolerable depression, sleeping twenty hours a day. By Thanksgiving, he started to consider suicide.

He came home for the holidays and grew panicky at the prospect of returning to Milton but was too paralyzed by fear of failure to speak of it. Vacation ended. It was time to go. He walked out the front door, down the knoll, and over to Stan Sheldon's house. He told Stan that if he went back to school, he was afraid he was going to take his own life.

Sheldon talked him into seeing a psychiatrist; James broke down in the doctor's office. He was put under observation at McLean.

Taylor's tenure at the institution was a numbing routine of medication, drab meals eaten with plastic forks (confiscated afterward), and weekly consultations with conservative psychiatrists; it lasted several months. He didn't relish the time he spent looking through 2,000-pound-test security screens on the windows, but he had committed himself to McLean willingly because he saw his "certified-crazy papers" as his best exit from Milton Academy—and the draft.

When the army finally beckoned, Taylor asked a husky attendant named Carl and a similarly formidable friend to dress up in trademark "little white suits" and accompany him to the draft board. They flanked James during his entire interview and answered all his questions for him. James received a clean bill of poor mental health.

Taylor eventually slipped out of McLean in a friend's truck and sped to New York, where he renewed his friendship with Danny "Kootch" Kortchmar and composed such cheerless ballads as "Don't Talk Now," "The Blues Is Just a Bad Dream," and "Rainy Day Man." He joined Danny's new group, the Flying Machine. They cut a demo tape, played in Greenwich Village clubs. Their prospects looked good, but James' heroin habit contributed to the premature breakup of the group in 1967. James called his father, who flew to New York, rented a station wagon, and took his son back to Chapel Hill. Six months later, James flew to England to start over as a musician. The trip resulted in his signing with Apple Records through the good graces of A&R man Peter Asher, who had once been one-half of singing duo Peter & Gordon.

In 1968, Taylor cut his first album in London, Asher producing and Paul McCartney and George Harrison playing on the homesick "Carolina on My Mind." The album failed to catch on, and James was still strung out on junk, so he returned to America and committed himself to Austin Riggs for a five-month stay. Asher had become his manager, and when the Apple label fell apart, he got Taylor a contract with Warner Bros. Taylor appeared at the Newport Folk Festival, where he was introduced to Joni Mitchell and began work on *Sweet Baby James*, his second LP, with Kortchmar, pianist-singer Carole King, and others. Released in 1970, it rose to the Top 10 on the album charts, and "Fire and Rain" became a hit. In the next two years, he became a national figure, the old Flying Machine demo was released in album form, and numerous magazine articles about the musical Taylor family appeared. Livingston had two albums out by the time of James' stardom, and Kate and Alex both recorded LPs (although with meager returns). James' *Mud Slide Slim and the Blue Horizon* enjoyed massive sales in 1971, and he had a No. 1 hit with Carole King's "You've Got a Friend."

In November 1972, Taylor married Carly Simon, and they built a home on Martha's Vineyard, commuting between there and a Manhattan apartment. James wrestled with his heroin problem for another six years. His next five albums for Warner Bros. (*One Man Dog, Walking Man, Gorilla, In the Pocket, Greatest Hits*) had steady sales but only one hit, a cover of Holland-Dozier-Holland's Motown chestnut "How Sweet It Is (to Be Loved By You)." In 1977, he jumped to Columbia and went on to issue *J.T.*, *Flag*, and *Dad Loves His Work*. He had a hit in 1977 with a cover of the Jimmy Jones–Otis Blackwell ballad "Handyman" and another in 1978 with a cover of Sam Cooke's "Won-

A wistful "Moose"
(Peter Simon).

derful World," singing on the record with Paul Simon and Art Garfunkel.

Much of 1979 and 1980 were marred by uncontrolled drinking and rowdy rampages in which he blacked out whole days of outrageous and abusive behavior. "Hour That the Morning Comes," a song on *Dad Loves His Work* that describes the behavior of four people at a wild party, documented his exploits:

"The first one is Carly, who doesn't get drunk and has a good time without hurting herself. The second guy, with his head 'kacked'—that's a junkie term—in his lap, is just someone who's miserable. The next person, the 'fool with the lampshade on,' is somebody else I know, and the 'secret agent man' is a dealer, or someone who has an angle he has to play out at a party. I don't have much moderation in my drinking. If I get intoxicated, I lose control. I've sometimes made mistakes when I was too high that I deeply regret. I can get real sad thinking about things I've said to people and ways I've made people I love feel because I was so out of it."

In between benders, he gave benefit concerts for New York's Parks Commission, appeared at the MUSE antinuclear concerts at Madison Square Garden, and did benefit shows for presidential hopeful John Anderson. "Her Town Too," a duet with John David Souther from *Dad Loves His Work*, was a hit in 1981.

James had resolved to curb his vices, especially drinking, in 1981, but it was too late to salvage his marriage. He and Carly were separated by year's end. In 1982, while James was gathering material for a new record and toying with the idea of opening a brewery with his older brother Hugh ("How does Taylor's Lighthouse Lager sound?"), Carly sued for divorce. In 1983, he swore off demon alcohol. Taylor was once more alone with his work.

BOB SEGER

DRESSED IN BLACK FROM HEAD TO TOE, HE HOWLS LIKE A man with his hand being pulverized under the pistons of one of the 460-cubic-inch behemoths that keep so many Motor City assembly-linemen in swill money and exhaust fumes. Bob Seger echoes the permanent anxieties and soiled but unshaken hopes of every River Rouge grease monkey who gets his paycheck on Friday night and his first hasty sex of that evening through the fly of his overalls.

It took two grinding decades for him to ascend to the rock pantheon. His beard and shoulder-length hair were streaked with gray by the time he got there, his high, nasty tenor growl ground to a fine edge from six-night-a-week stints playing in truck-stop strip joints and successive one-night stands in Tampa, Florida, and in Flint, Michigan, with nothing but diet pills and a station wagon to get him there on time and intact. Through the years and the beers and the close brushes with all-out stardom, Seger churned out scrappy records of matchless integrity, representative of the absolute best in American rock and roll, overflowing with the unsuppressed bullheadedness of the heartland.

Never a fop, never a faddist, his brawny stage presence suggesting a jock buccaneer, he's one of the seminal sources of the steam-whistle urgency and air-hammer ardor that burns through the best of John Cougar Mellencamp, Bruce Springsteen, the J. Geils Band, Foreigner, Tom Petty and the Heartbreakers—and he is the only white rhythm and blues–bred rock singer who deserves mention in the same breath with Van Morrison. Without pose or pretense, prone to mistakes but incapable of false moves, onstage never anything but his restless, caring self, Seger has meant every syllable of every song he's ever recorded. His catchy proletarian heart-pounders swing like lunch pails and have broadened the parameters of rock dreams to include every untimid Midwestern factory boy who's ever longed to aim his fuel-injected designs at the heart of the night. Whether detailing his teenage loss of virginity on a backroad in 1962 in "Night Moves," the dull ache of another Ramada Inn rollout in "Turn the Page," or the working stiff's susceptibility to self-corruption in "Hollywood Nights," he speaks for the spunky pilgrim. Bob Seger is the man who made rock and roll a blue-collar profession of ballsy merit.

HE WAS BORN ON MAY 6, 1945, IN ANN ARBOR, MICHIGAN, THE SECOND son of Stewart and Charlotte Seger. His father was a medic for the Ford company and a moonlighting orchestra leader who played guitar, piano, saxophone, and clarinet and also sang bass in a barbershop quartet. In 1955, he deserted his family; his wife and sons landed in a one-room flat with a hot plate. Bob's older brother, George, took a job with the Wrigley's Gum Company and his mother became a domestic.

When George entered the service, Bob held down dumb jobs to keep the creditors at bay, supplementing his income by playing rock with a group called

the Decibels in bars and at the frat parties of the well-to-do kids at the University of Michigan. In 1961, Bob made a demo of his first song, "The Lonely One," and got a local DJ to spin it. Once.

Going into music full-time, he played with the Town Criers and Doug Brown and the Omens. One morning, he stood out on Mack Avenue in Detroit, cleared his throat, adjusted his ratty leather jacket, tugged a comb through a Brylcreemed pompadour, and walked into the storefront offices of club owner/concert promoter Eddie "Punch" Andrews. While Andrews sized up the shabbily dressed young hitter, Seger launched into "East Side Story," a song about his life in the seamy section of town, set to a melody akin to Van Morrison and Them's "Gloria." Punch listened, shook Seger's sweaty hand, and they became partners for the next twenty years.

Together, Andrews and Seger raised the $1,200 necessary to press the tune for Andrews's own Hideout label in 1965. It sold 50,000 copies locally and got picked up by Philadelphia's Cameo-Parkway label. There were other singles on Cameo; the last was Seger's first national chart entry, "Heavy Music." Hurrying up and down the eastern seaboard, he and his band, the Last Heard, paused to pay his first visit to the company's New York offices. The firm had folded, and "Heavy Music" died with it.

Seger dropped out of the business for eleven months, seeking psychiatric help for his suicidal disconsolation. Andrews nursed his spirit by spending the next two years pitching demos of Seger's best song, "Ramblin' Gamblin' Man." In 1968, Capitol agreed to pick it up. Seger was grateful. Then, when he learned through the morning paper that a boyhood friend had been killed in Vietnam, he wrote "2 + 2 = ?," one of the first antiwar rock songs directly critical of the conflict, and insisted Capitol put it out before "Ramblin' Gamblin' Man." That record also died. Not long afterward, Bob learned that his father had perished in a fire; the man had been too drunk to save himself. By the end of 1968, Seger made it to the charts with "Ramblin' Gamblin' Man." He was pleased, but it was a kick undercut by the demise of his one-year-old marriage.

While at Capitol, Seger made four feckless albums, did three of the same for Warner Bros., and then rejoined Capitol on the rebound. *Seven*, released in 1974, showed a glimmer of better days coming with the ballistic "Get Out of Denver." But how was he to keep the meager momentum going? His friends were doing great. Glenn Frey, whom Seger had produced on Hideout Records ten years earlier, was now coleader with Don Henley of the Eagles, whose *On the Border* LP was fast establishing them as one of the biggest acts in rock. Wrung out, enraged, feeling stalemated, Seger made a wholly confessional last-shot LP in 1975, a peer into the abyss called *Beautiful Loser*. He wasn't sure himself if he had written a scenario for his own looming failure or a fond, accepting farewell.

Loser clicked, and Glenn Frey slapped Seger on the back and said, "Now, you're starting to catch on." When Seger collected the best of his old singles and album cuts in 1976 for *Live Bullet*, his new Silver Bullet Band shone brighter on every track. Seger had been searching everywhere but within for inspiration. Now, in two fell swoops, the reenactment of his disappointments had turned him into a million-selling artist. He'd gone to see *American Graffiti* late in 1974, and it made him realize that his own adolescent experiences had special merit. He spent the next year and a half writing narratives about an adolescence spent dancing before a row of headlights fifty cars long, parked deep in a Michigan cornfield with all the radios synchronized. These were "grassers," illicit outdoor hops endemic to the region, and the source material for his 1976 effort, *Night Moves*, one of the greatest rock albums about coming of age ever written by an adult. The title track and the enormously affecting "Rock and Roll Never Forgets" were huge hits and hailed as immediate classics.

Three more exceptional albums (*Stranger in Town, Against the Wind, Nine Tonight*) carried Seger into the 1980s; with each release the veteran gained ground over rockers half his age. An assessment of the man who went to work at keeping the boy in himself alive, *The Distance* was the masterstroke to complement *Night Moves*. While a cover of Rodney Crowell's "Shame on the Moon" produced a No. 2 hit, it was "Making Thunderbirds" that held the soul of the LP's triumph.

In 1964, Seger had spent time on a Ford assembly line and then quit, refusing to give up on rock and roll but wanting to make the kind of music that would help his co-workers feel good about themselves, too. Thinking back on it almost twenty years later, with the auto industry facing the most dubious future since its inception, he sat down at the piano in his Michigan home and wrote a song about a bygone, intractable pride in one's labor and in an impeccable finished product. "Making Thunderbirds" was scorching rock and roll of superior car-radio vintage. We made *Thunderbirds* once, he sang. And if we bust our asses hard enough, someday, in some way, we might rediscover the secret of doing it again.

Like Bob Seger. The Keeper of the Gearbox.

JOHNNY ROTTEN

HE BEGAN LIFE AS JOHN LYDON ON JANUARY 31, 1956, WAS born to Irish Catholic parents in North London, and grew up in Finsbury Park. He left school while in his early teens and did as little of anything as possible. He had no money, and his parents had none to give him. He had no plans for himself and refused any advice offered by others.

In 1975, young John was lolling around the jukebox in Sex, a barbarous boutique on the King's Road, being his usual uncouth, scurrilous, philistine self, when the shop's owner, hustler Malcolm McLaren, asked him if he wanted to sing in a rock group. John, blond, scrawny, deathly pale, and smelly, said he'd never sung a note in his bleeding life, so piss off, you wanker, all rock stars are faggots who eat dead babies.

McLaren smiled. He was accustomed to the niceties of screening talents like young Johnny.

IN 1971, McLAREN AND WIFE VIVIENNE WESTWOOD HAD OPENED LET IT ROCK, a dodgy little haberdashery serving London's duck-tailed teddyboy revivalists. Next came a place called Too Fast to Live, Too Young to Die. In 1974, McLaren was visited by five rouged, hangdog longhairs in scuffed platform shoes, halter tops, and body stockings. They looked like transvestite screamers who'd been hauled through a knothole. They were the New York Dolls, a rock group on the skids. Malcolm wouldn't let them leave the shop without him; he tailed them to Paris and then the States; he begged to be their major domo, proposing a new image build around something he called "the politics of boredom." They took the bait—and threw it back. When the Dolls disbanded in the middle of a performance in Florida, McLaren returned home to his wife's new shop, Sex. (Actually it was still the same dump they'd been running since 1971; only the names and, occasionally, the clientele had changed.)

JOHN SMILED BACK, SOMETHING HE SELDOM DID. McLAREN GOT AN UN-precedented peep at the youth's cheesy, crud-caked incisors and re-named him Johnny Rotten. This was it: the ideal lead singer for a group designed to insult. The rest of the band—which McLaren had dubbed the Sex Pistols—consisted of bassist Glen Matlock, drummer Paul Cook, and guitarist Steve Jones. They borrowed their antimusical sound from the head-splitting blare of the Ramones, a New York band noted for their three-chord dronathons, and sought an alliance with the thousands of unemployed and dis-affected English youth whose parents were on the dole. Their audience: the punks. Their creed: Oh, bollocks, let it all fall down; we've no bleeding future, rock and roll included; Mick Jagger is a rich twit; Rod Stewart is old and in the way; everything is irrelevant, especially us.

EMI Records signed them and released their first single, "Anarchy in the UK," in 1976. It sounded like four alley cats in a blender with the setting on "shred." Somewhere in the, ah, lyrics, Rotten claimed to be the Antichrist.

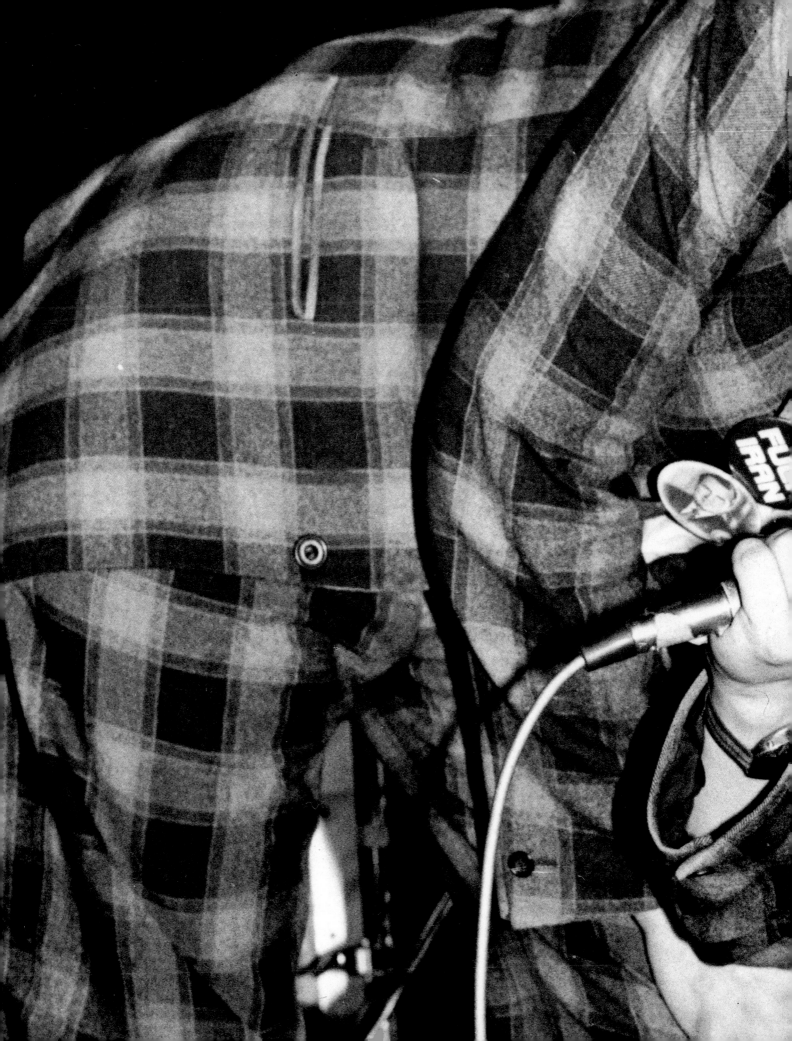

The Sex Pistols were invited onto *Today*, London's popular live television talk show, and host Bill Grundy asked Rotten to utter something outrageous. Johnny bared his moldy teeth and obliged with "dirty fucker" and "fucking rotter." By the next morning, the Pistols had been denounced in Parliament, damned on the front pages, and reviled in the streets. "Anarchy" was an overnight hit. Twenty-one concert dates were booked across the U.K. The Pistols were prevented from playing all but three, getting the plug pulled on them at their debut after ten minutes.

In January 1977, Steve Jones was accused of vomiting on an old woman in a lounge at Heathrow Airport, and EMI responded by dropping them. There was a stampede by other companies to sign the Pistols, and a thoroughly disgusted Matlock left, to be replaced by a thoroughly disgusting Sid Vicious, aka John Ritchie. A&M took them on, and seven days later called the deal off; the Pistols got £75,000 to go away. Virgin Records was next up, and issued "God Save the Queen"—in which Rotten commented, "She ain't no human being!"—just in time for the Queen's Silver Jubilee. Warner Bros. signed them for the States, and an LP, *Never Mind the Bollocks, Here's the Sex Pistols* reached the stores late in 1977, slapped with a sticker that read: THIS ALBUM MAY CONTAIN MATERIAL UNSUITABLE FOR AIRPLAY.

The Pistols couldn't get any gigs in their homeland, so they raced through Europe, one half-step ahead of vice squads and other civil authorities, then jumped a plane to America, showing up for a handful of *fortissimo* free-for-alls before chucking it in San Francisco on January 14, 1978.

JOHNNY CHANGED HIS NAME BACK TO LYDON AND FORMED A NEW BAND, the Carnivorous Buttocks Flies, who then became Public Image Limited (PiL, for short) and landed a deal with Virgin Records. It was a seven-man outfit. They drew up a list of principles to be distributed to the press: 1. PiL is not a group, but a wide-ranging corporation, which deals with other corporations; PiL produces music, images, and graphics. 2. PiL refuses to deal with middlemen, notably managers. 3. PiL is composed of individuals who make music separately, and the music of PiL is a collage of their individual work. 4. PiL does not tour. There is no question of becoming a production line. 5. PiL doesn't put out records, but objects.

PiL's first album, *First Issue*, sounded like seven alley cats in a blender with the setting on "grind." PiL released three more albums, *Second Edition* (issued as *Metal Box* in England and packaged in a film canister), *Paris au Printemps*, and *Flowers of Romance*. In 1981, Public Image, Ltd., did a show at the Ritz in New York City while standing behind a scrim, and irate fans responded with a bottle-throwing melee.

PiL was gone by 1983, and Lydon, broke and in debt, accepted $10,000 to appear in a low-budget film, *Order of Death*. He played Leo Smith, a wealthy schizophrenic cop killer who induces Officer Fred O'Connor (actor Harvey Keitel) to slit his own throat. Lydon/Smith was able to effect this without singing a single note. The movie, released in the United States as *Corrupt*, was universally panned, but the *New York Times* found Johnny convincing, especially in the scenes in which he eats from a dog bowl: "Mr. Lydon, who has just the right insinuating, runty quality for Leo, makes a strong impression."

CHAPTER

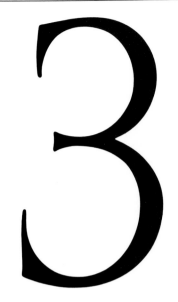

THE INHERITORS

FACING PAGE
Rickie Lee Jones, downbeat bohemian (Bonnie Schiffman).
OVERLEAF
Michael Jackson's "Thriller" video was an urban horror fantasy (Don Hamerman).

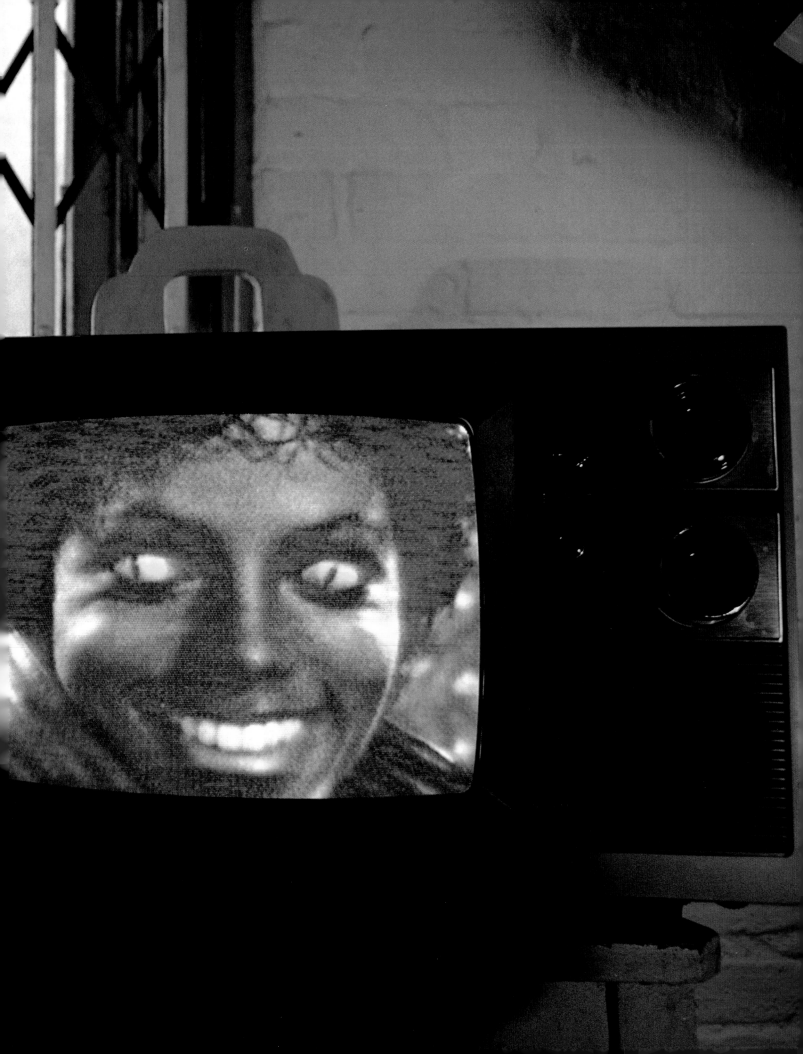

MICHAEL JACKSON

C HILDLIKE PLAYFULNESS AND TEMPERED METTLE HAVE RARE-ly blended so well in a performer's facial features: bright, sparkling, manchild eyes gazing out from beneath feathery eyebrows and fairly illuminating the gently rounded caramel lineaments. A gracefully sloping, mildly puggish nose strengthened by high cheekbones and a strong, angular jaw. A symmetrical halo of wiry hair hovering confidently over it all. Utterly beguiling, brimming with boundless curiosity, good humor, and clarity of purpose—and it is gone forever.

In its place is a disturbing mask, stark and skull-like, the physiognomy flattened and hardened in deference to a pinched skeletal nose that seems a hasty reconstruction, as artificial and undistinguished as the plucked eyebrows that form pencil-line arches above the now-cold stare. The mouth is a sullen fissure, unconvincing when smiling, ungainly when set in a frown.

No natural development could have so cruelly eradicated the former sub-tlety and charity of this countenance. It is a visage reassembled after a tragedy, or one deliberately distorted in a grotesque act of self-conscious folly. In 1982, for better or worse, a plastic surgeon forever changed Michael Jackson's face as Michael Jackson irrevocably changed the face of popular music.

I N THE BEGINNING, MICHAEL WAS A FRISKY SCAMP FROM GARY, INDIANA, leading a family fivesome consisting of older brothers Jackie, Tito, Jer-maine, and Marlon. Jermaine had been the lead singer when the Jackson Family was a trio, but when little Michael was added in 1969, the balance of power began to shift. After a year of basic training in the martial art of rhythm and blues shouting-cum-showmanship, thumping a set of congas and refining his piercing vocal punctuation, Michael was seasoned enough to take over as front man.

The first appearance of the Jackson 5 was a Christmas benefit at a hospital. The enthusiastic reception for their calliope harmonies, and for the adult agil-ity of the hyperactive pipsqueak who danced and sang center stage, led to more work at fireman's balls and school assemblies at their alma mater, Garnett Ele-mentary. The act was prodded and pruned by father Joseph Jackson. Shrewd, frugal, authoritarian, Joseph cast an appraising eye on the burgeoning bravado of his brood of six boys and three girls and sank money into instruments and equipment, drilling the Jackson 5 as a close-order soul revue. To this day, his children reportedly regard him as a hard-hearted taskmaster incapable of ex-pressing parental affection, and his wife, Katherine, has filed for divorce, cit-ing irreconcilable differences.

Berry Gordy rubbed his unbelieving eyes when he was confronted with the spit-polished act, and he signed them up for Motown. Few recording artists have made their initial splash with a sound as fresh and as forceful, an efferves-cent mixture of juvenile vocal histrionics and seamless funk fired by what their high-flying lead singer referred to as "poppin' soul." Often imitated since, the

Michael, pre-superstardom and pre-cosmetic surgery (Henry Diltz).

OVERLEAF
Jackson seems trapped inside a bubble created by two decades of showbiz single-mindedness (left, EA/Retna Ltd.; right, Bonnie Schiffman).

approach was virtually unheard of when their first album, *Diana Ross Presents the Jackson 5*, was released in 1969. The following year, millions of Americans were won over by the Jackson 5's tightly synchronized choreography and vocal cohesion after witnessing the fireworks on the *Ed Sullivan Show*.

"From Gary, Indiana!" boomed Sullivan in his introduction, taking nervous half-steps in several different directions. "Here's the youthful Jackson 5, opening with a medley of their hits that have sold over a million, each, er, each skit—hit!"

The camera lingered a moment too long on the traditionally tongue-tied Sullivan. Then the gaudily dressed Jackson boys burst onto the home screen to a thunderous *"ee-yaaaaaa!"* from the hordes of little girls in the studio audience. Tito, Jermaine, Marlon, and Jackie formed a frantic phalanx as the diminutive twelve-year-old Michael, decked out in a garish vest and matching bell bottoms, belted a segment of "I Want You Back" before swinging his exultant falsetto into "ABC." Michael's leaping vocals were live, as was the precision footwork, dance steps so spectacular that many observers later charged the kid was a thirty-five-year-old midget.

Throughout the early 1970s, the Jackson 5 continued to place singles in the Top 20 and became legendary as a torrid tour attraction, but things cooled off commercially after "Dancing Machine." The brothers grew restive under the combined yokes of Berry Gordy and Joe Jackson. Blood was thicker than contractual ink, and the Jackson 5 left Motown for Epic in March 1976. The split was acrimonious. Lawsuits erupted. Motown sought $20 million in damages from Epic parent company CBS Records. Eventually, they received $600,000 in damages and sole rights to the name the Jackson 5.

Michael had long wanted to issue his own album. Epic liked the idea and brought in studio veteran Quincy Jones to provide guidance. *Off the Wall* made heads turn... and then history. It featured Michael in a tuxedo on the cover; it gave him an older, more suave image; and it sold 8 million copies. But the Michael Jackson whom Jones came to know took, well, a lot of getting used to.

SEATED IN A DARK CORNER OF A MIDTOWN FRENCH RESTAURANT—A willowy wallflower dressed in jeans, polo shirt, and silver racing jacket—Michael was a mere month beyond his nineteenth birthday, yet poised on the very threshold of his ultimate pop ascendancy. As he struggled to comprehend the menu and the method of ordering, he behaved as if in a rarefied daze. Possessed of an awesome ignorance encompassing everything from recent political history ("Was Ford a *president?* Boy, I've gotta keep up on these things!") to common table etiquette and the use of silverware ("I don't know how everything works"), he seemed to be a textbook case of arrested development.

"I'm not as comfortable now as I am onstage, 'cause that's where I was raised," he explained in a squeaky hush. "All I did was sing, dance, watch other people do it, and then travel on.

"What I would like to do, what I would *love* to do, is to travel to India. It's very poor there, and I want to see what it's really like to starve. Like, all the different things I read in my schoolbooks about England and the Queen were okay, but when we did a Royal Command Performance there, and then after it I actually looked in the Queen's eyes, it was the greatest thing! And it's the same thing with starvation!

"I've never been scared of any kind of performing, even when I was the littlest kid," he continued, ordering some "qweech" lorraine for himself. "It's like the Scarecrow. There's so many smart people walking around that don't think they're smart, don't believe in themselves. In the film, these crows come and jive me every day, saying I'm dumb, don't know nothing, and I can't even get down off my pole and walk around. And they're so cool, they fly into my garden and take advantage of me.

"See, my character knows that something is wrong with the way he sees things," Michael Jackson concluded, "but he can't quite put his finger on it."

AFTER NEARLY TWO YEARS OF RELATIVE SECLUSION, MICHAEL REappeared as a solo performer. He was wholly transformed. He showed an altered aspect, and he was peddling a torrid album that boasted intoxicating terpsichorean fare about illegitimate children, gang violence, and youthful seduction. When *Thriller* hit the stores in 1982, its presence proved incendiary, luring legions of buyers into record shops. Vivid, dramatic videos shot for "Beat It" and "Billie Jean" helped accelerate the stampede to the cash register when they were shown on Warner Amex's twenty-four-hour MTV cable network. Consumer obsession with the lanky new superstar expanded beyond measurability after he appeared on a reunionlike 1983 TV special marking Motown Records' twenty-fifth anniversary. The gala program was taped and aired for the press, but not one reporter foresaw the reaction viewers would have to Michael Jackson's performance. After a Memory Lane medley with his brothers, he launched into a breathtaking song-and-dance rendition of "Beat It," his narrowed eyes flashing near-sinister sparks as he slithered through a sexually ambiguous *danse de force* highlighted by slippery "moon walk" pantomime, breakneck spins, and balletic toe stands. Home viewers' awe with the unexpected star turn swept the country by word of mouth, and kids flocked to buy the single.

His young fans screamed and swooned and bought more albums when director John Landis unveiled the *Night of the Living Dead*–inspired video for "Thriller." Then Michael's hair caught fire while filming a pyrotechnic sequence of a Pepsi commercial. He was rushed to the hospital with second- and third-degree scalp burns. Over 700,000 copies of the album were sold in a single week following the accident.

By the middle of 1984, *Thriller* had sold more than 30 million records worldwide, earning a place in the Guinness Book of World Records that demanded an almost daily update. He signed a $1 million deal for a photo book to be edited by Jacqueline Onassis. An 11-inch replica of himself was the sensation of the American Toy Fair. At the twenty-sixth annual Grammy Awards, Jackson collected an unprecedented eight awards for *Thriller*. During commercial breaks, millions saw the finished Pepsi ad. There was no place left to hide from Michael Jackson, and, very nearly, vice versa.

I N A CLIMATE OF EXTREME EXPECTATION, ANXIETY, ENVY, GREED, AND desperation, strained ties of old began to cut deeply, while more recent ones were broken off. Ron Weisner and Freddy DeMann, the management team hired by Joe Jackson, were summarily dismissed. Joe made racist asides about no longer needing "white help" as go-betweens with CBS Records. Michael denounced his father's remarks in a statement to *Billboard* magazine: "To hear him talk like that turns my stomach." Promoter Don King got flagrant in his boasts of control over Michael's destiny; he too was brought up short in a pointed epistle from Michael's office. He could take no actions concerning Michael without advance formal approval from the singer himself. Period.

Even Michael's heroes and role models faded into insignificance. The Emotions . . . Jackie Wilson . . . Sly Stone, whose funk-rock dance stylings fascinated Michael. Cynical comparisons of wealth, canniness, impact, and artistic contributions were drawn in the international press; the defunked Sly Stone was relieved of his connections to his musical legacy as Michael Joe Jackson officially acquired the rights to the dissolute soulrocker's publishing catalogue.

Resounding through all these actions was the icy echo of doors being slammed shut and sealed over, of the engineering of an autonomy and an exquisite isolation that beggars description. Michael passed more and more of his idle hours in self-enforced confinement. Michael is a Jehovah's Witness; the problems inherent in the public proselytizing his religion requires have rendered the practice all but prohibitive; there were fewer and fewer neighborhoods whose residents didn't own his records, didn't display posters of his likeness, didn't give their children miniature Michaels to play with, didn't send them to "Thriller" dance classes.

For all the silly innuendoes that dogged Michael Jackson, the fact remained that he had yet to have a romantic intimate with whom he might share his jagged peaks and valleys. Not since Elvis had a star been so alone, or so ill-equipped for the experience.

CARLY SIMON

JAMES TAYLOR FIRST GLIMPSED HIS FUTURE WIFE ON MARTHA'S VINE-yard in the mid-1960s, as Carly Simon and her sister Lucy performed at the legendary Mooncusser folk club. But some six years passed before they had so much as a casual conversation. Carly remembers the exact date that she first spoke to James: April 6, 1971. She was performing in Los Angeles when "Jamie" Taylor came backstage. She was attracted to Taylor and let him know it. "If you ever want a home-cooked meal..." she murmured.

"Tonight," he said.

When they married, in 1972, he was twenty-four and riding high with the commercial and critical triumph of *Mudslide Slim and the Blue Horizon* and its single, "You've Got a Friend." Carly, then twenty-seven, was soon to rival her spouse's successes with "You're So Vain," the monumental hit off her third album, *No Secrets*.

Considering her flirtatious ways and his roustabout inclinations, they seemed a plausible show-biz pairing. Stepping out of limos, locking arms in night clubs, they were two lanky aristocrats—he from the South, she from the North—embodying the talent, intelligence, self-conscious style, and sex appeal that characterized soft-rock stardom in the 1970s. James was the slyly reluctant ladies' man, sauntering around in the spotlight with an "Aw, shucks" self-deprecation that amplified his magnetism. And Carly was the brainy siren, the ultimate catch. But while everyone was chasing Carly, she was running after the one guy who just kept on walking.

Taylor was the right guy for all the wrong reasons. Clever, shy, reckless, aloof, gentle, and romantic in his own unreliable way, he was as casually self-absorbed as a man hooked on heroin for the better part of nine years could be. Drawing him out of *that* relationship and into hers, Carly found, was rough. Carly's "foxy lady" routine was just an act to build up her courage. She never wanted to be a rock and roll vamp, a mascaraed minx who snares only sweetly errant rogues or cold-hearted rakes. But she found herself living that script. Sadly, she realized that if she wanted to hold on to James, the act would have to become a way of life.

Although she could, occasionally, be a firebrand and a hell-raiser, there was a dreadful disparity between Carly's relatively austere existence and what she called James's "extravagant lifestyle." He did drugs. She *hated* them. He drank and partied with abandon. She was embarrassed for both of them. He roamed where he pleased, winging off to St. Maarten and St. Bart's to go on recording-related benders with singer Jimmy Buffett. She also followed her own impulses, but they always led her straight back to her children, her responsibilities at home, and so away from him.

For a while, however, they managed to keep the relationship from flying apart. There was a steady ebb and flow. Then James became more elusive, departing on bike rides that turned into weekend binges and recording sessions that led around the world. His behavior was not unlike that of his father, Dr.

Isaac Taylor. "It seems," said Carly after the breakup that led to divorce, "that sons cannot help following in their fathers' footsteps."

But, then, daughters can hardly profess immunity to the same sort of legacy. Perhaps one craves the safety perceived in imposed distances, while another clings to the hollow refuge of the hearth.

IN THE SPRING OF 1950, RICHARD SIMON, FOUNDER AND PRESIDENT OF THE powerful Simon & Schuster publishing house, and Andrea, his wife of fifteen years, packed up Carly and her siblings and moved from Manhattan to a stately red-brick Georgian mansion in the Riverdale section of the Bronx. Inside the house, the large living room functioned as the family agora for group entertainments and solo concerts on piano by Dick Simon, affectionately nicknamed "Big Man" by his spouse. It was also the social rallying point for the father's friends and business associates—noted writers, artists, thinkers, composers, and even baseball players.

It was a warm house, full of fireplaces and crackling expectations. It was also an often-troubled house, rife with undercurrents of frustration and grave apprehension.

By 1957, Dick Simon was a semi-invalid, and his career was in jeopardy. Back in the mid-1940s, he had been pressured by his partners to sell his interest in Simon & Schuster in order to accommodate the company's expensive move into the wave of the future—paperbacks. And because he hadn't been in favor of the change, he was eventually shunted aside. It was a severe blow to an already precarious personality. During the tragic mental disintegration that ensued, he paid little attention to his children, especially Carly (born June 25, 1945).

"I was close to my father for two years—1952 and 1953," she says. "We used to drive to Ebbet's Field almost every day the Dodgers were home and watch them play. We'd sit and talk RBIs, Texas Leaguers, and Carl Furillo's batting average. I did it to cultivate a relationship with my father. My mother was often giving me hints about how to win his love, because I felt he didn't love me. People have told me I'm wrong, but I didn't *feel* it.

"By the time I came along," Carly remembers, "my father wanted a boy. So, perhaps during an Oedipal phase in my life, I went after him in a very matter-of-fact way, thinking I *had* to win this man's love."

Carly was about ten and her father was about fifty-five when he was hospitalized with a heart attack. From the time he got sick to the time he died (of another heart attack, on July 31, 1960), she would knock on wood 500 times every night before she went to sleep. She was desperate that he stay alive at least until she could conquer his seeming indifference toward her. Carly was sixteen when her mother woke her in the morning with the news of her father's death. She says she was neither angry nor sad. But she became envious when she saw her sister Lucy doubled over in tears.

"With Dad's death," says Lucy Simon, "my sense of anguish was for the loss, because I had achieved all I hoped for in terms of being satisfied that I had his love and respect. Carly's relationship with him was never totally established, so his death made it impossible for her to complete her task."

Carly was, by her own admission, "a fairly neurotic kid" who grappled from an early age with agoraphobia (literally, "fear of the marketplace"). She had a strong aversion to leaving the house to go to school and often made the inevitable trip with stomach aches and a gagging constriction in her throat that she and her mother referred to as the "worry lump." In class, she often stuttered so badly she could scarcely utter a sound, let alone recite or read aloud. Carly needed extra attention and constant reassurance simply to function. She was about nine when the emotional damn inside her finally broke.

"I was eating a bowl of Cheerios," she remembers, "and I suddenly started shaking all over, feeling clammy and faint and utterly panicked and lapsing into palpitations—I didn't know what they were then. I ran upstairs and started whirling around the bathroom, thinking that I was gonna die and telling my mother to call an ambulance and get a straitjacket."

The worry lump kept recurring, as did the stuttering, the anxiety, the agoraphobia. At age eleven, Carly saw her first psychiatrist. She had to be excused from school each Tuesday and Thursday for her appointments, and the disruption in the classroom routine became a source of mortification that she later felt undermined any benefits the experience might have offered. It was the 1950s. Psychiatry was for misfits and malcontents. She felt indelibly stigmatized. And it eventually corrupted her own image of herself.

She also felt ridiculed for her "unusual" looks. "It seemed a very long period in my life where I felt ugly," she says, noting that she still feels homely one day out of three. Her father's blunt criticism and caustic wit did little to alleviate this notion of undesirability.

"He could be very thoughtful, but he could also be very cruel," says Carly. "One day I said, 'Daddy, do you have any good-looking friends who could come to the house?' because I was reading *Gone with the Wind* at the time and was in love with Clark Gable. He said, 'There's a man coming today who, in fact, looks just like Clark Gable!' I was so excited and got all dressed up, put on makeup, did my hair, the works. When the dinner guest showed up, I came down the stairs Scarlett O'Hara-style, and he was just a little old man with glasses. I saw my father laughing at me, and I was crushed."

Carly's early sense of herself as the ugly duckling in a bevy of swans was cemented in later years when Sloan Wilson, author of *The Man in the Grey Flannel Suit* and a frequent visitor to the Simon house, wrote a book of memoirs in which he remembered *all* the Simons as strikingly attractive—except Carly. "There it was," she says, "the horrible truth, finally confirmed."

CARLY INSISTS SHE NEVER PLANNED A CAREER IN MUSIC, THAT IT HAD been Lucy who dragged her, over the course of the summer before she went to college, into the spotlight. Dave Kapp caught the Simon Sisters' act at the Bitter End, and in the early 1960s, he signed them to a deal with Kapp Records that produced two LPs—*The Simon Sisters* and *Cuddlebug*—and a regional hit single—the syrupy "Wynken, Blynken and Nod." They even appeared on the popular "Hootenanny" TV program. After Carly left the Simon Sisters, John Cort (a partner with Albert Grossman in the firm that handled Bob Dylan) determined to guide Carly to a new professional plateau. "I remember feeling that I was being groomed as a female Dylan," Carly says. Dylan rewrote "Baby Let Me Follow You Down" for her; she cut it with most of the members of the Band and Mike Bloomfield, but Columbia Records declined to release it. Cort and Grossman made another half-hearted attempt to advance her career by creating an act called Carly and the Deacon. Eager-to-please Carly consented to the queer coupling. "He was going to be some short black man from the South who was going to sing duets with me." Fortunately, the act never made it off the drawing board.

Signed to Elektra in 1970, Carly Simon first tasted acclaim with the significant sales and airplay of "That's the Way I've Always Heard It Should Be," the single from her first album, and she found herself "driven" to acquire another dose. And another. "It made me feel in awe of myself," she says. The flip side of that sensation came many years later with the release of *Spy* in 1979. It promised to be the biggest album of her career: the timing seemed right; she had a nice body of work behind her; she was fairly aggressive about her career; she had worked hard and created a well-crafted product. But nothing happened. Nobody seemed to care.

"It plunged me into depression and a serious ego quandary. It seemed to hit me at a time when my self-esteem was precarious anyway. And it toppled it." Moreover, Carly was   prone to sudden acute anxiety attacks and finding it increasingly difficult to perform her music live.

While on tour in October 1980 to support *Come Upstairs*, everything began to fall apart in her life. She got weaker and weaker with each concert, became overwrought with self-doubt, and eventually developed a deep dread her own physical well-being. The grotesque denouement occurred as she was about to go onstage in Pittsburgh.

"When I got onstage, I was having such bad palpitations that I couldn't breathe at all, and I couldn't get the words to the songs out. I seemed to go to pieces in front of the audience. They were incredibly supportive, and a lot of them came up onstage to sit by me. It made me feel as if I owed them even more—that I should either pull myself together and do a great show or *die* and fulfill their expectations."

Afterward, Carly resumed seeing a psychiatrist for a time. In the autumn of 1981, she and James decided to divorce. At the same juncture, she began work on her eleventh solo LP. Entitled *Torch*, the record was devoted almost entirely to the kinds of songs she had grown up hearing: bittersweet love ballads that her father used to play at the Steinway in the Riverdale living room.

"Basically," reflected a somber Carly Simon, "you don't have to see somebody for a long, long time for them to still be inside of you. On my *Boys in the Trees* [1978] album, I had a song called 'Haunting.' 'There's always someone haunting someone' was part of the lyric. And some people have that effect on me. There's no way of killing it off; it's a kind of obsession. I have a good memory, especially for emotions, and I don't get over strong feelings.

"Sometimes, if you're in a complete relationship, feelings have a chance to die out. But if a relationship has ended prematurely for some reason, or it can't be fulfilled for another reason, the haunting goes on, the obsession, the dreams about the person. And the feeling that he is forever locked inside."

Following the cool commercial reception accorded the critically acclaimed *Torch*, Carly Simon dropped from sight to devote herself in the main to the raising of her children. She reemerged in the autumn of 1983 with an album that proved to be a modest popular success. Dedicated to her father, the record was entitled *Hello Big Man*.

BILLY JOEL

WILLIAM LEVITT HAD AN AMERICAN DREAM. HE wanted to strike the first bold blow in defeating the massive housing crunch of the years 1945–1949. Men who had risked their lives to eradicate the Nazi threat were returning home to rebuild their lives, get married, and detonate a baby boom—but there was no shelter for the swarm. These men, who by now had learned to fight more than one kind of battle, were being forced to live in coops, lean-tos, and stables; and a nationwide revolt of disturbingly uncertain proportions was in the air. Politicians warned of the impending shame of new Hoovervilles, the Washington, D.C., shanty-towns from which General MacArthur's tanks routed thousands of unemployed and impoverished World War I veterans and their families in July 1932. The Senate held hearings on the problem but did little.

William Levitt seized the initiative. Looking at the massive stretches of potato fields on his native Long Island, he saw land easily convertible to housing developments and conceived the idea of mass preparation of the site, putting in all the utilities, hardware, and so on, for some 17,500 Cape Cod houses, the same way a spud farmer might install a sprinkler system for an anticipated crop. There would also be ball fields, village greens, schools, and even a shopping center to make the community self-sustaining. Paring the construction schedule of the entirely uniform homes to twenty-six steps, he trained his civilian crews accordingly, convinced the government to underwrite the mortgaging for the strapped vets, and the greatest tract-housing sprawl known to man was born—Levittown, New York.

That was the good news. The bad news was, as William "Billy" Martin Joel, who grew up in the West Village Green section of Levittown, phrased it, "The houses looked so much alike that if you stumbled home drunk, you never knew where you'd end up." Once the vets got over the thrill of owning their own homes, while at the same time not having to fret about keeping up with the Joneses (who had the same house right down to the daintiest detail), they began to be oppressed by the stupefying and terribly alienating sameness of the development. This reaction took a while to take shape. It was the children of the vets who really hated Levittown, and they hated it with a flagrant, sometimes fatal vengeance. One native elevated his ire to the level of a lively art, turning his characterizations of suburban American alienation amongst the products of the postwar baby boom into superbly acerbic anthems: this was Billy Joel.

BILLY'S FATHER TOOK THE LONG WAY HOME FROM THE RAVAGES OF HITLER and the war. A Jew born in Nuremberg, Howard Joel survived confinement in the Dachau concentration camp and escaped to New York City by way of Cuba. He married, fathered two children while he and wife Rosalind lived in the Bronx, then got sold on Levittown.

Billy was born on May 9, 1949. At the age of four, his mother lost patience

with the boy's constant banging on the Lester upright piano in their tiny living room and dragged him to formal lessons, so that he might emulate his father, a classically trained pianist. The Joels' economic status was mildly middle-class until the parents divorced when Billy was seven, leaving his mother to muddle along on a meager secretary's salary, supplemented by small support checks from her ex-husband, who'd moved to Vienna.

By his early teens, Billy's thorough disdain for the impersonal landscape of Levittown and his fury with the way in which he stuck out in it, had hardened and found expression in crime. Attired in the standard night-spree garb of leather jacket, purple shirt, chinos, and matador boots, he and other members of the Parkway Green Gang took to robbing stores, fighting with rival gangs, drinking wine, and sniffing glue.

During Billy's high-school years, the Beatles arrived in America, followed by the Dave Clark Five and the scruffy, defiant Rolling Stones. Playing in a band was now as important as being ballsy in a punchout. The time he'd spent at sissy piano lessons became valuable, and he formed a group called the Echoes. Dressed in blue jackets with velvet collars, the Echoes were the hit of the Teen Canteen at Hicksville High. The group changed its name to the Emerald Lords, then the Lost Souls. Sneaking backstage after a Young Rascals concert to meet keyboardist Felix Cavaliere, Joel became a convert to their blue-eyed Long Island soul. Staying up all night playing bars and roadhouses became a routine, and the 7 A.M. wakeup alarm for school became a nuisance. Scheduled to graduate from Hicksville High with the Class of 1967, he was informed that spring that his diploma would be denied due to absenteeism. Running away from home, he found himself sitting on the stoop of some anonymous home in Hicksville, wondering where he'd sleep that night, when a patrol car pulled up. The house had been broken into earlier that day, and he was arrested on suspicion of burglary. Spending the night in jail, he imagined what it must have been like for his father in Dachau and panicked.

The charges were dropped the following morning, but Joel's sense of being trapped, in Levittown, in shabby economic circumstances, took root. Just turned eighteen, he saw that many of his friends in the Parkway Green Gang were in jail, strung out on drugs, or dead from toppling off train trestles while intoxicated and playing "Chicken." An offer came to join the Hassles, a major club band, and he took it; the band recorded two albums for United Artists Records, *The Hassles* and *Hour of the Wolf*, in the late 1960s before being dissolved. Joel found work dredging oysters from a barge. At roughly the same time, his longtime girlfriend broke up with him. He attempted to commit suicide by drinking a bottle of furniture polish, then committed himself to the mental ward of the Meadowbrook Hospital in East Meadow, Long Island, for three weeks of observation.

Convinced by his stay "with a cast of characters out of *One Flew over the Cuckoo's Nest*" that he was not crazy, he redoubled his efforts to make it in rock and roll. He and Jon Small, the drumer in the Hassles, formed Attila, a two-man psychedelic band inspired by Cream and the Lee Michaels Band. The two were pictured on the album jacket dressed as Huns and standing in a meatlocker.

In 1971, he fell in with entrepreneur Artie Ripp's Family Productions and cut a solo album, *Cold Spring Harbor*, for ABC-Paramount Records. When it was released in 1972, the mismastered LP made Joel sound like one of the

Chipmunks. Worse, Joel had sold off much of his publishing royalties to Ripp. Embittered by the consequences of his naiveté, Joel left town, hiding out in Los Angeles for almost two years under the pseudonym of Bill Martin.

Ripp realized the blanket contract with Joel would have to be renegotiated if either party was to get anything out of it, so a settlement was reached wherein Ripp's Family Productions would receive twenty-five cents from every dollar Joel made from all subsequent albums. Joel signed with Columbia Records, and "Piano Man" was released in October 1973. Although it rose no higher than the Top 20, it established Joel as a songwriter. "The Ballad of Billy the Kid" also received considerable FM attention. The song was a deliberately inaccurate retelling of the outlaw's life story, the singer's point being that anyone has the power to reinvent himself if he dares.

Piano Man was the work of a completely novel rock practitioner. Unfortunately, though it sold over a million copies, Joel reportedly made only $7,763 on the album. Appalled, he asked his wife, Elizabeth, a graduate of UCLA's School of Management, to sort out his affairs. She did well by him. His next album, *Street Life Serenade*, yielded a Top 40 hit in 1974 with "The Entertainer," a song simultaneously cynical and stirring. Then, in 1976, Joel issued *Turnstiles*, which contained "New York State of Mind," a song he wrote on a plane returning to the city; he pictured Ray Charles singing it at Yankee Stadium—the quintessential pop standard. Instead, Joel himself made it a standard, and Frank Sinatra sang it at Carnegie Hall.

The Stranger arrived in 1977, with five huge hits, all of them omnipresent in the American pop music repertoire. This album accentuated Joel's uniqueness in rock and roll—he'd successfully merged the vernaculars of Hollywood sound stages with those of Shubert and Tin Pan Alley, along with the warm ambiance of Sinatra saloon albums, 1950s car-radio pop, the sound of the Beatles-led British Invasion, and the rich melodicism of post–New Wave rock. It was a remarkable feat, making his pissed-off, polyglot music the most widely accepted since that of the Beatles, yet completely his own.

Glass Houses and *52nd Street* produced more hits, and *Songs from the Attic* did well in 1981 with its reprise of little-known songs from the early stages of his career. In 1982, Joel unleashed what was generally considered to be his masterpiece, *The Nylon Curtain*, which contained "Pressure," "Goodnight Saigon," and "Allentown." At the beginning of 1983, Joel and his manager-wife Elizabeth filed for divorce, and he began dating model Christie Brinkley. *An Innocent Man*, released in 1983, was Joel's final farewell to the reckless romanticism of his youth, distilling the distinctive sounds of the acts he thrived on when he was a glue-sniffing gang pug—the Four Seasons, the Tymes, Little Anthony and the Imperials.

"Here we are, having fought our way to adulthood in the aftermath of the baby boom, while rising up through the traditional values of our parents, protesting and testing them," said Joel. "Now that we're prepared to go forward with our heads screwed on straight, all the possibilities are being closed off. What happened to the everyday workingman's dreams—small modest dreams, not big ones—that always came true in America? An unspoken promise has been broken."

STEVIE NICKS

IT IS SAID THAT THE DOOR TO THE OTHER SIDE OF THIS EXISTENCE, TO THE Spirit Corridor and the Plain of Souls, has no knob on it and can only be opened from the outside. You, on this side of the door, must answer the spectral knock with a beckoning, for the Darkness cannot cross your threshold unless it is invited in. And so, on a cool spring night in 1981, in an ancient château outside of Paris, there was no rest for a believer.

Fresh from finishing *Bella Donna*, her first solo album, Stevie Nicks had met up with her band, Fleetwood Mac, at Le Château, the legendary studio-retreat where Elton John recorded *Honky Château* in 1972 and where the Mac were laying down tracks for *Mirage*. Retiring for the night, Stevie turned off the light in her huge shadowy bedroom. Suddenly, she was startled by the sound of rapidly flapping wings in the blackness. The noise abruptly ceased. Then came a queer whir, and something brushed against her cheek. She froze. The light she had just extinguished sprang on, and she was so petrified she could not scream, could not even speak. Ten minutes passed as she cowered in mute terror; then she stumbled down the damp hallway to the room of her secretary, who calmed and reassured her. Stevie eventually made her way back to bed and fell into a troubled sleep.

The morning found her still frightened, and as she tried to orient herself, the French doors across from her bed swung wide open with such force that they toppled the desk standing in front of them.

"I just sat there and watched as these paned doors, two stories high, flew open," Nicks recalled that autumn. "The glass doors opened on a wrought iron balcony overlooking a wishing well. It was quite dramatic, and the desk went over like *whamp!* I went into the kitchen, and the people who worked there said it was the ghost of the château. 'He is a good ghost, he will not hurt you, he just wants to make himself known,' they said. 'Nothing was broken was it?' " It was then that Nicks realized nothing had been damaged, not even a slender jade-colored candle, which would have snapped if it had been dropped even at arm's length.

The prospect of communicating with the dead has considerable appeal for Nicks, who believes she was a monk in a previous life and who named her publishing company Welsh Witch Music.

"If ghosts are friendly and willing to talk, I am ready to sit down at any time. I would *love* to."

SHE LOVES FAIRY TALES AND BELIEVES IN SPIRITS AND WILL-O'-THE-wisps and things that go bump in the daytime and the night. She would like to build her own pyramid and live in a little "witch house" on a cliff overlooking a turbulent sea. Halloween is her favorite night of the year, and although she can't explain the coincidences, certain symbols and words constantly crop up in her life. One is Maya, also known as the Shakti goddess Devi, who represents in Hindu the illusory world of the senses. It's the name of her clothes designer's studios and of the cobbler's shop where she has her out-

moded platform boots made. She finds the symbols even invade her sleep.

In fact, the cover of *Bella Donna* was the result of one of her somnolent brainstorms. It looks like a greeting card from the Good Witch of the North: an ethereal assemblage of crystal balls, blue mists, silver tambourines, and mystic trinities of white roses, with Stevie and a white bird in the center.

To understand Stevie Nicks, it's important to be aware of the yin and yang of her muse. For instance, the original cover for *Bella Donna* was not quite so...visionary. Her more grounded nature was in command when she and photographer Herbert Worthington conceived a double-exposed portrait of the two sides of her personality. The photo depicted Stevie's threatening, take-charge yin fiercely scolding the idle, preoccupied yang. Nicks confides that "these two personalities are constantly fighting each other," and she adds that she was prejudiced against the first cover because it looked "too heavy, too real." Most of us would like a temporary respite from life's serrated edges, and a few of us have secret gardens of the imagination into which we occasionally steal. The difference between Stevie Nicks and the rest of the world is that, given the choice, she usually opts for never-never land—and she brings along a lunch pail and a pup tent.

Stevie says that her favorite fairy tale is *Beauty and the Beast*. She loved the fable as a child, but when she saw the Jean Cocteau film rendition years later, her fascination was cemented. She'll recount her version of the yarn at the drop of a hat, claiming that, at the end of the fable, "Beauty became the Beast, and he became the beautiful one."

A rather gothic variation on the Cinderella myth, *Beauty and the Beast* seems to transcend mere allegory in Stevie's mind. (The trappings of this fable entranced Stevie so much that while she was at Le Château, she rode a borrowed white steed around the phantasmal grounds, her black cape flowing behind her, and almost fell off when the runaway horse threatened to tumble headlong into the crowded parking lot.) Bewildered by the infinite number of possibilities in life, part of Nicks lets such fairy tales overtake her.

PRECEDING PAGE
Stevie Nicks, spacey rock queen (Neil Preston/Camera 5).

FACING PAGE
Few female pop singers display such fateful fantasy (Scott Weiner/ Retna Ltd.).

OVERLEAF
Nicks's "After the Glitter Fades" tells of the heartbreak of a doomed rock dreamer (John Bellissimo/ Retna Ltd.).

S HE WAS BORN ON MAY 26, 1948, IN PHOENIX, ARIZONA. HER FATHER HELD positions as president of General Brewing, executive vice-president of Greyhound, and president of Armour Foods. With each promotion, he was obliged to uproot his family, and he moved them from Arizona to New Mexico, Texas, Utah, and California over the course of more than a decade. Stevie had just completed her sophomore year at a Los Angeles high school and was singing in Changing Times, a foursome modeled after the Mamas and Papas, when Mr. Nicks was summoned to San Francisco. While growing up in the Bay Area, Stevie blossomed as a beauty and came out from behind her granny glasses long enough to become first runner-up as homecoming queen in her junior year at Menlo-Atherton High School. When the family headed for Chicago in 1968, she stayed behind to play with boyfriend Lindsey Buckingham in an acid-rock band called Fritz, working (for one day) as a dental assistant and then as a hostess at a Bob's Big Boy restaurant. Fritz stayed together for four years, and she and Buckingham recorded an album, *Buckingham-Nicks*, for Polydor Records in 1972.

Stevie credits her late grandfather, Aaron Jess Nicks, with her will to sing. An ardent but failed country crooner, he taught Stevie to warble the female parts of call-and-response country songs like Goldie Hill and Red Sovine's

*Wild hair, wild heart
(Ebet Roberts).*

"Are You Mine" while she was still a toddler. Living out of two trailers in the Arizona mountains, A.J., as he was called, was a bona fide eccentric but also a talented guitarist, fiddler, and harmonica player, He took Stevie along with him to gin mills to sing and dance as he played. She was about five when A.J. had an argument with her parents, who forbade him from taking their daughter on the road for a small tour, and he stormed out of the house.

"He went away for two years, and we never saw or heard from him," says Stevie. "I was very upset." About a year before he died in 1973, she wrote a song for him called "The Grandfather Song."

When Fleetwood Mac, the British blues-band-turned-rock-act resettled in California in 1974, producer Keith Olsen played *Buckingham-Nicks* for members John McVie, Christine McVie, and Mick Fleetwood. It was Olsen's way of establishing his credentials. Fleetwood Mac contacted Nicks (who was now waiting tables in Beverly Hills) and Buckingham, and they invited the duo to join the group.

Among Nicks's personal contributions to the remarkably successful *Fleetwood Mac* LP was "Rhiannon," a surging, mesmerizing song about a Welsh witch, which, aided by Stevie's nasal incantations, became a huge hit single in 1975. And Stevie herself quickly became a concert cynosure of the rock-queen mode, floating spacily across stages in gossamer black chiffon, midnight-suede boots, and a top hat. In 1976, her live-in relationship with Buckingham ended and the McVies divorced, but Fleetwood Mac remained a unit, and their 1977 LP, *Rumours*, sold 15 million copies.

Nicks was a sex symbol and the most popular member of the group; but she was also the shakiest, plagued with problems with her eyesight and nodes on her throat from singing too hard. Nasty press notices followed many of the shows in which her formidable vocal cords faltered or cut out altogether. Prior to joining the road-hungry group, she had never had to push her voice. Four-month outings grew into trips triple that duration, and her ravaged vocal cords never had time to heal.

She began to have nightmares in which she would come onstage and open her mouth but nothing would come forth, the huge crowd and the band staring at her in silence. She was near despair when a friend guided her to a Beverly Hills specialist who prescribed a routine of rest between concert stands—three days on, two off—and of constantly speaking a bit higher, at a decidedly *un-*gravelly pitch. She got into the habit of hurrying from plane to hotel room, shutting all windows and doors, putting cotton in her ears, and napping for as long as possible before the sound check.

All was well. Her voice became stronger than ever before, but then she learned that a woman in Grand Rapids, Michigan, was suing her for the rights to Stevie's favorite composition, "Sara." The woman claimed she had written it and sent a copy of the lyrics to Warner Bros. in November 1978.

The suit raged for months, despite Stevie's numerous witnesses (including singer Kenny Loggins) and a demo of the song cut at producer Gordon Perry's Dallas studio in July 1978. It was only in the middle of 1981 that the woman's lawyers finally gave up, stating, says Stevie, "We believe you."

When band members began to consider side projects, Nicks signed with Modern Records, a small label distributed by Atlantic, and she released *Bella Donna*, a solo album, in 1981. It hit No. 1 and yielded two Top 10 singles, both duets: "Leather and Lace," with former Eagle Don Henley, and "Stop Draggin' My Heart Around," with Tom Petty. And in 1983, she released *Wild Heart*, which contained the hits "Stand Back" and "If Anyone Falls," as well as "Beauty and the Beast," a song she'd been working on for two years.

ON JANUARY 29, 1983, STEVIE NICKS MARRIED KIM ANDERSON, A MEMber of the Hiding Place Church, a community of born-again Christians whose liturgy stresses the supernatural and the charismatic. Anderson had previously been married to Nicks's best friend, Robin Anderson, to whom *Wild Heart* was dedicated. Robin died of leukemia in 1982, giving birth to a child a week before her death. Stevie was the child's godmother.

Nicks's marriage lasted only a few months before divorce papers were filed. Phillip Wagner, the minister who performed the ceremony, had earlier expressed "trepidation" about the pairing, not knowing "where Stevie was at with God." Following the news of the breakup, Nicks went into seclusion. The divorce came through in April 1984, and Stevie began work on an album she planned to call *Rock a Little*.

"I can't believe that the next life couldn't be better than this," she said in 1981. "If it isn't, I don't want to know about it. I think that if you're reincarnated, you're probably reincarnated as many times as you want to come back."

BRUCE SPRINGSTEEN

I N THE BEGINNING, BRUCE SPRINGSTEEN WAS A LOQUACIOUS PUBLIC CELE-brant of the highly mechanized American landscape of his adolescence. The niftiest attraction in this sprawling panorama was the car. He came of age in a generation where any guy could own or at least temporarily control a car while still in his teen years, acting out rites of freedom and fulfillment while cruising the Miracle Mile. In the past ten years, Springsteen has perhaps written more songs about late-model jalopies and the untrammeled mobility (poignantly real and pointedly imagined) of the kids that drive and ride in them than any other rocker. His first album, 1973's *Greetings from Asbury Park*, introduced a dialogue-starved young parkway philosopher who could not hold back his verbosely drawn observations on the suburban curbside buffet. In songs like "Growin' Up" and "Blinded by the Light," the music was a muddled mix of folk-based English rock and starchy blue-eyed soul. *The Wild, the Innocent and the E-Street Shuffle* appeared later the same year, almost as a vociferous afterthought, smoothing out the contradictions of the first record, straining to make its musical intentions clear, the singer's vision of the workingman's automotive urban ballad now pleasantly stylized, thanks to able instrumental support from a show band in the Memphis-soul tradition of Otis Redding and Sam and Dave. It was the work of an impatient, abruptly lucid romantic who had stayed up all night to square it away, an impulsive visionary with plenty of time to kill.

Two years later, after much anticipation from fans and dread from over-committed American critics, Springsteen let go of *Born to Run*, an ambitious album he had been reluctant to release. The dreamy zeal with which it had been created was apparent in cinematic songs like "Meeting Across the River" and "She's the One," the writer's *West Side Story* plotlines providing the singer side of himself with ample room to act them out in the studio and (with greater, grander improvisation) onstage. The staunchly unkempt Springsteen became well-known for his last-ounce-of-effort performances, which demonstrated enormous energy and warmth toward his highly appreciative fans.

He was equally renowned for the legal hassles surrounding his songwriting and recording. His career was stalled when a lawsuit was filed against manager Mike Appel for "unconscionable exploitation" of his career and writing output, Springsteen charging Appel with fraud and breach of trust. The case was settled out of court, and music critic Jon Landau took over the guidance of Springsteen's career as well as production chores (Landau had assisted on *Born to Run*). Springsteen also branched out as a songwriter, writing hits for other artists, or seeing their covers of his work do well. The Hollies charted with "Sandy," Manfred Mann scored with "Blinded by the Light," the Pointer Sisters did well with "Fire," and rock poet Patti Smith reached the high point of her short singing career with the success of the co-written "Because the Night."

Between 1978 and 1982, Springsteen released three more albums, *Darkness on the Edge of Town, The River, Nebraska*, each one progressively more

PRECEDING PAGE
Bruce Springsteen,
"the Boss" (Ebet
Roberts).

FACING PAGE and LEFT
Springsteen's music
expresses the loneliness
of the long-distance
rocker (Photo Trends,
Frank Driggs
Collection,
respectively).

OVERLEAF
Springsteen and
horn man Clarence
Clemons (M. Weiss/
Sygma).

bleak, barren, distraught. In the broadest sense, the songs addressed with histrionic "road warrior" metaphors the OPEC oil embargoes and the gas crisis they precipitated. He came off like a marooned hot-rodder trying to make peace with the diminished possibilities for long-range cruising that empty gas tanks seemed to promise. The resignation in his music remained after the OPEC threat had faded. Some interpreted Springsteen's austere outlook as a back-to-basics approach to rock and roll; others, focusing on the themes of defeat and disjunction, saw the man as running out of ideas and a fresh perspective on his own very finite concerns.

HE WAS BORN ON SEPTEMBER 23, 1948, IN FREEHOLD, NEW JERSEY, HIS father a bus driver, his mother a housewife. His parents would have preferred their son to pursue a career in law, but he'd been bitten by the garage-band bug and then got a salty taste of provincial glory in the clubs on the boardwalks of the Jersey shore. His early groups had names like the Castiles, Earth, Child, Steel Mill, Dr. Zoom and the Sonic Boom. The E Street Band, its personnel changeable, became his V-8. Dates were secured along the Eastern seaboard and on the West Coast, and he dropped out of a local community college to explore the band's showcase potential. The record contract came from Clive Davis at Columbia Records, under John Hammond's patronage. It was June 1972.

Then it was 1984, and Springsteen released *Born in the U.S.A.*, a record about cars and nightfall, one that aimed for a commanding depiction of their modest potential for conquering new horizons. He sang in gravelly bursts, like a souped-up Chevy skidding away from the soft shoulder of the road, and on the album jacket he stood before a massive Stars and Stripes like a puckish Patton; but his music was the sound of a defeated rebel, stuck in a small town, afraid to leave home.

RICKIE LEE JONES

SHE CALLS THEM PIRATES, BECAUSE THEY ARE PEOPLE WHO "CAN steal something from you." They sit down next to you in bistros or on late-night bus rides, lighting your cigarette or buying you a drink or simply offering conversation when you're so lonely you could jump out of your skin. So you become their friend or lover, and they, of course, become your benefactor, and everything in life suddenly seems enticing again.

The days are full of safety and a hazy reassurance, and the nights are vast marketplaces where you dare to go on mad spending sprees of the spirit, because now you've got a warm body, a pirate, whom you can fall back on. And once you start falling, you almost grow to like the sound of the wind in your ears and your exhilarated shrieks as you pick up speed. And other pirates look on and smile. They blink from the shadows and wave you in.

You fall through places you've never been before, secret rendezvous on the fringes of public squares, railway stations, and night clubs, and you see faces you didn't know existed: soiled, smeared, chiseled, and grizzled masks slapped on the heads of those who have decided not to tow anyone's line. They are the types of souls you encounter in such books of photography as Brassaï's *The Secret Paris of the 30's*: hungry, self-absorbed creatures who, whether crowded together or coupled in corners, all seem to stand out equally, as in a diorama. They are the sort of people Rickie Lee Jones sings about on *Pirates*. Not coincidentally, the album features a Brassaï photo on its cover.

These people have become pirates, Rickie Lee is saying from the back booth of a Greenwich Village bar one night, because they've gained power over others. It doesn't necessarily make them bad people; it just makes them bad for the powerless—or the ones who surrender to that illusion.

"It's about being caught in time," she says, "getting sabotaged and not being able to get out. But it has a positive and a negative context. It's like you're on your way somewhere and something gets *hold* of you before you get there."

Rickie Lee wears an earring some fans gave her when she was in New Orleans. It's a battered old coin with a Spanish cross on one side and a seal on the other.

"These fans found out what hotel I was at," she says, "and they came bearing gifts. They found the coin on a sunken ship; it's a treasure, and they had it cleaned and put it on an earring for me because they wanted me to be a pirate like them. But they didn't need to do that."

Why not?

She pulls her white beret down over her eyebrows and flashes a strange smile.

"'Cause I already *am* a pirate."

S HE CAME FINGER-POPPIN' INTO THE FOREGROUND OF ROCK AND ROLL IN the spring of 1979, a jazz-hinged hussy arrayed in a white beret and Frederick's of Hollywood splendor. Swaggering, slur-voiced, she sang in an anguished alto that contained eccentric shadings of Laura Nyro, Van Morrison, Beat poetry, and café jazz. Too severe to be considered romantic, too droll to be described as plaintive, her songs were bohemian vignettes of what she referred to as "the jazz side of life." In fact, they were a savage journal of one young woman's stoned soul picnic in purgatory—all of it from her own baroque, downbeat background.

Bettye Jane Jones met her husband, Richard Loris Jones, in Chicago after World War II. She was a waitress. He was a soda jerk fresh out of the army. His mother had been a chorus girl, his father a one-legged vaudeville dancer who went by the name Peg Leg Jones. Rickie Lee was born on November 8, 1954, the third of the Jones's four children. The family moved frequently, from Chicago to Los Angeles and back, then on to Phoenix, Arizona, and finally to Olympia, Washington, as Mr. Jones, hellbent on upholding the slim show-business traditions in the family, divided his energies between a small singing career, acting classes at the Pasadena Playhouse, and work as a long-shoreman, gardener, and day laborer. There was little time left for his family, Rickie Lee getting most of what he had to spare because she was interested in his music; he reciprocated by teaching her to play piano and guitar. The parents separated while Rickie Lee was in her teens, and Mr. Jones continued his vagabond life.

At the age of twelve, Rickie Lee had a premonition about her sixteen-year-old brother Danny being in danger; this was followed by a motorcycle accident in which Danny's leg was torn off. He was in a coma for months, and Rickie Lee spent all her free time with him at the hospital, taking breaks in which she would ride the elevator to the top and sing into the shaft. When Danny came out of his coma, he took to kidding his sister that she was a witch.

At fourteen, Rickie Lee became a chronic runaway, her initial flight involving a boyfriend and a car they stole in Phoenix; they got nabbed en route to San Diego and spent the night in a juvenile detention home. An LSD fancier who would later get into STP, cocaine, and more or less "every drug you can do," she had no interest in the straight life and was expelled from the Timberlane High School in Olympia for insubordination. She relocated to Los Angeles at nineteen, taking a waitressing job in an Italian restaurant in the seedy Echo Park section. Her boyfriend, a guitar player she'd been living with, ditched her. Jones then lost both her job and her apartment. She took to sleeping on friends' floors and couches, in parks and behind the HOLLYWOOD sign, passing afternoons writing songs on a piano in a coffee shop in Venice.

What money she earned came from gigs in Venice beaneries and bars like the Comeback Inn, or the occasional Hoot Night at the Troubadour on Santa Monica Boulevard. She got friendly with the club's cook, Chuck E. Weiss. Singer Tom Waits caught her act in the fall of 1977, and the three grew close, Jones becoming Waits's lover. The trio seemed inseparable. When Weiss disappeared for a spell, later phoning Waits at his quarters at the Tropicana Motel to say he'd been dating a cousin in Denver, an excited Waits hung up, and told Rickie Lee, "Chuck E.'s in love!" and she wrote a song based on the incident. In the meantime, an early manager had sent Warner Bros. a four-song demo originally done with financing from A&M Records. It contained "Easy Money" and three other originals, "Company," "Young Blood," and "The Last Chance Texaco." A&R man Lenny Waronker got staff producers Ted Templeman and Russ Titelman interested, and the three coordinated *Rickie Lee Jones*, her first LP, in 1979. When the finished product was released, "Chuck E.'s in Love" went Top 5, and Rickie Lee Jones was hailed by critics as the most original talent in recent memory.

The bulk of the brilliant *Pirates*, released in 1981, did not sparkle like her debut. Slower, more somber, with references to death and the supernatural, the songs flowed into each other like the slow dissolves of a sad love affair. A new version of "So Long, Lonely Avenue," a grief-stricken good-bye to past attachments, was included. Many of the more melancholy tracks concerned the end of her relationship with Tom Waits, which by all accounts had evolved into an obsessive and destructive one for both parties. Combined with her inability to cope with sudden success, she had a breakdown, and it was months before she could function again.

"My mother was taking care of me," she has said, "because I couldn't eat or get out of bed. I was real sick at heart, actually close to dying from heartsickness and fear. I finally let go of it when I was lying in bed in Washington. I was looking up at my mother and she looked at me, and there was so much pain and dread for me in her face that I barely recognized her—it was *that* distorted. That's when I knew I had to get out of bed and go on living."

Rickie Lee did one of her infrequent tours to promote *Pirates*, confounding some reviewers with her disjointed between-song musings, and startling others by presenting her works in an unflinchingly visceral fashion that rendered them as personal outpourings, the concert being less a performance than an intimate showdown with her illusions and expectations.

Girl at Her Volcano, a seven-song, ten-inch EP was issued in 1983 while Jones wrote material for her next full-length studio album. She spent a good deal of time in Paris and with her mother in the state of Washington, keeping a low public profile, trying to come to grips with her black moods and grievous "gypsy" heritage. In 1984, she released *Magazine*.

As a child, her father used to tell her, "You come from a long line of people who are Welsh and Irish, and you should be proud of them because they were singers, dancers, and poets, and they believed in *magic*." Withdrawn, enigmatic, she took his counsel to heart, clinging to two imaginary playmates named Baslau and Sholbesla. She was in her mid-twenties when her mother asked her what had become of them. Rickie Lee grinned oddly, saying, "But Mom, they're *still here*."

RICKIE LEE JONES HAS COME TO THE REALIZATION "THAT I WAS DEPRESSED all my life. I was very, very unhappy, and I don't want to be like that again. If your inspiration, say, for writing, comes out of pain, and only out of pain, and you find yourself in a position where you don't feel that pain, you may not be able to write. I don't think you have to deliberately suffer to create. I think you *will* suffer. Period."

HIS MOUTH IS A TIGHT SLIT, AND HE SPEAKS SOLEMNLY— almost to himself: "I knew I would never be a part of normal society, but if I didn't find some freedom, I think that eventually madness would have interceded."

Sting's boyhood home of Newcastle—a once-thriving coal and shipbuilding city in the north of England that never bounced back from a recession in the 1930s—is his idea of Hades, the adjacent Tyne River as close to a Stygian watercourse as he can envision. In his memory, it is a dingy, permanently overcast tableau of sagging rubble, petty scheming, and dull defeat, thoroughly loathsome in every sense. Indeed, it resembles the world of Gormenghast, the gigantic castle community in British novelist Mervyn Peake's postwar fantasy trilogy.

The first installment of the gothic, allegorical Gormenghast series was published in 1946, when Britons suffering through the first cruel days of peace had their noses buried in *Animal Farm, 1984*, and *Brideshead Revisited*. Sting purchased the film rights to the trilogy in the early 1980s and wrote the script himself. The central theme revolves around the mad, immensely stagnant life of the castle, its inhabitants choking on the ponderous observance of its arcane traditions, guided one numbing half-step at a time by the Warden of the Immemorial Rites.

But trouble is brewing. Down in the Great Kitchen of Gormenghast— which is kept clean by eighteen slaves called the Grey Scrubbers, virtual automatons who have surrendered to their destiny—a destroyer emerges. He is young Steerpike, the disrespectful kitchen boy who rises above his station to torch the castle's hall of records, murder its leaders, and invoke a season of depravity and—most ghastly of all for the staunchly inert community—irreversible change.

Sting was drawn to the books because of what they had to say about England after the war: "the change that happened when the old empire had decayed, and the working class had a new consciousness and began to rise, destroying the old order." He awarded himself the role of Steerpike, the cunning catalyst from the lower depths, as an exercise in self-exploration. "I have a genuinely destructive nature but not necessarily a *self*-destructive one. I'm just opposites. I'm creative and I like beauty, elegance, grace. But I also like destroying things in order to build them up again."

His own supreme creation is Sting, the stunning Aryan Adonis who cast out the depressingly ordinary Gordon Sumner and became the vaguely sinister rock ringmaster who puts the most popular band in the world through its paces.

Sting delights in ambiguities, the Janus-like nature of humanity, and professes fascination with the idea, for instance, that evil can be a catalyst for good. The band's 1981 *Ghost in the Machine* album was inspired by a 1967 study by behavioral psychologist Arthur Koestler of what Koestler considered the

source of man's greatest predicament: the human mind. Koestler urged the world's scientists to undertake global research studies to find a psychopharmacological "vaccination" to restore the integrity of the split hierarchy of the human brain—the divided house of faith and reason—and rescue the species from the tragic paranoia implanted by evolutionary mutation.

The next Police LP, *Synchronicity* (1983), was, like the previous record, largely Sting-authored, and it took its themes from the writings of C.J. Jung. The theory of synchronicity was an attempt by Jung to explain the noncausal relationship between the prophetic dreams he'd had throughout his life and their actual fulfillment; he employed the term to describe the mystical roots of coincidence.

Sting feels that the huge success of the album and its single "was a synchronistic prophecy, because as a people we've all gotten to Orwell's 1984 a year early—that book is no longer science fiction but a sublime aggregate of the world's current atrocities. The fact that the album has been at the top of the international charts proves the point. My God! It's absolute poison! People don't know what they're hearing!"

IN 1977, GORDON SUMNER, THE TENOR SAX–LIKE JAZZ VOCALIST AND BASSIST with a faltering British band called Last Exit, quit that group to become part of a London-based rock quartet called the Police. The group had recently been founded by drummer Stewart Copeland, third son of an ex-CIA agent. Soon afterward, Corsican rhythm guitarist Henry Padovani departed and the band became a threesome, with classically trained Andy Summers, late of Eric Burdon's Animals and the Soft Machine, on lead guitar. With a loan of £800, they recorded and pressed their own record, a single called "Fall Out." Released by Illegal Records, a label founded by Stewart's older brother Miles, it eventually sold 70,000 copies. Sting talked the other members into bleaching their hair blond for a Wrigley's gum commercial, a move engineered by his wife's theatrical agent. That led to modeling jobs for Sting and more commercials hawking gold chains and Triumph bras. ("I was an extra in the background, *not* the featured attraction.") The real breakthrough was their signing to the major A&M Records on the strength of a tape of "Roxanne." Sting's reggae-flavored serenade to a French whore became a global hit.

The turnabout in Sting's fortunes was dramatic. The son of a taciturn, work-impassioned milkman (Eugene Sumner eventually came to own the dairy) and his stoic hairdresser wife, Gordon had been desperate to leave Newcastle ever since he'd spent the summer of his seventeenth year working for Princess Cruises as a member of the Ronnie Pierson Trio, a shipboard dance band. After that eye-opening taste of travel, he found himself back in bleak Newcastle, digging ditches for a construction crew, filing tax records as a clerk in the Inland Revenue office, and then teaching English and serving as soccer coach at St. Catherine's Convent School, a Catholic school for girls. During a side gig as a bassist for a theater troupe, he met his Belfast-born wife, actress Frances Tomelty. There seemed no escape from Newcastle until lanky American Stewart Copeland showed up, scouting talent for his group. Sting immediately moved to London, where he and his family slept on the floor of a friend's flat. Among the things he left behind was his Catholic religious background, although he remains grateful to its traditions of magic, ritual sacrifice, ghostly presences, and blood-drenched dogma for firing his imagination.

By 1980, the Police found they had risen above embattled Britain's punk-rock upheaval—on the strength of Sting's haunting reggae-fired songs of loveless prostitutes, mass alienation, and the specter of apocalypse—to become one of the most popular mainstream rock attractions on either side of the Atlantic. Yet Sting, a young, handsome, rich chap with a pretty wife and a kindergarten-age son, found himself full of the foulest sort of contempt for life itself. He says he was "catatonically sullen for a full twelve months," very difficult to be with, very aggressive, plagued by the idea that he was just treading water artistically, full of an awesome feeling of negativity and a detestation of everything.

"In a sense, my son Joseph created my nihilistic period in that I felt that if I died tomorrow, I'd had a good life with a lot of vivid experiences—but my child was entering a world that was increasingly small, increasingly polluted, increasingly mindless. Especially if we were all going to be blown up next week by a tactical nuclear device. I felt he was being cheated out of a full life, and so what was the fucking point?!"

His first marriage did not survive the first wave of chaos in his own private Gormenghast, and Sting adopted a new attitude toward his son. "I'm very aware that everything I say to him has to go through the father-son filtering process, which means that he has to reject almost everything I stand for. In order to become himself, my son must in fact destroy me.

"I don't intend to leave him *any* money. I don't intend to give him a nest egg or a head start. If, for example, at the age of twelve I had been given a million dollars, it would have harmed me greatly. I'm his father and that's it. I will *not* create a cocoon for another human being."

HE BEGAN WRITING KNIFE-EDGED QUASI-REGGAE SONGS WITH TITLES like "Bombs Away," "Don't Stand So Close to Me," "Driven to Tears," and "When the World Is Running Down, You Make the Best of What's Still Around." *Zenyatta Mondatta*, the album on which these songs appeared, was a huge commercial and critical triumph, easily selling over a million copies in the penny-pinching winter of 1981 and spawning two singles that ruled the Top 10 charts for months. Sting, however, regarded the record as an artistic failure, felt he was out of ideas, and developed a suicidal attitude. The only thing that pulled him back, he is sure, was a mere book—one he had first chanced upon years before, but in his callowness had not grasped and appreciated. Yet, on a second reading of *Ghost in the Machine*, he was more prepared to heed its urgent message, and he fervently believes it not only gave him the strength and guile to push his stardom to a new plateau but probably saved his mortal ass. An act of synchronicity.

Koestler, guru to the dehumanized and the damned, believed that the human race was hurtling itself past a last-ditch opportunity for redemption. His thesis, predicated on neurological evidence, was that during the course of human evolution, something went awry in the brain; in its rapid growth it developed an inbred imperfection, a paranoiac impulse that corresponded to the creative one. So that lovers of beauty and order, for instance, became the orchestrators of destruction, Hitlers who commit genocide, American presidents who dub a thermonuclear weapon "the Peacemaker."

"Through reading *Ghost in the Machine*, I became more spiritual in a very scientific way. Rereading it, it spoke to me, and in a logical way it ended my lazy grip on logic. After reading Koestler, I started to read Carl Jung and the *I*

Ching, and I got very interested in Tarot cards. I met a clairvoyant, who is now a great friend of mine. He's not some end-of-the-pier entertainer but a clever, well-read, and intelligent man. He told me that I was indeed a machine in terms of my behavior, one with no heart—emotionless—and that I would have to work to alter this. But he said the fact that I could write songs, play music, and be creative showed that I had at least the potential to be a larger person than I was at the time.''

Sting's favorite Tarot card is Death, which for him symbolizes "ultimate change and the end of illusion." He also says he has few illusions about his own demise, having been given information about the hour of his passing by another prescient personage. "I think that rock and roll is dead," he adds, "but the Police are having a fucking good time dancing on its grave."

ON JUNE 6, 1961, AT THE AGE OF EIGHTY-FIVE, C.J. JUNG DIED AT HIS home in Switzerland during a fierce thunderstorm, lightning striking his favorite tree in the garden. On March 3, 1983, Scotland Yard revealed that the bodies of Arthur Koestler, seventy-seven and his wife, Cynthia, fifty-five, were found in their elegant flat in the Knightsbridge section of London. Both were dead from a barbiturate overdose in an apparent suicide pact. A note near the bodies instructed the maid to "phone the police." In 1983, following widespread rumors of a breakup, the Police reemerged with a new album and tour that established them as the most popular and successful rock band on the planet. As Sting sang in the record's title song: "A star falls, a phone call, it joins all—synchronicity."

THANKS TO KOESTLER AND JUNG, STING'S SOLE RELIGION IS AN AGGRESsive drive toward self-realization, an all-consuming code whose tenets guide his expanding career as a film actor. When, in 1978, he landed the role of Ace Face, the icy-cool mod ladykiller in the feature film version of the Who's *Quadrophenia* concept album, he became a cult star and a solid screen presence. This fact has been reaffirmed in his subsequent films—*Radio On*, *Artemis '81*, *Brimstone and Treacle*, and director David Lynch's screen adaptation of Frank Herbert's *Dune*. In each case, Sting has been determined to confront the dark side of himself—the "shadow," as Jung termed it, "which personifies everything the subject refuses to acknowledge about himself," lest he become whatever it is he's resisting—a Milquetoast or a monster. Thus far, he's thoroughly convincingly portrayed a snot, an arrogant punk; a determined adolescent demon; a suburban fiend; and a celestial prince of evil named Feyd-Ravtha.

As for the Police, Sting constantly flirts with disbanding them, their destruction holding an irresistible allure for him. "It's all so easy, I'm bored with it, not interested anymore. The game is won. My ambitions are wide, which is why I'm interested in film—another game, with still more chaos."

Sting sees himself as "the man on the highest tightrope in the circus tent. The spectators want to see me fall—or fly!"

ANNIE LENNOX

THE WORD "EURYTHMICS" IS GREEK IN ORIGIN. THE TERM suggests well-arranged proportion and harmony in design, an excellent disposition of the human pulse, a graceful carriage of the body when moving in rhythm. Stated simply, the ancient Greek esthetic behind the word is that the artistic figure, as well as the artistic rhythm, must be beautiful. The beautiful figure is said to be symmetrical; the beautiful rhythm is described as eurythmic.

Regarding the attainment of this august state of temporal consonance, the Greeks were less specific, except to stress that discipline is required. Conceivably, that discipline can emerge from a joyous unity of purpose or from the spiky depths of neurosis or distemper. In the case of Annie Lennox and David Stewart, it was a mixture of both.

SHE WAS BORN ON CHRISTMAS DAY, 1953, IN THE SCOTTISH PORT CITY OF Aberdeen. The only daughter of a boilermaker who played the bagpipes, Annie Lennox grew up in a two-room tenement; her father encouraged her to study the piano and the flute to dispel the gloom of their existence. At seventeen, she left Aberdeen High School for Girls and entered the Royal Academy of Music in London to continue her studies. For three years she strained to find new life in the classics, then gave up in a rage just prior to final exams. She turned to waitressing by night, by day setting strange poems to music at a large, ornately carved harmonium in her tiny flat. Annie Lennox became one more eccentric pauper in a city noted for its forlorn youth fringe.

IN 1966, DAVID STEWART ATTENDED A CONCERT BY THE AMAZING BLONDEL— his first live exposure to the high-volume mayhem of rock—and stowed away in their van after the show. Fifteen-year-old David was returned to his parents (who were then divorcing), but he was eager to leave home for good. David had captured Blondel's fancy and was able to spend subsequent school holidays traveling with the band. By 1969, he was part of Longdancer, a group on Elton John's Rocket label; but Longdancer blew their six-figure advance on cocaine and speed, and David went on to blow his mind on a year-long LSD binge. The last psychedelic straw came when he and his teenaged wife swallowed the better part of eight tabs of Sunshine obtained from Grateful Dead roadies. When the kaleidoscopic maelstrom finally wound down, he'd sworn off acid and his wife had sworn off him, running away with the lead singer in an all-girl band called the Sadista Sisters.

IN THE MID-1970s, TWO CALLERS CAME TO HEAR ANNIE'S MUSIC. THEY WERE Peet Coombs, a destitute London singer-songwriter, and a disheveled David Stewart. As they sat and listened to the wan blonde woman run through her harrowing repertoire of harmonium hymns, Stewart told himself that she was akin to the Phantom of the Opera, striking cathedral-sized chords of de-

spair in the subterranean bowels of the City of London sewers. He also decided that he loved her, and they moved in together.

Annie, David, and Peet joined forces and began to write music. But it wasn't until their Australian friend Creepy John Thomas offered them some free demo sessions with German producer Conny Plank that they found their basic sound. In 1978, they formed the Tourists, and, in 1979, their devious, crackling cover of Dusty Springfield's vintage pop torch song "I Only Want to Be with You" became a hit. After two highly active years, the Tourists disbanded, dead broke. Lennox and Stewart came undone, both as individuals and as a couple. Reluctant to leave her home, wracked by a list of irrational phobias, Lennox succumbed to nervous exhaustion and went into therapy. Stewart drifted back into drugs.

After a year of intermittent estrangement, Lennox and Stewart found the will to function again. At the zenith of the punk onslaught, they had gone halfies on what punks considered the most loathsome of appliances, a synthesizer. They now reunited, platonically, around the electronic keyboard; and their noodling moved on to earnest experimentation. Conny Plank loved their revived enthusiasm, as well as the operatic range and aloof sensuality of Annie's voice. Lennox wrote words; Stewart supplied music and arrangements. Together they stirred it until the end product came to a low sizzle. Lennox and Stewart had decided to scale down the normally grandiose presentation of rock, juxtaposing the bare ambient essentials in the studio, and employing a componentlike roundelay of musicians when on the road. Thematically, the songs were mind-movies of duality and detritus, disjointed love ballads set to predatory time signatures, moments of ecstasy signaled by a mechanical snarl.

THE EURYTHMICS CUT THEIR FIRST LP, *IN THE GARDEN*, IN THE bucolic tranquility of Plank's studio outside of Cologne. *In the Garden* was issued only in Europe, and it defined the Eurythmics' philosophy: a precise, symmetrical intermingling of mood, image, and narrative steeped in emotion and sexual conundrums and sophistry; this, filled with a mystique that suggests benign hedonism masking a nagging menace. It was music that identified a pleasure factor in mental confusion and suffering, and it had been masterminded by two people whose last few years had been delineated by a maze of misfortunes that ranged from Stewart's multiple car crashes to the periodic breakdowns and incapacitating depressions they shared.

As the Eurythmics ventured into live performances in clubs, Annie presented herself as thoroughly feminine, in a smart smock and a wig of jet-black tresses. Then one night in 1981—while the Eurythmics were holding Heaven (a London dance club) in relative thrall—a randy audience member thought he recognized Annie as the blonde stage decoration from the late Tourists. He lunged toward her and tore away the shimmering wig. Beneath it, to the crowd's dumbfounded surprise, was a tangerine-colored boot-camp cut, flat on top and greased on the sides to an umber sheen. In that instant, the comely known quantity became the biggest sexual wild card in all of London. Word traveled fast. She was a man. He was a woman. She did it with mirrors. He did it with herself.

The drag balls and dress-up poofery of the cult-of-fashion Blitz scene in London were then beginning to heat up, milliners from Soho consorting with mod rockers from Ladbroke Grove to create a stylish musical alloy dubbed the

New Romantics. Steve Strange, mascaraed cofounder of the floating Tuesdays-only Blitz club, had put down permanent roots in a place on Great Queen Street, and found George O'Dowd (then a strapping whelp in warpaint, soon to be the ever-glamorous Boy George) to check wraps at the door. For a generation that had missed the loutish Teddy Boy Edwardian primping of the mid-1950s and had recently rejected punk scatology by reviving the faddish mohair splendor and biker leather of the 1960s Mods and Rockers, the outré frippery of pansexual eurythmia was definitely *de rigueur*. To use the parlance of the preening new beau monde, Annie Lennox became an "ace face."

Borrowing money, she and Stewart cut a number of demos at an eight-track studio in the dreary Chalk Farm section of London. These demos became *Sweet Dreams (Are Made of This)*, the hit album RCA released in 1983. Both the title track and "Love Is a Stranger" were huge hits. *Touch* appeared at the end of 1983, scoring again with the compelling "Here Comes the Rain Again."

Lennox experienced some throat problems as extensive concert commitments placed unprecedented strain on her voice, and she flew to Vienna in December 1983, to consult a specialist. After a checkup and rest, the Eurythmics hit the States for a sold-out twenty-six-city tour. The tour was preceded by Lennox's guest appearance on the Grammy Awards. While the Eurythmics were passed over in the awards, Lennox (who was a guest presenter as well as a nominee) caused considerable commotion when she strode out as a sideburned siren, done up as a dead ringer for a gender-bent Elvis Presley.

Though the "sideburned siren" turns up in a video, Lennox temporarily shelved the Presley look after Grammy night ("I just wanted to be perplexing"). She toured with her familiar carrot-top thatch, enhanced by a black leather military uniform, or a white tropical suit with leopard sash, pillbox hat, and shoes. Gesturing elegantly in blood-red gloves, she generated mystery on all levels from the libido to the frontal lobe. In performance, each facial expression is arresting for the emotion it epitomizes, and the nuances in her forceful singing are the perfect complement. But it is a triumph of effect, much like a slender mannequin come to life and responding to flashcards. There is one semiconsistent display: a delighted, and oddly delightful, joker's grin.

She was married in England in March 1984 to, she said, a West German fellow named Robert. She would not divulge his full name, how she met him, his profession, or if she wore white at the ceremony. "He's a very special person who has provided me with a great deal of support and stabilizing," she stated, discounting rumors in the British press that she had eloped with a Hare Krishna cook named Rhada. "The whole thing was kept unannounced because we wanted our privacy to remain unspoiled."

OVERLEAF
David Stewart and Lennox. The art of severe contrast (Kees Tabak/Retna Ltd.).

HER ELUSIVE PERSONA MIRRORS HER MUSIC: A SPACIOUS, GRIPPING soundtrack to a sci-fi arabesque of pursuit and intrigue, irresistible for dancing, irresistible for secret fantasy. An exquisite rhythm. Annie Lennox has been asked about the velvety venereal contortions in her music. "You might say I've had a love affair with pain," she responds. "Much of my creativity has derived from that."

IT IS DIFFICULT TO IMAGINE. BUT THE BIG BROWN MORASS THAT CHURNS and eddies its way out of Lake Itasca, 446 miles up in the cloud country of northern Minnesota, is the beginning of the lazy Mississippi. By the time it sweeps past the port of Minneapolis, bending this way and that, shifting and twisting, slack and taut, placid and propulsive, forty-one dams have done their damnedest to moderate its onrush. And by the time it disgorges itself beneath the lusty delta country made notorious by Robert Johnson, the sense of relief it exudes is intoxicating.

Up around Duluth, the Mississippi is plenty bottled up. The parameters of its flowing passion are so narrow that you can't navigate it with anything bigger than a rowboat; looking down its curvaceous length, however, to where the headwaters surge into the Gulf of Mexico, it's wide enough to handle an aircraft carrier. It's not a pretty river by most standards, but there are those who find its changeability alluring, its protracted thrust a stimulating metaphor. Some iniquitous blues shouters of bygone days compared the wriggling Mississippi to a bedded woman in heat; others likened it to an amorous libertine at the peak of his powers. For a malefactor with an imagination, the snug font in the Northwest was high promise of the deep South finale.

THE YEAR WAS 1973, THE SEASON WAS SPRING, AND THE SWOLLEN MISSISsippi had exploded its banks for the first time in half a century, inundating whole communities. All along the river, everything, to borrow a phrase from Prince's erotic first single, was soft and wet. Thirteen-year-old novice guitarist Prince Rogers Nelson, son of mulatto bandleader John Nelson and his white wife, left his Minneapolis home for good.

His father bade his mother adieu when Prince was about seven. His mother remarried, and Prince's stepfather made it plain he didn't care for the boy's wanton ways—or the piano that he pounded with impunity. So Prince tried living with his father for a while. John Nelson, in his moonlighting heyday, had led a snazzy jazz combo; but he had largely put his music career behind him, only occasionally adding keyboard accompaniment to downtown strip shows. His stage name, Prince Rogers, he bequeathed to his son.

The boy moved on and was ultimately befriended by Bernadette Anderson, mother of his buddy Andre. By his sixteenth year, Prince had acquired a reputation as something of a freakish free spirit, ignoring school and leading a band called Grand Central, which included Andre Anderson on bass guitar, Andre's sister Linda on keyboards, and Morris Day on drums. At the beginning of Prince's lackadaisical high-school years, the group was expanded and renamed Champagne; they began adding unusually lewd songs written by the olive-skinned front man with the feminine, "fuck-me" eyes. Practice sessions were held in Andre's basement, as were postpubescent orgies that—thanks to commemorative songs like "Soft and Wet"—remain notorious to this day.

Prince's first album, *For You*, was released by Warner Bros. in 1978. Barely eighteen at the time (if you believe his claim of a 1960 birthdate; others

say he was born in 1958), Prince played all the instruments on the first LP. Sales were spotty. Prince tried living in New York with his sister for several months, then returned to Minneapolis to form a touring band with Andre Cymone (as Anderson now prefers to be known) on bass. When *Prince*, the second album, was issued in 1979, the steamy "I Wanna Be Your Lover" secured a No. 1 berth in the black market, and "Why You Wanna Treat Me So Bad?" also did well. All of the singles had the synth-funk textures then popular in urban dance clubs, and the themes were suggestive, agitated, ribald, foretelling the perfect ending to a perfect evening on the town.

No one was quite prepared for the third album, *Dirty Mind*, a concept work about sexual discovery that many interpreted to be at least partly autobiographical. The songs were sung with the tremulous breathlessness of a newly aroused adolescent; and the storylines, though blatant in their delivery, somehow maintained an innocence that augmented their erotic appeal.

Live, Prince was far more than even his most rabid devotees had bargained for, initially performing naked but for a loose-fitting mackintosh, later opting for a studded purple greatcoat, black Lycra jockey shorts, legwarmers, and knee-length black boots. The explicit shows Prince unveiled were a wild ride in a category all their own. Sliding down a gleaming firepole, shedding clothing along the way, pouncing on a brass bed, and panting as he arched his bare back, he compared the seductive proceedings to the landing of a jumbo jet. "We are now making our final approach to satisfaction," he sighed in short-winded gulps. "Please bring your lips, your arms, your hips into the up and locked position—for landing!"

Prince kept the temperature rising with *Controversy*. Three of his four albums were gold, with sales of 500,000, when he released the two-record *1999* in 1982. This record yielded his first mainstream Top 10 success, "Little Red Corvette." This foggy-windows rock raver pared the Robert Johnson–pioneered personification of woman as hot car down to a sleek, hair-curling homily to internal combustion. While in "Terraplane Blues" Johnson had leaned over the hood and assured his shapely conveyance that "I'm gonna get deep down in this connection / Keep on tangling with your wires," Prince was a driven man. His guarantee: "I'm gonna try to tame your / Little red love machine."

PRINCE NO SOONER GAINED FAME THAN HE SHUNNED PUBLICITY, BECOMing a total recluse when not performing, shutting himself away in his lakeside mansion in northern Minnesota. But he could be reached, and he was pretty forthcoming on "not-so-private" topics, saying that as a twelve-year-old he used to sneak into his mother's bedroom to borrow her vibrator, and that when he's traveling he's afraid of using hotel bathtubs because "a maid could walk in." In the summer of 1984, Prince starred in *Purple Rain*, an autobiographical film released with a companion LP of coital doxology.

Obviously, little has changed at either end of the murky Mississippi since Robert Johnson went down to the crossroads at the midnight hour, shook hands with the Old Deceiver, agreed to an early grave, and was duly empowered to rock the blues in a ring of hellfire. It may not be everybody's idea of a square deal, but for those who feel the mighty tug of its torrid fringe benefits, there really is no choice. Voltaire said it best: "You must have the Devil in you to succeed in any of the arts."

INDEX

ACKNOWLEDGMENTS

I would like to thank the editors and writers of *Crawdaddy*, *Rolling Stone*, *The New Musical Express*, *Sounds*, and *Musician* magazines for their friendship, inspiration, and assistance over the years. To acknowledge them is to appreciate colleagues and friends who are among the finest music journalists of the last twenty years. In particular, I thank Chet Flippo, Cameron Crowe, Mitchell Glazer, Charles M. Young, Ben Fong-Torres, Robert Palmer, Peter Guralnick, David Felton, Paul Nelson, Nick Tosches, Vic Garbarini, Dave Marsh, Greil Marcus, Kurt Loder, Barbara Charone, John Swenson, Debby Miller.

Thanks also to Joel Whitburn, Alan Greenberg, Bruce C. Fishelman, Esq., Frank Management, Shelley Ryan, Leora Kahn, Judy McGrath, Bob Merlis, Jerry Wexler, Deborah Drier, John Sturman, and all the photographers whose work appears herein. Much thanks to my editor, Roy Finamore, to my agent, Erica Spellman, and to my fellow conspirator, J. C. Suarès. Finally, gratitude to Gloria Marie White, for encouraging me to write, and to John Alexander White, for encouraging me to rock.

We have endeavored to obtain the necessary permission to reproduce the illustrations, lyrics, and music in this volume and to provide proper copyright acknowledgments. We welcome information on any error or oversight, which we will correct in all subsequent printings.

The book was set in Plantin Light by TGA Communications Inc., New York, New York.

The book was printed by Toppan Printing Company, Ltd., Tokyo, Japan.

HOUND

Medium Bright Rock

(et)

Bb

ain't noth-in' but a Hound Dog,